BECOMING HUMAN

"Just saying you're human doesn't do it"

Leticia Robles Amador

Daniel S. Amador

EXISTOLOGY PUBLICATIONS, INC.

EP1

Becoming Human
"Just saying you're human doesn't do it."

Cover and text design by Kathryn E. Campbell

For permission write to:
Existology Publications
13110 NE 177th PL # 217
Woodinville, WA 98072

Library of Congress Control Number 2009940134
ISBN 9780615331003

Printed by Gorham Printing

CONTENTS

Part I: Our Interactive Foundation

Part II: Transitioning Out of Animal Nature

Part III: Our Animalness: Cultured and Civilized

Part IV: Animal Beings Threaten the Survival of Our Species

Part V: On Becoming Human

ACKNOWLEDGEMENTS

BIOPHILIA by Edward O. Wilson, p. 18, Cambridge, Mass.: The Belknap Press of Harvard University Press, Copyright © 1984 by the President and Fellows of Harvard College. Reprinted by permission of the publisher.

ON HUMAN NATURE by Edward O. Wilson, pp. 24, 46, 71, Cambridge, Mass.: The Belknap Press of Harvard University Press, Copyright © 1978 by the President and Fellows of Harvard College. Reprinted by permission of the publisher.

SOCIOBIOLOGY: THE NEW SYNTHESIS by Edward O. Wilson, p. 3, Cambridge, Mass.: The Belknap Press of Harvard University Press, Copyright © 1975, 2000 by the President and Fellows of Harvard College. Reprinted by permission of the publisher.

THE ANTS by Bert Hölldobler and Edward O. Wilson, p. 197, Cambridge, Mass.: The Belknap Press of Harvard University Press, Copyright © 1990 by Bert Hölldobler and Edward O. Wilson. Reprinted by permission of the publisher.

HERITAGE: CIVILIZATION AND THE JEWS by Abba Eban, pp. 141, 148, 180, 268, and 297 © 1984 by Abba Eban. Used by permission of Simon & Schuster Adult Publishing Group.

ABOUT CERN copyright from CERN. Reprinted by permission.

"In Praise of Feeling Bad About Yourself" from VIEW WITH A GRAIN OF SAND by Wislawa Szymborka, Harcourt Brace and Co. © 1995. Reprinted by permission of the publisher.

Part I:

Our Foundation

 From Nonliving to Living

Message to the Reader

"Unless there is a new mind there cannot be a new line, the old will go on repeating itself with recurring deadliness."
WILLIAM CARLOS WILLIAMS

Our species has accomplished all kinds of wonders, from discovering new planets and galaxies to using stem cells to create parts for our body, to creating synthetic cells. It seems like there is no end to our species' range of interactions (feelings, beliefs, behaviors, etc.).

Yet, why do we kill each other? Why is our caring for the welfare of others woefully retarded in comparison to our technological capabilities? Fortunately, science can now answer such questions and many others relating to the nature of our species. This advancement in our understanding has been achieved by taking into account our species' nonliving foundation and inherited animal nature. In other words, the "new line" stresses that much of what we are is a result of our species' vast inheritance.

Becoming Human explores our species' animal nature mainly through United States cultural practices since it is the authors' culture and also our species' most powerful. The animal nature of our species is apparent in our culture's capitalistic system. The glorification of individualism, greed, and constant exploitation of global resources for the wealth of a chosen few are all hallmarks

1

of animal nature. These cultural practices don't even provide for the welfare of all U.S. citizens, and they certainly don't provide for the welfare of our species.

In addition, for thousands of years myths via religions have been "belief realities" for most of us. Religions are divisive among peoples, and continuously cause wars. The practices involved in religion are also a result of our species' inherited animal nature.

Realizing our species' inherent animal nature makes us aware that, at best, our species is a transitional species, a species still much like an animal species, but one that's evolving to a level of caring beyond that of animals. For of all our inherited interactions, it is our level of caring that is separating us from animal nature. In other words, the *new line* should awaken you to understand why most of us interact as *Animal beings*, and why only a minority of us interacts as *Human beings*. "Human" is not used indiscriminately to simply mean members of our Homo sapient species. This hypothesis, that our species is in a transitional status, serves to explain many issues concerning our interactions.

Becoming Human will provide you a broad view of our species' living and nonliving evolution that gave rise to our extraordinary potential. Chapter 1 begins with the foundation of nonliving microcosmic entities that created the living cell, the foundation of life and its interactions. Chapters 2 through 4 explore animal nature's interactive evolution from which our species emerged. Chapter 5 explains why *Animal beings* are a danger to the welfare of our species. Chapters 6 through 7 explore the dominant practices of our culture and Judaic-Germanic civilization by focusing on how they are shaped by a belief-language core. In Chapter 8, race, a dominant factor in our U.S. culture, is examined for what it is and what it is not. Chapters 9 through 11 focus on racism, capitalism, and religion as our culture's practices of limited caring for the welfare of others. Chapter 12 explores the nature of being Human and how our U.S. culture's dominant practices hamper our species' Human evolution.

Revisiting Carlos Williams quote, the "new line" is more difficult to understand and accept than the old line that has programmed us to ignore our genetic animalness. Yet, the new line is crucial in understanding that the way we interact is because of our animalness and our species' transitional status.

Of course, the "new line" on our species is not enough for a complete answer as to why we interact the way we do. However, an understanding of the "new line" will expand your understanding of your own interactions and those of others. We hope the new line on our species' nature will not leave you with the thought of "I feel no different," but will awaken you to participate in the humane evolution of our species.

Becoming Human is written to provocatively satisfy your intellect. You are advised to read the chapters in the order presented. This will facilitate an understanding of the authors' hypotheses and conclusions, permitting you to reasonably agree or disagree. The writing of this book would not have been possible without the research of such scientists and intellectuals as Charles Darwin, Karl Marx, E. O. Wilson, Noam Chomsky, Michael Parenti, Ernst Mayr, and notions from the scriptures of Christianity and Judaism.

Please read on...

1

From Nothing to Something

"There are no unnatural or supernatural phenomena, only large gaps in our knowledge of what is natural...We should strive to fill those gaps of ignorance."

ASTRONAUT EDGAR MITCHELL, APOLLO 14

For thousands of generations we have stared out to space and wondered: "What's it all about? Why don't I have more to say about it, and why do I care?" Most of us have such thoughts. But it took billions of years of quarks, photons, electrons, protons,... and many more "nonliving" entities' interactions to create the cellular potential for us to wonder about it all.

The fundamental source of our species' enormous potential to behave, feel, think, and so on began billions of years before life evolved. Paleontologist Dr. Richard Fortey, president of the Geological Society of London, tells us: "The great outward explosion of time and matter at the 'big bang' was a factory of creation" (Fortey, 1998, 27). All that was to evolve (nonliving entities and living entities) into existence was initiated at the moment of creation. It took some nonliving entities billions of years to evolve into life via the living cell. "That vital spark from inanimate matter to animate matter happened once

5

and only once, and all living existence depends on that moment" (Ibid. 37). In other words, nonliving entities' interactions (bonding, rejections, attractions, etc.) are at the roots of our potential to interact—to behave, feel, think, and so forth.

From here on, "dead entities" will be used to mean *nonliving entities,* and the term "entities" rather than *particles* is used. The term *entities* is preferred because it gives the impression of units with the potential to interact. According to physicists, dead entities display innumerable interactions. It is vital to have some scientific knowledge about dead entities' interactive potentials at the foundation of our interactions. The reason for this is that the greater our ignorance of our species' interactive foundation, the more susceptible we are to rely on super-unnatural beliefs from stories of organized religions to explain our being and interactions.

From Nothingness To Something

For thousands of years we have instinctively believed in the existence of entities that we cannot detect with our senses. We have believed in the existence of spirits, ghosts, and gods as entities we cannot touch, see, or hear. They forever loiter about in an infinite domain of nothingness. Instinctively, we have thought of them as nonmatter things that do not take up *time* (duration) and *space* (size, area). In some god beliefs this is the domain called "heaven," where nothing ever happens.

A domain of nothingness may seem ridiculous, but not to some physicists who speculate that existence burst from a domain of nothingness. Such a domain is void of scientific data because scientists need time and space ("timespace") to theoretically explain or predict the existence of anything. Therefore, speculation is that a domain of nothingness would be a domain of forever—a domain without time, without space, without interactions. Scientists tend to agree that "nothing is forever," and perhaps they will come to agree that *only nothing* is forever.

Tiny Dead Entities

The interaction between time and space may have triggered the instant when nothingness became something via the big bang. This was "a factory of creation" of microcosmic entities such as quarks, photons, neutrinos, and many other dead entities. Such tiny dead entities eventually evolved the atom and, billions of years later, the living cell. They maintained the evolution of the cell into countless of living forms and their interactions, and they continue to interact in the cells of all living entities. They are the foundation of our being and of our interactions.

Scientists have discovered that microcosmic entities do not interact the way things interact in our world of matter. A neutrino, for example, barely interacts with entities of matter because it has no electric charge and barely any mass. Massive amounts of neutrinos from cosmic space pass through our entire planet and emerge untouched by anything. According to physicists, more than a million of them zipped through your body in the time it took to read this sentence. They are so tiny that they go through our cells and atoms without crashing into anything. Our bodies are like galaxies to neutrinos. If they were searching for life, they wouldn't see anything that looked alive as they went through us.

Other microcosmic entities (particles) seem to disappear. For example, physicist Dr. Richard Morris (1990, 7) explains that as soon as a positron and an electron meet, they "annihilate one another." (Physicists tell us that for every particle there is an "anti-particle," and a *positron* is a "anti-electron.") An electron ceases to exist when it is broken down, but a proton turns into three quarks when it is broken down. The three quarks cease to exist when scientists try to separate the trio. It seems that when microcosmic entities reach the depths of zero timespace they cease to exist in our world of matter.

According to superstring theories, microcosmic entities creating existence are like strings rolled to a size of about 10^{-33} centimeters. This fantastically tiny size prevents scientists from detecting such entities because of the energy needed to go to that depth of the microcosm. Princeton University physicist Dr. John Archibald Wheeler stated that when we are able to explain what quantum theories are trying to tell us we will exclaim to each other, "How could we have been so stupid for so long?" (Wheeler, 1986, B4)

Scientists discover and study microcosmic entities' interactions with a massive entity collider. The new Large Hadron Collider (LHC) is 27 kilometers long and 100 meters underground. The collider is part of the Conseil Europeen pour la Recherche Nucleaire (CERN), which is located in France and is the largest particle physics center in the world. With such a machine scientists expect to find other microcosmic interactive entities that are at the foundation of our existence and everything else. They especially hope to find the Higgs boson, also called the God entity.

> Scientists have found that everything in the Universe is made up from a small number of basic building blocks called elementary particles [entities], governed by a few fundamental forces. Some of these particles are stable and form the normal matter; the others live [exist] for fractions of a second and then decay to the stable ones. All of them coexisted for a few instants after the big bang. Since then, only the enormous concentration of energy that can be reached in an accelerator at CERN can bring them back to life [existence]. Therefore, studying particles collisions is like "looking back in time," recreating the environment present at the origin of our Universe. What for? To understand the formation of stars, earth, trees, everything you see around and, finally, us! (Internet Web site: *About CERN* 2007)

Although physicists consider microcosmic entities to be the basis of matter, most of us consider the atom to be the basic entity of matter. Atoms are made up of microcosmic entities, or subatomic entities. Some atoms are composed of many microcosmic entities and some are composed of only a few. There are about ninety-four natural occurring atoms. (We are composed of an infinite number of atoms.) We will take a glimpse at the makeup of one of these atoms.

The tiny atom is a huge place for its microcosmic entities. To help us visualize its spaciousness we use Riordan and Schramm's description from their book, *Shadows of Creation* (1991). They ask readers to imagine a hydrogen atom, made up of a nucleus and one electron, enlarged by a factor of a trillion. They explain that this would make the atom about the size of a U.S. football field. Even in this enormous enlargement, the nucleus of the atom would only be the size of a housefly hovering around the center of the stadium at the fifty-yard line. The electron of the atom, tinier than a flea, would be circling the nucleus at the distance of the goalposts and side stands. If we were in the middle of the football field we might be able to see the nucleus of the atom, but not the electron circling us some fifty yards away. Riordan and Schramm's imagined scenario gives us some idea of the huge space within an atom in relation to the size of the microcosmic entities creating an atom.

The idea of a tiny basic unit of matter came up thousands of years ago. Around 450 B.C. Greek philosopher Democritus was triggered to think that something could be cut up to a point where it could not be cut any smaller and coined the term *átomos*, which means "uncuttable" in Greek. Several hundred years before Democritus, Indian philosophers of the sixth century B.C. had also thought about the concept of the atom. Both Indian and Greek philosophers had connected their concepts to religious ideas. Not until chemistry developed as a science in the 1600s did studies of atoms begin. Several hundred years later, in 1945, under the supervision of the United States government, an international team of nuclear scientists, experts in interacting with dead entities, created the atom bomb with uranium atoms. A uranium atom is made up of many subatomic entities. The power of annihilation with such a weapon enticed the U.S. to drop two atom bombs on the civilian populations of Hiroshima and Nagasaki, Japan, during WWII.

Dead Matter's Transition to Living Matter

For billions of years atoms created all kinds of dead molecular entities. Then some three to four billion years ago the molecule that changed a dead existence to a living one was created. This was the deoxyribonucleic acid (DNA) molecule of the "living" cell. Everything creating the cell complex including the DNA molecule consists of dead entities. Yet, science identifies the cell's interactions as living interactions because the dead entities' interactions via the cell transition to living interactions. In other words, dead matters' awesome potential is displayed in the awesomeness of life.

Scientists display this vast potential in their ideas, inventions and discoveries. This is why Russian biochemist Dr. Aleksandr I. Oparin's potential was triggered enabling him to understand that the transition from dead matter to living matter was a natural occurrence. In his book, *The Origin of Life on the Earth* (1952), Oparin explains that there is no fundamental difference between a living entity and a dead entity. The interactions and properties of dead matter in the cell transition into the interactions and properties that characterize life.

It is shocking when we understand that a bunch of dead, but wise entities maintain living entities and their interactions (including ours). They are wise because they did not create life, but evolved themselves into a living cell. According to cell biologist Dr. Bruce Lipton (2005, 37), "There is not one 'new' function in our bodies that is not already expressed in a single cell." Each nucleus-containing cell has systems that function like our nervous, digestive, respiratory, circulatory, skin, and reproductive systems. Cells organize themselves and communicate with each other to perform a myriad of functions that maintain all life forms and their interactions. Of all its interactions, however, scientists consider the living cell's potential of reproduction as the key trait of life. Yet, whenever a cell reproduces itself it is actually the cell's dead entities reproducing themselves. In summation, the cell evolved as a "minibrain" with the potential to interact with the environment and evolve infinite complex living entities.

Thus, when we are asked, "What is life?" we can answer, "Life is a notion of a bunch of dead entities interacting inside a cell." Could the wise dead entities in the form of a cell be the closest thing to what we think of as the "Creator" of life?

The Environment and Genetics

The "dead" environment evolved the "living" environment via the cell (minibrain). The cell became the entity that the environment could trigger to evolve the complexity of life. The evolution of the living cell was the evolution of reciprocal interactions between the genetic complex (DNA, cell's membrane, and everything else in the cell.) and the environment (everything in and about us, including timespace). This relationship has continued from the first bacteria through the evolution of our species. This means that the environment continuously triggers interactions from living entities. In turn, living entities' interactions, especially ours, trigger interactions from the environment. The authors call this reciprocity the "genetic-environment (G-E) complex." It is difficult for us to become aware of the G-E complex in our life because it is the continuous occurrence of being alive—we are in the midst of it. It is like not seeing the forest for the trees. It is difficult for us to become aware of how the environment triggers our interactions and how our interactions trigger changes in the environment because we have difficulty perceiving our culture, parents, friends, children, pets, plants, and so forth as part of the environment. As a species, our vast G-E complex has triggered an immense diversity of inventions and discoveries, which have been both good and bad for life.

The interactions of the first single-celled bacteria illustrate the continuous reciprocity of a living entity with the environment and the effect of such reciprocity. Some 3.4 billion years ago the bacteria were triggered by photons from the sun to begin changing the earth's gaseous atmosphere of carbon dioxide into carbon and oxygen. The bacteria took in carbon dioxide from the environment for nourishment and excreted oxygen into the environment as a waste product. This reciprocity went on for millions of years resulting in enough oxygen to make earth's environment hospitable for the evolution of a vast diversity of living forms (Fortey, 1998, 30). Or, we can say that the G-E complex evolved Mother Nature's infinite ways to feel, taste, smell, hear, see, and care for the environment. It is our vast collectivity of cells interacting with the environment that makes it possible for us to experience the joy of living and the fear of dying.

Some scientists consider genes the most important dead entities of the cell. For example, socio-biologist Dr. E. O. Wilson explains that the genes' most important mission is to dictate their continuation through living entities' sexuality. Wilson explains that "In a Darwinist sense the organism [plant, animal, person] does not live for itself. Its primary function is not even to reproduce other organisms; it reproduces genes and it serves as their temporary carriers" (Wilson, 1975, 3). However, genes do not exist for themselves either. They are "temporary carriers" of the atoms and microcosmic entities that they are made of.

Some of us might question whether the environment or genes are more important. It can be reasoned that genes need the environment to exist, but the environment does not need genes to exist. Both, however, are equally vital for all living entities. How they look and how they interact is brought about by how the environment triggers their genetic complex.

In 2008 a genetic study at North Carolina State University showed how lifestyle and geography strongly affect our genetics. The study found these environmental factors could activate or deactivate some of our genes. According to the scientists involved in the study, "The same gene can be expressed in the city but not in a rural place because of the environment. So you must look at the environment when studying associations between genes and disease" (Internet, *Science Daily*, April 23, 2008). This suggests that even in a wealthy nation (as the U.S.) poverty can trigger certain diseases that would not be triggered in a non-poverty neighborhood.

No matter how any living organism interacts, it is the genetic-environment (G-E) complex at work. For example, the potential of man or beaver to cut down a tree is triggered by the environment. It is not man or beaver versus the environment (nature). When we create music, or dance, apply calculus, kill, eat, surf the Internet, search for quarks, and wonder what life is all about it is the environment triggering our genetic complex potential. Thus, man versus nature is primitive thinking. It is time to understand that we did not evolve from a source separate from the environment. Our interactions exist because of how the environment triggers our genetic complex.

※   ※   ※

Our planet might not be the only place in the vast cosmos where dead entities created life. Dr. Cyril Ponnamperuma, director of the Laboratory of Chemical Evolution at the University of Maryland, explains: "The genetic code in life on earth may reflect a universal chemistry—one essentially consistent throughout the cosmos," and that "if there is life elsewhere in the universe, chemically speaking, it would be very similar to what we have on earth" (Raloff, 1986,

182). Ponnamperuma found all five chemical compounds needed for cellular life in a single meteorite. It seems that meteorites dart about cosmic timespace like sperm searching for a hot, wet ovum like Mother Earth to impregnate.

It is logical to think that dead entities would create millions of planets with earth's potential and then plant life on as many of them as possible. That may be why the wise dead entities did not give our species the potential to populate the universe. We cannot travel zillions of miles at speeds faster than the speed of light or survive horrid temperatures and spectacular cosmic collisions. Yet, these wise dead entities have had the potential to survive these interactions for billions of years through zillions of miles.

Quest for "What's It All about?"

Since billions of years of interactions are encoded in our cells, it is reasonable to think that we, as a species, are triggered to search for our dead and living evolution. After all, we are part of that which we observe and wonder about.

Theologians and scientists made it their quest to answer our questions on existence. Hence, we are given a diverse range of answers, from the primitive belief that a god created existence in seven days to the complex idea that some 13 billion years ago timespace triggered the evolution of everything that was to exist.

Theologians simplify the complexities of existence with god's word captured in one or two books such as the *Old* and *New Testaments*. It is comforting to god believers to think that "what it's all about" can be found in one or two holy books. They read and reread, listen and re-listen to the same old stories about "holy" men and their stories. The more god believers read and hear the stories, the more convinced they become of their "validity." For believers therefore the stories replace our species' evolution that began billions of years before there was anyone to make up such stories. This is not to say that theologians don't speak the truth, but it is a truth based on the beliefs of primitive people of thousands of years ago.

At the extreme opposite of theologians' simple notions we find scientists' complex notions, which have caused repercussions from religious institutions. Even up to several hundred years ago, scientists were tortured or killed

"Science is the light illuminating roads towards the reality, The end of road not led by science is dark."

Hacı Bektaş-i Veli, the great Turkish thinker, 1248

if their findings disagreed with their culture's religious beliefs. For example, once upon a time theologians held that the earth was motionless at the center of the universe. In 1600 Dominican friar Giordano Bruno expressed his scientific idea that the earth orbited the sun. He was burned at the stake. In the 1930s the Catholic Church denied French Jesuit priest Pierre Teilhard de Chardin, who was also a philosopher and paleontologist, the right to publish his now classical nonfiction book, *The Phenomenon of Man.* He was denied publication because it included the concept of evolution. The book was published after he died in 1955. God beliefs have a long history of conflicting with scientific findings and theories.

Scientists' complex notions emerge from their ongoing task of accumulating and updating information on our origins and environment. While theologians can quickly tell us what it's all about, scientists cannot. Scientists are aware there is always much more to know and they keep on accumulating information. (The word "science" comes from the Latin verb "to know.")

For centuries scientists have been accumulating information on all aspects of the environment in order to know all they can about life. In 1828 German chemist Friedreich Wohler surprised his contemporaries when he created organic matter needed for the emergence of life from a mixture of oxygen, carbon, nitrogen, and hydrogen. In 1957 biochemists Sydney W. Fox and biochemist A. I. Oparin, independently from each other, created dead molecular entities, which exhibited interactions that had been considered only possible by living entities. Scientists began referring to Oparin's and Fox's molecules as *pre-life* entities. Their research suggests that such pre-life entities' interactions were precursors to the living cell's interactions. However, no matter how much information scientists have gathered about the dead entities that create and maintain life, the phenomenon of the emergence of life remains a mystery. But it is the nature of scientists to keep on trying to decipher the mystery.

Most of us prize scientific achievements, but scientists generally annoy, bore, or frustrate us with their expanding, complex information. In addition, scientific information comes to us in fragments. Scientists tend to focus on particular fields of study. Physicists focus on our evolution from subatomic entities and atoms; chemists focus on our chemical makeup; biologists focus on our evolution from the living cell; anthropologists focus on our evolution from the apes; and psychologists focus on why we feel, think, and behave so ape-like. But there has been a trend in merging scientific fields to create such studies as biochemistry, sociobiology, astrophysics, and others. Although most of us cannot understand scientists' information, nevertheless, they are the reason we have some facts on "what it's all about."

Perhaps a new field of science such as "existology" would help us perceive the genetic-environment complex of all entities. Existology would link all fields of science, giving us a glimpse of the multi-dimensional interactions that create existence. This would help us perceive the inseparability of dead and living interactions creating existence. It would help us perceive that our species and all living entities are unified by the G-E reciprocity. In other words, existology would unify interactions traditionally considered unrelated to each other. Existology would make the interactions of electrons, atoms, chemicals, insects, apes, Jesus, Marx, Darwin, Picasso, and so on relevant to each other.

Summary

It is speculated that barely existing microcosmic entities were ejected from a domain of "nothingness" into existence by the interactions of timespace, and that some of these entities were encoded with a general blueprint of how they were to evolve life. It is not known if dead entities' interactions were once living interactions, but we know that living interactions were once dead interactions. It can be further speculated that living entity's interactions, from the first bacteria's potential to produce oxygen through to our species' potential to evolve humanness, emerged from the genetic-environment complex. The reciprocity of genes and the environment continuously shaped new interactions. This was the creation of countless of different species.

For now we may say that our species' genetic complex holds "inside" what is "outside." What is in the genes is the microcosmic potential of what creates the macrocosms. We are part of that evolution from "nothing to something." Teilhard de Chardin explains: "To decipher man is essentially to try to find out how the world was made..." The authors are two more in what seems to be a *Don Quixote de La Mancha* quest.

Although dead entities are fundamental to the interactive potential of life, in the next chapter credit is given to animal nature. For it was in the evolution of animal nature that many of the ways of how we feel, think, believe, and behave took shape.

2

Animal Nature

The reciprocity between genes and the environ-
ment created an infinite pool of animal interactions
for the foundation of our species' interactions.

A glimpse at animal nature's interactions gives us a reality check of the precursors of our interactions (feelings, behaviors, beliefs, etc.). For our Homo sapient species evolved from the animal kingdom and is classified in the Order Primates and the Subfamily Homininae, which includes African apes.

The Nature of Animals' Interactions

Animal nature as a whole is an infinite pool of interactions, but each animal species is genetically programmed with fixed interactions creating a stagnant potential. This means that all members of a species interact much the same way generation after generation for the duration of the species.

For example, millions of years ago a bug species was triggered to create something round and to know the advantage of something round. A bug of this species, millions of years later, lays her eggs in dung and rolls it into a ball many times her size and weight; she knows she can easily move it. The bug did not have to learn any of the skills involved in making her nest mobile. The environment triggers what she knows from her genetically programmed potential just

Scientists have classified the diversity of life into five kingdoms: Monera (bacteria), Fungi (mushrooms, mold, yeast, etc.), Protista (single-celled creatures invisible to the naked eye), Plantae (plants), and Animalia (animals). The authors refer to the Animalia Kingdom as "**animal nature.**"

as it triggered the same know-how from bugs of her species millions of years ago.

Animal nature's rigidity and stagnancy of interactions exists in all animals, but is most obvious in primitive species. Evolutionary biologist Ernst Mayr explains: "In most invertebrates the parents die before their offspring hatch from the eggs. The entire behavioral information available to the newborn is contained in its DNA" (Mayr, 2001, 253). In other words, newborns believe, know, feel, and do what the oldest members of the species believe, know, and do. Both old and young interact the same way the species has been interacting for millions of years. The more primitive the species the less it doubts on how to interact in the environment.

Mammals exhibit more variety in their interactions than primitive animals do, but they still interact within their species' genetically programmed potential. In advanced mammals such as dolphins, elephants, and apes some modeling from parents or older siblings is needed to trigger or turn on necessary genetic interactions in the young. For instance, baby chimps are triggered to observe their mothers and learn from them how to get termites from a termite nest without disturbing the nest. This is not an easy skill to learn. It takes the baby chimps some practice to learn to choose an appropriate stick, insert it into the nest and give it just the right twist in order not to knock off the clinging tasty morsels.

Although advanced animals exhibit flexibility in their interactions (i.e., they can be trained to perform programmed behaviors at specific times), they are restricted to their species' programmed interactions. Thus, no young chimp in the wild will develop a significantly better way to get more termites from a nest than how its species has done for eons. A wolf pack's hierarchy of social inequality will not change into social equality. And, an adult wise chimp will never carve out one commandment for his group. In other words, members of animal species live and die never deviating significantly from interactions that were encoded in their species' genetics millions of years ago. All animals are born with little or no doubt in how they are to respond to the environment.

Although stagnant potentials are characteristic of animal species, even a glimpse at various animals' interactions of technology, organization, communication, and caring will show the incredible interactive potential of the whole of animal nature. This incredible interactive whole seems to be encoded in our species' genetic potential. (This will be discussed in a later chapter.) We call attention to technology, organization, and communication because, according to ethologists, these primitive animal instincts are at the roots of our cultures and civilizations. We, as a species, especially glorify technology, organization, and communication and have markedly expanded these interactions beyond any animal species' potential. In fact, our expansion of these interactions is a dominant indicator of our cultures and civilizations' evolution.

We also call attention to animal nature's caring because our species evolved genetically programmed with animal nature's whole range of caring. (Animal nature's caring does not have the broad range of interactions found in technology, communication, and organization.) A noticeable level of caring indicating altruism for others evolved with the advanced mammals. Therefore, as a recent arrival to animal nature, we, as a species, are genetically programmed to interact dominantly with the advanced animals' level of caring. Even in this brief glimpse at some of animal nature's interactions it is easy to recognize the genetic roots of our species' interactive potential.

Technology

The ways spiders, termites, and honeybees construct their homes and other things to cope with their environment are some of animal nature's best examples of technology.

The Nephila claipes spider weaves its web with stretchable and waterproof silk strands. According to scientists, the web's silk strands are finer and lighter than our hair, but ounce-for-ounce are stronger than our steel. The strength and toughness of this spider's silk is unmatched by any of our synthetic fibers.

However, scientists have matched the technological principle of this spider's silk strands. They have created steel "strands" (cables) that have the strength and toughness to hold up tons of steel and concrete as in the construction of San Francisco's Golden Gate Bridge.

Another spider species called the "giant trap-door spider" exhibits its technological know-how in building a trap door to capture its meals. The spider selects a site, digs a round hole, lines it methodically with silk, and then makes a round lid of soil particles held together with silk. The spider has the common sense to make a silken hinge and attach additional gravel to the underside of the lid to make it heavy. *Voila!* The lid drops quickly, trapping an insect that wanders into the spider's hole. This spider's genetically encoded technology was passed on to our species' genetics, and we have expanded it in many forms and for many uses.

In the world of insects, termites seem to be architectural masters. The bellicose termite species evolved knowing how to construct multistory nests with indoor fungi gardens, nurseries, and built-in air conditioning systems. For millions of years the species has used dried mud for its building material because it evolved knowing that dried mud absorbs moisture. The dried mud absorbs moisture as it goes through the top of the nest, and the evaporation cools the bottom levels. This creates a flow of fresh air that maintains a comfortable temperature (30 to 31 degrees centigrade) throughout the massive nest. The nests have up to six-foot-deep cellars and a cluster of towers sometimes as high as twenty feet. Such technology would require superior thinking by members of our species, yet it is encoded in tiny blind insects. If our builders could mimic such structures in relationship to the size of man, they would end up with nearly a mile-high building. Nevertheless, this genetic potential is being triggered in our species. Our builders have already constructed a skyscraper in Dubai, United Arab Emirates that is a little over one-half a mile tall (2,717 feet or 828 m).

The magnetic termites evolved knowing how to use sun power to warm their huge nests. They build rectangular wedged-shaped nests, measuring about fifteen feet high and about ten feet wide, with a thin edge at the top aligned to point north and south. In this way, both sides of the tall nests get the full warmth of the sun as it rises and sets. Similar instincts were triggered from members of our species thousands of years ago in Egypt, and today's architects continue to design structures in relation to how sunlight will filter into rooms.

Honeybees' technology is evident in their hive construction. These insects evolved knowing six-sided-shaped cells fit together neatly and easily in confined places. Each cell (room) of their hive is a hexagon with cell walls meeting at exactly 120 degrees. The construction of their hive seems to require the mathematical and technological skills of an engineer. Their technology also includes a system of air conditioning using evaporation. The honeybees bring in droplets of water and make puddles around the cells containing the larvae, which are sensitive to overheating. In teams, they fan the water with enough force to create a cool, light breeze as the water evaporates. Their fanning maintains the temperature around the cells at about 35 degrees centigrade and removes stale air from the hive.

Having briefly explored some of animal nature's primitive technological interactions, it is important to remember that dead entities' interactions are at the foundation of these animal interactions. How else would animals "know" about heating, cooling, condensation, and geometric patterns? Most of us are ignorant about primitive creatures' vast technological know-how. Yet, much of what our specialists do in technology is because these primitive creatures' interactions are encoded in our species' genetics.

Organization

Drs. Bert Hölldobler and Edward O. Wilson's ant studies (1990) indicate that ants' interactions make them the social masters of the insect world. They evolved with the common sense to have well-disciplined cultures, which includes being neat, clean, and orderly. Their cooperative livelihood depends on a high level of social organization.

Ant species manifest a collectivity of interactions resulting in different organized lifestyles. Even the few examples given here show that social insects' interactions were the prelude to many of our cultural interactions.

For example, some ant species have been observed to interact as farmers, *vaqueros* (cowboys, cowmen), and slave owners. Farmer ants live deeply underground, grow fungi for food in gardens and know when to harvest it. The species that interacts as vaqueros herd their "cows" (aphids or plant lice) and transport them to better plants for grazing when necessary. Yes, the ants also "milk" them. They extract nectar from these insects by stroking them with their antennae. In contrast to these ants' seemingly cooperative and tranquil cultured life, there are ants that violently take other ants as slaves. These aggressive "slave owner" ants evolved with the potential for chemical warfare. They spew out chemicals at their prey to confuse and kill them. Then they kidnap their victims' fertilized eggs. Ants hatching from these captive eggs become enslaved domestic workers for the slave owner ants. The slaves clean and take care of their oppressors' baby ants never knowing that their work helps perpetuate the killing and enslavement of their kind. The programmed instincts of both ant species maintain their reciprocal relationship. Similar genetic interactions created the relationship between European and African peoples. Throughout the ages, animals' social interactions have been evident in the various lifestyles of our species and continue to be evident.

Hierarchies are animal nature's organized inequality. In a hierarchy, one animal or a few animals have a "chosen few" status over other members of their colony, flock, troop, pack, etc. This means there is a "top rooster," "top baboon," "top dog," and so on of a group. The top animal can slime, slobber, peck, claw, kick, grope, or bite all others of the group without consequence. Top animals' aggressive behaviors ensure their status, which gets them the best food, best sleeping or nesting places, and best mates. Those at the bottom of the group's hierarchy suffer from limited food, limited social interactions, and overall limited benefits.

For example, once the hierarchy is organized in a chicken coop, the rooster and top chicken peck on all other chickens. Only the rooster can peck the top chicken, and only the rooster and top chicken can peck on the second highest chicken. The ranking goes on throughout the flock to the bottom chicken. Every chicken in the coop knows who it has to respect or fear as well as who has to respect and fear it. The rooster and top chickens are entitled to the best benefits of coop life. The bottom chickens look and behave sickly because they are pecked by most and get to peck only the ground. Coop life is painful and stressful for low-status chickens.

It is impossible for most low-status animals to overcome their lowly status because they are genetically programmed to accept it. Whether an animal is aware or unaware that it is being exploited, it suffers. For example, a team of medical scientists led by a psychologist found that low-status monkeys had high levels of stress hormones and their cells' immunity was functioning at low levels.

Animal hierarchies or pecking orders are of special interest to social scientists because social hierarchies are dominant in the organization of our species' cultures. As it is in animal nature, our culture's lower status groups tend to have more stress-related illnesses, injuries, and social interactive difficulties. (In the United States these groups' illnesses and social difficulties are blamed on race or on foreign ethnicity rather than on low social statuses brought about by the culture's racism.)

Animal nature's interactions of organization created a strong genetic foundation for our species to interact collectively in cultures.

Communication

Honeybees are animal nature's masters of communication because their waggle dance is identified as "the closest approach known in the animal kingdom to a true symbolic language" (Wilson, 1984, 18). Their "symbolic language" indicates that complex communication was in primitive animals millions of years before the primates evolved.

A worker bee performs the waggle dance inside the hive after scouting for resources. With wing vibrations and other body movements, she communicates to her attentive hive mates where to find nectar, water, mud, and possible new home sites. Her waggle dance gives them an estimate of the distance and how far left or right of the sun to fly when leaving the hive to find sources of food. With such communication, "members of the hive can harvest nectar and pollen from flowers three miles or more from the hive" (Ibid.). Their communication indicates a high level of awareness and identification of the environment as well as excellent recall of immediate visual spatial memory and visual sequential memory. Educational psychologists evaluate these skills in children to determine their intellectual potential. Honeybees would score better in some of these skills than most of us would.

Caring for "Our Kind"

Animal nature evolved a vast range of caring, from individualism, or caring for only one's self…to caring for the welfare of others perceived as one's own kind. Caring for those perceived as one's own kind is the ultimate level of caring in animal nature.

Animal nature's most limited level of caring, caring for only one's self, is found in primitive animals such as slugs and flies. Parental caring is nonexistent—a mother lays her eggs and simply swims, crawls, flies, or slithers away. Each baby creature that makes it out of its cocoon or egg is immediately in charge of its own safety and needs. At this primitive level of caring, it is a "survival-of-the-fittest world." The more primitive the creature, the more rigid and limited are its caring interactions. This is the case no matter how advanced the creature may be in communication, technology, and organization.

Social insects' caring is more advanced than it is in other insects, but their actions still show the limitation of their programmed caring instincts. Honeybees' seemingly cooperative lifestyle involves limited caring for the welfare of members of the same hive. For example, when the queen no longer needs drones (males), a group of workers perform their patriotic duty by kicking the drones out of the hive to starve to death. The time also comes when the queen starts to kill "babies" that can become queens. Wasps also show a limited degree of caring for the welfare of their babies. A worker wasp might bite off the tail of a baby wasp to feed it to a nearby hungry baby wasp. Ants of a certain species also show limited caring for their babies. The babies are served as food to an invited guest in exchange for its sweet feces. The adult ants purposely bring a moth in its larva stage into the nest to leisurely eat the colony's baby ants. As the larva devours the babies, adult ants enjoy the larva's feces. Most of us may think of such primitive animals' caring as "real animal." However, variations of such primitive levels of limited caring exist in our species. For example, the queen bee's deadly, selfish instincts have been triggered in our species for thousands of years in members of royal families such as those of England. Family members in line for royalty were known to murder each other in order to hasten their turn as king or queen.

From animal nature's most limited level of caring, we move on to its ultimate level of caring for the welfare of others found in mammals. Caring at this level extends to those perceived as of their kind (one's own kind).

Protecting members of one's group, pack, troop, or herd is a form of advanced caring. This level of caring is observed in a troop of baboons as it walks in open country. The mature males position themselves in front and at the flanks of the group in order to be the first to meet an attack. The very young and the females are positioned to walk in the center of the group. The troops' young males instinctively imitate the adult males' communication and organization in protecting the troop. Similarly, in an elephant herd, blood- and non-blood-related members organize themselves to protect members of their herd, especially the calves, from attacks. Members of the herd share responsibilities in caring for the safety of the calves by "baby-sitting."

Sharing food with one's kind is also advanced caring. African wild dogs' food sharing is a dominant trait in caring for the welfare of the pack, especially for the pups. For example, after a hunt the dogs share the kill back at the den. They regurgitate meat for pups and for adult dogs left behind as caretakers. When the pups are old enough to go with the hunting group, the adult dogs let the pups rush up to the kill and be the first to eat. The pups are the pack's top priority of concern. The adults eat the remains, if any, or return to the hunt. (This is unlike lions and most other animals where the animals at the top of the group's hierarchy eat first and the most. Their caring is markedly limited in comparison to the African wild dogs' caring.) Ethologists have observed that these caring dogs' sharing extends to disabled adult members of their pack. In one observation a lame dog arrived after all the meat had been eaten. The dog went around as if begging until a dog regurgitated some meat for him. In this species, a dog exhibiting individualism, selfishness, and greediness would be a sick dog and would probably be banned from the pack. The pack's altruism indicates that for them it is not a dog-eat-dog world, but an advanced level of caring for their kind.

Vampire bats also exhibit food sharing by regurgitating blood to bats that did not get their daily consumption. A five-year observation of bats documented that 70 percent of bat regurgitation was between mothers and their pups. The rest of the regurgitations were by adult females feeding pups other than their own. They also gave blood to related adult females as well as to non-related females. Sharing blood is crucial among vampire bats because they will die if they fail to feed for two consecutive nights. Getting blood is not always easy, especially for the young because it takes practice to make a quick and painless bite on the host animal. Food sharing is a form of charity that most of us think of as an ultimate level of caring for others, especially during holidays such as Thanksgiving and Christmas in the U.S.

Some mammalian species such as porpoises, dogs, and apes can perceive and care for others that are not of their species. Such caring is observed when a dog identifies itself as a protector or caretaker of a member of our species. It identifies the person as a member of its pack. This is apparent in the relationship between a police officer and his police dog. The dog identifies the police officer as its leader and other uniformed officers as members of its pack. Female dogs are usually not used because in running after a suspect it seems that maternal caring is triggered. A female dog tends to divide her attention between the chase and checking that her partner (police officer) is safe and keeping up. Caring for others perceived as one's own kind is animal nature's most advanced and ultimate level of caring.

Since animal nature's ultimate level of caring evolved with the advanced mammals, it has a short evolutionary history. This could be why our species evolved dominantly with advanced animals' level of caring. Animal nature's advanced level of caring feels so natural for most of us that we are awed by apes in zoos exhibiting their level of caring. But apes' caring should no longer perplex us. Instead of screaming, "My god, they behave just like people," we should know they are simply behaving like the advanced caring animals that they are. By now, it should be common sense that it is not apes behaving like us, but us behaving like them. It is depressing to become aware that too many of us, in an eyeball-to-eyeball affair with an ape at the zoo, are as ignorant as the ape about our genetic relationship. Our species' inherited animal nature came with a diversity of caring levels ranging from the limited caring of primitive creatures to the advanced mammals' caring.

Sexuality

Heterosexuality, adultery, incest, and homosexuality are part of the animal kingdom's range of sexual activities.

Elaborate courting rituals for heterosexual lovers evolved in animal species. Animals' "song and dance" or *macho* toughness and feminine movements trigger appropriate responses from potential mates. Our species evolved with these interactions, and our environment triggers us to act similarly. We use enticing scents, seductive movements, and "preen" ourselves with all kinds of cosmetics and apparel to lure or seduce someone we find attractive. Our heterosexual mating rituals can range from the tender love and passion that occurs between a Don Juan and a feminine woman to the robotic passion of a rooster mounting a chicken. No matter how females and males entice each other for intercourse, heterosexual instincts are triggered in common animals and in us primarily to perpetuate life.

Our adultery activities are also part of animal nature. In some ape species only the alpha male of the group fertilizes all the females of his group. Although the alpha male of a group guards his females closely, they still commit adultery. Females willfully engage in sexual activities with other males when the alpha male is sleeping, eating, or fighting. They are instinctively creating genetic diversity for the troop's longevity, according to ethologists.

Incest and rape are also inherited animal instincts. Incest occurs in apes, but they have some instincts to prevent it. For example, in chimpanzee groups the maturing males are instinctively pushed out of the family group. Since maturing females are not pushed out of the family group, incest does occur with most ape species. Similar to ape groups, our cultures try to prevent incest with taboos and punishment.

Homosexuality is also an animal instinct. Some apes are genetically prone to interact as homosexuals, and their environment activates this instinct. Scientists find that homosexual interactions are triggered in bonobo apes to reduce their stress and aggressiveness. This animal instinct is in our species and is activated in some members of our species. Most people consider homosexuality as a bizarre and deviant behavior. Yet, unlike incest, homosexuality is not perceived as an animal instinct that should *not* be reinforced in Homo sapiens.

Cultures should realize that it is bizarre to program their citizens to perceive the partnership of homosexuals the same as the partnership of heterosexuals. Cultures that are making the partnership of homosexuals legally the same as heterosexual couples are not only causing animosity against homosexuals, but they are also creating a berserk cultural practice. This is not to say that homosexuals don't deserve equal rights, but they should not be made to appear as normal heterosexual couples. This is because, while heterosexuality perpetuates life, homosexuality serves to limit the perpetuation of life. Homosexuality might also serve to eventually eliminate one of the genders (female or male).

Since homosexuality is a genetic instinct in our species, the environment can activate it in some members of our species. Therefore, similar to bonobo apes, homosexuals do not see using a rectum as a vagina as bizarre sexual behavior. Similar to bonobo apes, they cannot identify their sexuality as being deviant. Some day genetic engineering will be able to inactivate such genes causing deviant sexual behaviors in members of our species. If not, the diseases and social problems they contribute to our struggling species will only increase.

It is difficult for most of us to understand that these and many other animal interactions were not only precursors to our species' interactions, but that they are also programmed in our genetics.

A Genetic Belief-Reality

The environment creates every new species by triggering the cell complex. It is in response to the environment that species selectivity is triggered; the environment selects the species.

All species evolve from the reciprocal relationship between the environment and the cell complex. This relationship makes it possible for members of a species to be born knowing how to interact with the environment. After all, every animal is a creation of the environment. The relationship gives the animal a packaged "ready-set way" to interact with the environment. This is what the authors refer to as the animal's *belief-reality*. It is a creature's way of coping with the environment. All animals have in their belief-reality the interactions that enable them to interact as members of a particular species.

In primitive species, every animal is born with its species' entire DNA programmed pool of interactions in their belief-reality. All of a species' interactions are in each animal's belief-reality ready to be triggered by the environment. Therefore, there is little to zero interactive variation among members of primitive animal species. We recall what Dr, Mayr said about primitive animals: "The entire behavioral information available to the newborn is contained in its DNA" (Mayr, 2001, 253).

Advanced animal species are also born with their species entire DNA programmed pool of interactions. However, unlike primitive animals, advanced animals do not have their species' entire pool of interactions in their belief-reality. Advanced animals seem to have progressively evolved *without* their species' entire DNA programmed pool of interactions in their belief-reality. A baby of an advanced species, for example, is born with its species' entire interactions encoded in its genome. Yet, this does not mean that the baby's belief-reality is ready to interact with its species' entire pool of genetic interactions. However, as the baby interacts with the environment genes are activated from its species' programmed interactions. These interactions are added to the baby's belief-reality. In other words, the more the baby interacts with the environment, the more interactions will be activated from its species' genome. In this way the baby's belief-reality to cope with the environment expands.

Similarly, things and events in the maturing baby's environment can deactivate interactions in its belief-reality. For example, certain interactions that helped it cope with the environment as a baby will not be needed as it matures. In time interactions such as seeking its mother for nourishment and protection will be deactivated. Eventually, the animal has a packaged belief-reality to interact with the environment as a mature member of its species. Similar to how changes occur in the belief-reality of a baby as it progresses to maturity, changes occur in a mature individual's belief reality as it continues to interact with environment. Its *individualized* belief reality continues to change.

The more interactions that can be triggered from a species' genetically programmed potential the more options its members have in dealing with the environment. In other words, the broader the species' potential, the more the environment (other animals, trainers, etc.) can activate or deactivate specific interactions.

A police dog is a good example of how an advanced animal's interactions can be modified to make it interact very differently than other dogs. Yet, no matter how awesomely a police dog performs its skills, it interacts with police officers with its *individualized* belief-reality. The dog's belief-reality was modified to identify policemen in uniform as members of its pack. It does not think of the runaway suspect as a criminal, but as a despised creature who is not of its pack. In short, the police dog performs its major interactions in the line of duty because its environment, trainers, police partner and other police officers, modified its individualized belief reality to cope with a "different" environment.

The phenomenon of an individualized belief-reality is especially apparent in our species. Members of our species have a vast genetic pool of interactions from which the environment can activate or deactivate. In other words, the environment, through research, experiments, and so on can activate or deactivate genes through "learning." Therefore, there are marked differences in perceptions, conceptualizations, altruism, and so on among members of our species.

The more limited creatures' interactions forming their belief-realities, the more righteous they are about their interactions (awareness, beliefs, perceptions, etc.). They have little doubt about what they believe is the right thing to do. Poet Wislawa Szymborska captures animals' programmed righteousness in one of her poems from *View With a Grain of Sand.*

> The Buzzard never says it is to blame.
> The panther wouldn't know what scruples mean.
> When the piranha strikes, it feels no shame.
> If snakes had hands, they'd claim their hands were clean.
> A jackal doesn't understand remorse
> Lions and lice don't waver in their course.
> Why should they, when they know they're right? ...
> On this third planet of the sun among the signs of bestiality
> a clear conscience is Number One.

Summary

Animal nature is a vast range of interactions. However, each animal interacts with its species' stagnant interactive potential. The more primitive the species, the more narrow and stagnant is its interactive potential. The interactions of technology, communication, and organization emerged in primitive creatures over 250 million years ago, and they are most glorified and expanded by our species. (Most of these primitive interactions remained latent throughout later animal evolution until the emergence of our species.) Altruism, on the other hand, was late in developing. It was not until the emergence of mammals that significant levels of caring emerged. The advanced animals evolved animal nature's ultimate level of caring for those perceived as of *one's own kind*. This is the dominant level of caring that our species emerged with.

It is impossible for scientists to become fully aware of animals' vast range of interactions forming animal nature. However, even the range that scientists are aware of is staggering. The amazing thing about animal nature is that it shaped and created an enormous pool of living interactions in its reciprocity with the environment. This vast interactive pool created the foundation of our species' enormous potential.

3

Our Last Animal Ancestors

"My dear, descended from the apes!

Let us hope it is not true..."

Praying Helped

In 1859, when news of Charles Darwin's book, *On the Origin of Species by Means of Natural Selection,* reached the wife of the Bishop of Worchester in England it is said she whined: "My dear, descended from the apes! Let us hope it is not true, but if it is, let us pray that it will not become generally known." Well, it was true. But praying helped, because for over 150 years most of us have remained as ignorant as apes about our close relationship. Now, scientists tell us our Homo sapient species is 99.8 percent genetically related to chimpanzees and that this makes us as close to chimpanzees as horses are to zebras. But if this is so, why are we so much smarter and better looking?

Although chimpanzees' genetics and our genetics are almost identical, the evolution of our species' last animal ancestors reveals how we got so much wiser and better looking.

Our species' ancestral hominid (wise ape) species split from the chimpanzee branch about 7 million years ago. The authors refer to hominids as "wise apes" to keep in mind they were still ape species, still animal species. However, the evolution of our species' wise ape lineage was different from that of chimpanzees. Evolution created little changes in the chimpanzee species in comparison to changes made in our species' wise ape lineage. Today's chimpanzees have almost the same appearance and interact with the same belief-reality as did their ancestors of millions of years ago. (A *belief-reality* is a creature's "ready-set way" to interact with the environment.) In contrast, the emergence of our species involved some six wise ape species. Each wise ape species evolved less ape-like and a little smarter. It took about 6 million years for our species' wise ape lineage to evolve the genetic foundation for the emergence of our Homo sapient species. (Other wise ape species not of our lineage also evolved during the evolutionary era of our species' wise ape lineage.)

Although our species' wise ape lineage is far from complete, there is ample evidence indicating it evolved from particular wise ape species. Evolutionary biologist Ernst Mayr bluntly explains, "No well-informed person any longer questions the descent of man from primates and more specifically from apes" (Mayr, 2001, 235). What is questioned is—which wise ape species are of our species' lineage, and when did our species evolve from its last wise ape ancestor? The intent here is to show that it took a series of wise ape species' genetic changes to evolve our species. Each wise ape species in our species' lineage evolved with a more advanced level of intelligence than its predecessor and less ape-looking.

Our Wise Ape Lineage

The emergence of our wise ape ancestors took millions of years. To begin with, paleontologists think there was a transitional species between monkeys and apes some 16 million years ago known as Proconsul. This species' bones indicated its transitional status. Its anklebones were like those of monkeys, but its first toe was like an ape's toe, and its pelvic area resembled a combination of monkey-ape anatomy. Scientists speculate that it took some 10 million years for apes to evolve from the Proconsul species. Once ape evolution separated from monkey evolution, several ape branches (gorillas, chimpanzees, etc.) emerged. DNA experts estimate that our wise ape genetic lineage branched off from the chimpanzee genetic branch about 7 million years ago.

Our species' wise ape lineage of some six species went through an evolution that created a potential that progressively advanced with the emergence of each ancestral wise ape species. In other words, each ancestral wise ape species evolved genetically "smarter" with a greater potential of awareness, feelings, thoughts, and behaviors than its predecessor had. This unique 6 million-year evolution of a series of wise ape species produced our species. Such an evolution did not occur with the chimpanzee or any other ape species.

Although the apish look lessened and interactions expanded with the evolution of each wise ape species in our lineage, all our ancestral wise ape species were animal species. Their interactions never left the realm of animal nature. Each species' interactions remained stagnant for the duration of the species. Just as every spider of a species spins the same kind of web and every bird of a species builds the same kind of nest, every wise ape's interactions were limited to its species' programmed instincts. When a wise ape species evolved to do something in a certain way, all its members did it the same way throughout the species' life span. When members of the species evolved believing in a certain way, they believed that way for the life span of the species. Although each wise ape species in our lineage got smarter, each species lived out its life span with the same feelings, thoughts, and behaviors that it had evolved with because they were animals.

Scientists continue to look for more evidence on our species' wise ape lineage. As of this time, fossil evidence indicates that the following are most likely to have been in our species' lineage: Sahelanthropus tchadensis, Ardipithecus ramidus, Australopithecus afarensis, Homo habilis, Homo erectus, and Homo sapiens idaltu. The Ardipithecus and H. idaltu species are relatively new discoveries. Ardipithecus bones were first discovered in 1994, and it was identified as our species' oldest ancestral wise ape species when analysis of the species' bones was completed in 2009. H. idaltu skulls where found in 1997, and in 2003 the species was introduced as most likely our species' last wise ape ancestor. Archaic sapiens and Neanderthal species are discussed because of their interest to Germanic ethnicities, but these species have been genetically ruled out from our species' ancestral lineage. The following section goes through the six wise ape species included in our species' lineage.

Sahelanthropus tchadensis Species

Some scientists believe Sahelanthropus tchadensis might be the transitional species that emerged when the environment triggered a major genetic change in some chimpanzees and began the evolution of our species' wise ape lineage. Remains of this species (a skull, jaw fragments, and some teeth) were found in Chad, Africa and were estimated as being over 6 million years old. The remains indicate that they are of a transitional species between common apes and our ancestral wise ape species because they appear to have both chimpanzee and wise ape characteristic traits. For example, scientists determined that the hole where the spinal cord enters the skull indicates that the species' standing and walking posture was more erect than that of chimps. Some scientists, however, question if this is the species that branched off from the chimpanzee.

Ardipithecus ramidus Species

Scientists are much more in agreement about this species being of our lineage. The skeletal remains of this wise-ape species were of "Ardi," a 110-pound, 4-foot tall female found in Ethiopia, Africa. Her species roamed the woodlands walking upright about 4.4 million years ago. The development of this species' arms and legs indicates its members spent most of the time on the ground. Yet, they could climb carefully along tree branches on all fours. An analysis of Ardi's tooth enamel suggests a diet of fruit, nuts, leaves and invertebrates. Ardi's hand and wrist were a mix of primate traits and a few new ones. She had short palms and flexible fingers indicating she could manipulate objects better than a chimp can and that she could carry things while walking. Her pelvis and hip indicate gluteal muscles were positioned to walk upright. Her feet were rigid enough for walking and had a grasping big toe still useful for climbing. By studying Ardi, paleoanthropologists believe that the species' brain may have already been positioned to expand interactions involving visual and spatial perception. Details of her skull indicate her brain was positioned in a way similar to our species' brain, but only one-fifth the size. Paleoanthropologists believe Ardi represents a genus ancestral to Australopithecus because some of Ardi's primitive features appear more modern in Australopithecus, which lived a million years after Ardi's species.

Wise ape species' cerebrum expanded greatly during a short evolutionary span. Three million years ago the Australopithecus species evolved with a cranial capacity of about 400 cubic centimeters. Two million years later, Homo erectus species evolved with a cranial capacity of about 1,000 cubic centimeters. One million years later our Homo sapiens species evolved with a cranial capacity of about 2,000 cubic centimeters.

(E.O. Wilson 2000, 548).

Australopithecus afarensis Species

A minor genetic change in Ardi seems to have evolved this species. In anthropological circles, there is a popular story of an A. afarensis family out for a walk. The story is based on 3.2-million-year-old footprints. The prints are of a family walking with the male ahead of his mate. Her prints indicate she usually stepped inside the male's larger footprints. (At this period of our wise ape ancestry males were much larger than females.) A third set of much smaller prints indicates that a child darted in and out from the larger footprints, stopping at one point to face west and then turning to follow its parents. Traces of this ancestral walk were discovered by a group of anthropologists led by Mary Leaky. The walk took place on freshly fallen volcanic ash in Africa, and the family's footprints were preserved as the ash turned into volcanic rock.

Scientists detected markings inside A. afarensis skulls indicating the development of a change in blood flow for upright walking. They believe walking upright created new blood vessels from the heart to the brain, which helped cool the brain. This facilitated the enlargement of the brain and freed the hands for complex activities. Upright walking also took less energy than quadruple walking. Bipedal walking was a huge factor in this species' advancement in its interactive potential. Some scientists identify the evolution of walking on two legs as the cornerstone of interactions leading to the creation of our species.

Chimpanzees use rocks and sticks as tools. So it is likely that members of the A. afarensis species also used such objects as tools and for more complex activities.

The Homo habilis Species

A genetic change in A. afarensis evolved the Homo habilis species about 2.5 million years ago. Homo habilis was the first of our ancestral wise ape species to have evolved with the technological instincts to create and use stone tools. Thus, this ancestor was honored with the name Homo habilis, which means handy man in Latin. Although some chimpanzees use leaves, twigs, or rocks as tools, no ape had ever created stone tools. The Homo habilis species created simple flake and pebble stone tools. These early tools were so primitively made that an untrained observer would not identify them as tools. Also, the same tool-making traits were programmed in all members for the duration of the species. Anthropologists found that the species' tools were all made as if by one individual. Throughout Homo habilis' existence of nearly one million years, the species could only make stone tools of flakes and pebbles. In other words, the species' tool-making interactions were stagnant for the duration of its life span. This also suggests that its other interactions were just as rigidly and narrowly programmed. Nevertheless, males of the Homo habilis species walked upright carrying their stone tools. It is likely that some males would accidentally bang their kneecaps as they walked with stone tools in hand because of their long arms. From the Homo habilis species onward, each wise ape species' stone tools increased in complexity.

Stone tools have lasted for millions of years and can be scientifically dated. They are anthropologists' criteria for measuring wise ape species' advancements in interactions. Although tool technology indicates that each wise ape in our lineage was getting smarter, each species' interactions remained stagnant for the duration of the species.

Species' advancement in stone tools, however, indicated an overall advancement in their interactive potential. For example, according to paleoneurologists Dr. Dean Falk of the State University of New York and Dr. Phillip V. Tobias of the University of South Africa, the evolution of Homo habilis indicated more than the creation of stone tools. Studies on H. habilis skulls revealed markings in the cranium's inner surfaces indicating the physiological development of an area needed for speech. Scientists can only speculate if H. habilis had the potential for any degree of language. It is likely that members of the species communicated with varying grunts, gestures, and facial expressions.

The Homo erectus Species

It is believed Homo erectus (Homo rhodesiensis) evolved from the Homo habilis species about 1.6 million years ago. This species lived until as recently as 200,000 years ago in Africa and Asia.

This species' appearance and interactions varied markedly from previous ancestral wise ape species. Homo erectus men and women had larger brains and shorter arms than their Homo habilis ancestors. There was also a significant reduction of sexual dimorphism in the species. Size difference was like that between today's male and female chimpanzees. It was also the first wise ape species to evolve with the bony labyrinth of the inner ear (as in our species) needed for good bipedal balance. Therefore, it evolved with the potential to walk erect, so it was named Homo erectus.

Homo erectus species made significantly more advanced tools than had the Homo habilis species. H. erectus teardrop-shaped stone scrapers and axes could make deep cuts into meat. However, anthropologists' consensus is that "although style varied somewhat from area to area, the products [tools] were remarkably uniform regardless of where they were made"(Lewin, 1982). Their tools were the same not only from cave to cave, but also from Africa to Asia wherever Homo erectus species roamed. As expected of an animal species, the species' life span of some one million years began and ended with the same teardrop-shaped tools without separate handles.

Homo erectus members began cave life. This was another advancement in the species' potential in coping with the environment. This primitive form of community household life increased caring for the welfare of the family group. Personal relationships may have expanded because of living together in close quarters for long periods of time. For example, a deformed 400,000-year-old H. erectus skull found in Morocco, Africa suggests that a severely deformed adult (probably disabled) had not been abandoned or killed by his family or group, as many animal species instinctively abandon or kill deformed or unhealthy offspring. Instead, he or she was cared for and lived to adulthood. Since the male's main role was to find food away from the caves, such advanced caring was probably first triggered in females.

The Homo erectus species added meat and bone marrow to its diet in contrast to its ancestors' vegetarian diet. Meat eating put the species in competition with the big cats and other meat-eating animals. Researchers have found bones in caves with both big cats' teeth marks and Homo erectus' stone-tool cut marks. Sometimes the tool marks are over tooth marks, and sometimes the tooth marks are over tool cuts. However, indications are that H. erectus' hunt for meat was mostly for leftovers. Nevertheless, scavenging for meat was no doubt due to the species' advanced awareness of its environment. Besides its increased awareness for meat hunting, the species was also aware of taking care not to become meat for the big cats. Whatever meat H. erectus ate was raw because the species did not evolve with the potential to make or use fire. However, it did evolve with the potential to expand its living environment. Eating meat and having more body fat, thicker body hair, and erect posture made it possible for members of this species to walk out of fair-weather-chimpanzee environments. H. erectus members were the first to migrate out of Africa to Asia.

Just as with other wise ape species and all common animals, Homo erectus' interactions remained noticeably stagnant for the duration of the species. Although Homo erectus created more advanced tools than its predecessor's tools, had a larger brain, lived in caves and exhibited advanced caring for others, added meat to its diet, and walked out of the jungle with good posture and balance, it was still an animal species.

A Hypothetical Pre-Homo sapient species

At the time the authors were researching our species' anthropological evolution, most anthropologists believed that our Homo sapient species evolved from the Homo erectus species some 200,000 years ago. The authors' research, however, led them to believe that another wise ape species evolved from H. erectus and that our species emerged from this unknown wise ape species only about 65,000 years ago. In relation to other wise apes' longevity, this unknown wise ape species had a short life term prior to our species' emergence. The authors therefore call this hypothetical wise ape species *Pre-Homo sapiens.*

The authors' hypothesis on the existence of a Pre-Homo sapient species is based on the following reasons. Some bones found and dated to be between 200,000 and 70,000 years old were identified as belonging to our Homo sapient species. However, no evidence, such as tools, has been found from that era indicating our species' interactive potential had arrived. The authors speculate that the bones belonged to "Pre-Homo sapiens" and that the species' interactions were still those of an animal species. For example, anthropologists found evidence in Afro-Asia (in Israeli caves) indicating that Pre-Homo sapient ancestors made similar tools and butchered animals similarly to how other wise ape (hominid) species of that era did. (These other wise ape species, not of our lineage, were the Archaic sapient species and the Neanderthal species.) The tool-making ability of the hypothesized Pre-Homo sapient species indicates only a slight increment over the tool-making ability of its ancestor Homo erectus species, but no better than those of Archaic sapiens and Neanderthals. In other words, tools found of that era indicate they were made by wise ape species, which were still animal species.

There is also evidence indicating Pre-Homo sapiens lived in the same areas with these other wise ape species. Anthropologists have discovered several 92,000-year-old skeletal remains of Pre-Homo sapiens, 60,000-year-old remains of Neanderthals, and 45,000-year-old skulls of Archaic sapiens in the area of northeastern Africa. In other words, remains of these three wise ape species in the same area indicate they might have lived peacefully cheek-to-cheek, keeping to their own kind, without killing each other. This is similar to how various kinds of apes still live in the wild. (The peaceful neighborhoods changed when our Homo sapient species evolved about 65,000 years ago.)

Pre-Homo sapiens species' bones might have been identical to our species' bones, but its static interactions—no advancement in tools beyond other wise apes of the period and staying in Africa for the duration of its life span—refute the assumption that it was our Homo sapient species that emerged from Homo erectus some 200,000 years ago. We Homo sapiens are a much younger species than most anthropologists think we are.

The authors hypothesize that 65,000 to 70,000 years ago, in Africa and in Asia, the environment triggered the genes of some Pre-Homo sapient mothers to give birth to our Homo sapient species. (If this hypothesis proves correct, then both the African and Asian races form the genetic racial foundations of our species.) The genetic change might have been microscopic, but it unleashed an awesome cerebral interactive potential. Decades ago anthropologist Dr. Milford H. Wolpoff pointed out that exceptional increments in the type and range of interactions took place with the emergence of our species. There is no evidence of exceptional interactions prior to some 65,000 years ago.

Once our Homo sapient species evolved, its potential indicated a significant advancement of interactions beyond wise apes' interactions. Our species began designing and making different tools with handles and using fire. It began migrating to all livable land areas of earth. Its oldest stone tools–dated to be 45,000 years old–were found in Australia. These stone tools had markings indicating that our species had evolved with the potential to attach handles to their tools. It is as Wolpoff suggested, that thoughts and behaviors rather than the alignment of bones marked our species' emergence.

It seems that Mother Nature created an "interim" Pre-Homo sapiens species with something like a "time release" genetic potential. The species' brief existence could be considered the final touch that triggered our species' emergence.

Homo sapiens idaltu species

Some years after completing research on our species' ancestral wise ape lineage, the authors were pleasantly surprised by the discovery of the *Homo sapiens idaltu species* whose life span seems to match that of their hypothetical "Pre-Homo sapient" species. The Homo sapiens idaltu species' existence fills the gap in our species' evolution from 200,000 to some 65,000 years ago. The discovery of 160,000-year-old skulls of the Homo sapiens idaltu has led paleontologists to think that they belonged to a species of the era when the "transition from Pre-Humans [Homo sapiens idaltu] to modern humans [Homo sapiens] took place" (Wilford, 2003). But no matter what the species is called, the important point is that the discovery of idaltu skulls seems to be leading scientists to believe that it was not our species that evolved directly from H.

erectus, as most anthropologists have believed.

Unlike the authors, however, paleontologists are not saying that this newly discovered species was a wise ape (hominid) species (an animal species). But, since the skulls are dated 160,000 years old, and since tools between 200,000 and some 65,000 years ago still indicate the interactive potential of an animal species, we are left to believe that the Homo sapient idaltu species was still an animal species. The skull fossils were found in Africa in Ethiopia by Tim D. White's team of the University of California at Berkeley and were assigned to the new *Homo sapiens idaltu* species.

According to paleontologists, H. idaltu skulls indicated that these ancestors' features were much like our species' appearance, except for some features such as their wide-spaced eyes. In the article "Skulls Reveal Dawn of Mankind" published in *Nature*, 11 June 2003, anthropologists point out that the skulls' overall "morphology, size and facial robusticity" resemble "some Australian and Oceanic individuals." Their Australian appearance is not surprising because the Australian race retains much of our species' original appearance due to its long period of isolation on the island continent.

The authors speculate that H. idaltu evolved genetically from Homo erectus about 200,000 years ago in Africa and in Asia. Then about 65,000 years ago, there took place a genetic merger between African and Asian members of the H. idaltu species. Their merger might have changed only a gene or two. However, the genetic change evolved a species that was no longer restricted to animal evolution's restrictive potential. It seems to have unleashed a potential that had been accumulating in living entities over billions of years. In other words, our Homo sapient species evolved from H. idaltu's genetic changes some 65,000 years ago or less.

This could explain our species' large populations and early advanced accomplishments in the areas where Asian and African H. idaltu people met in southwest Asia to Afro-Asia. This might be why the Chinese, Indian, and Egyptian civilizations were the earliest manifestations of our species' interactive potential. These civilizations existed thousands of years before the Greek civilization.

The genetic interchange between Asian and African H. idaltu members seems to have been a huge variable in triggering interactions from our species' potential. The manifestation of our species' potential, as it was concentrated in southwest Asia and Afro-Asia, did not occur in areas of southern and eastern Africa as well as in Australia. In other words, the genetic changes that occurred from the merger of African and Asians H. idaltu did not reach these populations until thousands of years later. It seems that these populations lacked the genetic potential to increase their individualized belief-realities from our species' programmed interactions. In sharp contrast, the achievements in southwest Asia and Afro-Asia are evidence that a significant number of people of these areas during that period were able to increase their individualized belief-realities' potential. They were able to significantly expand their interactions with the environment.

Germanic Affinity to Neanderthals

For centuries European (white) racists rejected information pointing to our species' African origins. Then in 1856 the remains of a wise ape species were discovered in the Neander Valley of Germany. The species was named Neanderthal. The discovery of a wise ape species in Germany was a big boost for Europeans' notion of having separate genetic roots from the African race. European anthropologists all over the world were ecstatic because they immediately assumed that the European race had evolved from this wise ape species. By the 1900s they claimed Neanderthals' brains were larger than Homo sapiens' brains and that Neanderthals were physically superior. Thus, Roger Lewin wrote, "Anthropologists began to recognize the 'real' significance of the Neanderthals and placed them into human [Homo sapient] prehistory as directly ancestral to modern European people" (Lewin, 1988, 115). However, the German discovery of the wise ape species "ancestral to modern European people" was false. Molecular archaeologists have provided ample evidence that the Neanderthal wise ape species evolved from a genetic branch separate from our Homo sapient species' wise ape lineage 200,000 years ago.

The Neanderthal species' had an apish physiology and appearance. Paleontologists Dr. Philip Lieberman of Brown University and his colleagues identified the species' vocal tract as being like that of common apes. So, like all common apes, Neanderthals could breathe and drink at the same time without choking. They were hairy, large-browed, and more muscular than Homo sapiens.

Nevertheless, some anthropologists of Germanic cultures persist with the myth that the Neanderthal species, one way or another, is at the genetic foundation of the European race. For example, in the 1960s some European anthropologists insisted that if Europeans were not the sole direct descendants of the Neanderthal species then they were created from a genetic mixture of Neanderthals and Homo sapiens. These anthropologists use the term "hybridization," which implies that Europeans are descendants of a wise ape–Homo sapient mixture. However, in the event that perverted sexual intercourse occurred between Neanderthal members and Homo sapient members, it is improbable that a half-breed European baby would have resulted from the sexual perversion. Laboratory experiments show that embryos produced by interspecies fertilization do not develop. It would therefore be improbable for such half-breeds (animal/Homo sapient) to be "ancestral to modern European people."

Yet, today there are still many in the U.S. culture persisting in the belief that the Neanderthal species gave birth to the European race. It is not surprising that life-sized figures of the species were exhibited in the Museum of Natural History's Hall of Human Biology and Evolution in Washington, D.C. The figures were made with pale skin, blond hair, and light-colored eyes. The Neanderthal heritage myth continues into the twenty-first century in the United States because racism is intrinsic to the culture.

However, the fact is that the Neanderthal species mysteriously disappeared only some 30,000 years ago without leaving any descendant species. Homo sapiens probably killed members of this species on sight and completed their extinction by taking over food sources and the best environments. It is too much to expect that our species could have lived and mingled peacefully cheek-to-cheek with Neanderthals or with any wise ape group. Our species was no longer that kind of animal. By 30,000 years ago, our species had already been wondering and wandering about an expanding environment for some 35,000 years and had literally gotten a handle on things. Homo sapiens discovered Australia some 55,000 years ago and migrated to the continents of Europe and North America about 40,000 years ago. By the time the Neanderthal species disappeared, our species had already settled in all livable areas of earth.

Ignorant as Ancestral Apes

There is truth in the statement that those ignorant of our genetic past are destined to think and behave as those of our genetic past. This ignorance prevails among us in spite of what scientists have been telling us for hundreds of years. However, scientists are not above causing confusion. Today many of them refer to our species as "humans," as if they did not know that a scientific term for our species exists, *Homo sapiens.*

In the mid 1700s Swedish scientist Karl Linnaeus identified our evolution from apes and named our species *Homo sapiens*, meaning "wise primates." Then in 1859 the English naturalist Charles Darwin offered rationale as to why we are of the animal kingdom. In 1973 Austrian zoologist and founder of ethology Dr. Konrad Lorenz explained, "Behavior is simply not intelligible on the basis of the life history of the individual, but only against the background of the long history of the species Homo sapiens, a history which for enormous periods of time was shared with the mammals and all other vertebrates" (Lorenz, 1973). In 2001 evolutionary biologist Dr. Ernst Mayr indicated that we are quite the same as other primates, except for the quantity of neurons in our brain. In other words, the time came when intellectuals and scientists debated on the significance of Linnaeus's and Darwin's findings. Heated debates on how unlike apes we were turned to how ape-like we are.

However, since the times of Karl Linnaeus (1707–1778) and Charles Darwin (1809–1882), much of what scientists have found out about our species is still far from being common sense. This may be why Tielhard de Chardin wrote: "Not much more than a hundred years ago man learned to his astonishment that there was an origin of animal species, a genesis in which he himself was evolved" (Chardin, 1959, 263). By "man" Chardin was referring to the few intellectuals and scientists of his day. To the present it is still natural for only a few of us to understand the significance of what it means to be members of a species coming out of wise-ape evolution.

Summary

Julian Huxley once wrote, "Man is not abruptly marked off from all other animals, but represents the accumulative of a process that can be clearly traced among other primates" (Huxley, 1970). Primate genetic research indicates that most traits thought to be unique to our species such as our specialized brain hemispheres and language are traced to primates of millions of years ago. We should, however, not fool ourselves by thinking that the chimps at the zoo are as closely related to us as horses are to zebras. Much more complex apes than chimpanzees were our last wise ape ancestors.

Scientists continue the difficult task of trying to piece together various wise ape species in our Homo sapient species' lineage. Our wise ape lineage was accompanied by other wise ape species. Disagreements as to which ones are and are not part of our lineage continue. Several important points, however, are for certain. Our species is descendent from a unique series of wise ape species whose interactions increased in complexity with each species. Our Homo sapient species' evolved only some 60,000 years ago, and it is the only living descendant of wise ape (hominid) species. Our ancient grandparent ancestors, some of who left footprints on volcanic ash, would have reason to be proud of us. Some of us have become aware of them and have come to care about them.

In short, a unique series of wise apes' evolution triggered our species out of the realm of common animal evolution. In other words, our species seems to be transitioning out of animal evolution. Our species appears to be what anthropologists refer to as a "transitional" species.

Part II:

Transitioning Out
of Animal Nature

Why we feel, think, and behave

the way we do.

4

Our Transitional Species

Throughout animal evolution there have been many transitional species, but they have transitioned from one kind of animal species to another. Our species is unique because it evolved with an awesome potential that is transitioning it out of animal nature. This awesome potential is made up of primarily three wide-ranging factors that do not seem to exist in any other species.

1. Our species' *multispecies* **potential**: This potential seems to include the entirety of evolution's interactive potential. Our species' **belief-reality** is a small part of our multispecies potential and it programs us to interact as Homo sapiens. However, our species' belief-reality potential varies among members of our species. (As discussed in Chapter 2, a belief-reality is a species' "ready-set-way" of interacting with the environment.)

2. **Gifted interactions:** Gifted individuals are not only programmed with our species' belief-reality, but they can also retrieve interactions from our species' multispecies potential. They keep our species' interactions from becoming stagnant. Therefore, their interactions accelerate our interactive evolution, as a species.

3. ***Human caring:*** This is an advanced level of caring for others
    beyond the ultimate level of caring found in animal nature. It is not
    programmed in all of us as part of our species' belief-reality. Human
    caring appears to be the major factor transitioning our species out
    of animal nature. The authors remind readers that "Human" is not
    used indiscriminately to mean all members of our Homo sapient
    species. (Human nature is the topic of Chapter 12.)

The Multispecies Factor

Although our species' multispecies potential seems to encapsulate the entirety
of evolution's interactive potential, we focus on our species' animal ancestry.
Our species' ancestral genetic potential shows up in our physiology and in
our interactions.

In our Physiology

Our inherited multispecies genetics is detected throughout our physiology.
To begin with, a Homo sapient embryo in its early stages looks much like
embryos of other mammals as well as like the embryos of fishes and reptiles.
Our brain, the essential organ of our being, can be traced back to different
phases of animal evolution beginning with the emergence of reptiles (the age
of dinosaurs). The brain stem, the first part of our brain to develop while in
our mother's womb, resembles the whole brain of a reptile. Monkeys evolved
our cerebrum and cortex. As infants, like other primates, we can suckle milk
and breathe simultaneously without choking. However, we lose this ape ability after infancy because there is a change in our throat, which enables us to
produce our sounds for speech. The change causes us to choke if we inhale
air and drink at the same time. But the possibility of choking is insignificant
considering that we ended up with the potential for complex speech.

We have all kinds of hormones and chemicals that are in countless animal
species, and they produce similar interactions (behaviors, emotions, etc.) in us
as they do in animals. For example, chemicals called leucosulfakinis are found
in detestable cockroaches. These chemicals are similar to hormones found in
us and in other mammals, and they serve a similar function. Our hemoglobin,

which has highly complex molecules, is virtually identical to that of chimps, according to evolutionary biologist Ernst Mayr (2001). Oxytocin is a hormone in our brain as well as in the brains of most mammals.

Oxytocin is of special interest because it appears to regulate caring for others and sexual bonding in us and in other mammals. Neuroscientists studied this hormone in two kinds of voles and found that the amount of hormone affected their level of caring for their offspring. Montane voles, which have few oxytocin receptors, avoid each other except during mating season. They are promiscuous, and mothers abandon their pups soon after birth. In contrast, prairie vole mothers, which have more oxytocin receptors, nurse and care for their pups. According to the scientists, the amount of the hormone in our brain may also determine how much or how little we care about our young and for the welfare of others. Scientists have also discovered that oxytocin helps us deal with stress. Women tend to have more oxytocin than men have. It might be that women need more of this hormone to help them cope with their children and husbands.

In our Interactions

Our multispecies potential profoundly influences our interactions. Our multispecies potential is like having a menu of infinite programmed interactions for the environment to trigger. Ethologist Dr. Konrad Lorenz (1981) explains: "Whether we behave morally or not; reasonably or unreasonably; or go berserk, it is because we are still subject to all the laws prevailing in all phylogenetically adapted instinctive behavior." For example, similar to how many territorial animal species claim their area with urine, feces or by clawing on trees, we are territorial and are also triggered to mark our claimed area. We mark our territory with rocks, walls, graffiti, fences, flags, and posters of our leaders to warn others from trespassing. Our religious activities can be seen as displays of animal submission to someone or something that we have identified as forever powerful. We close our eyes and lower our head; clasp our hands and make begging gestures; kneel or take prostrate positions and wail, chant, grovel, or scream. We react similarly to dictators, queens, kings, judges, celebrities, and wealthy individuals as people to look up to. In other words, similar to some animals (dogs, wolves, and others), we perceive those above us as individuals to fear or respect and to "lick up to."

When our interactions are triggered, they can be like a combination of different animals' instincts being triggered. For example, when our interactions of fear are triggered they are not like those of a gorilla, a rabbit, or a deer. They are a combination of these species' instincts of awareness, feelings, thoughts, responses, and more. Similarly, it is not surprising that the speed, skillful coordination, and other "specialized" instincts of certain animals are triggered in athletes. For example, let's take a frog's instincts in capturing and eating flying insects. In a split second it calculates the speed and distance of the insect darting by. It seems that such instincts are triggered in a tennis player such as Rafael Nadal in returning a 130-mile-an-hour serve just inside a corner of his opponent's court.

Neurologist Dr. Judith L. Rapoport (of the National Institute of Mental Health) suggests that some of our obsessive-compulsive disorders (OCD) are possibly the result of over-triggering inherited animal instincts. She indicates that the obsessive compulsion to wash our hands or face is triggered from inherited animals' grooming instincts. Such animal interactions can be triggered in us to such a degree that they incapacitate us. Rapoport describes such OCD as being like small computer programs left over from the primitive common ancestor of dogs and Homo sapiens. In the United States, it is estimated that yearly about four to six million people are diagnosed as suffering from OCD. In addition, the millions of individuals with addicted interactions of gamblers, sport spectators, Internet surfers, food gorgers, shoplifters, pedophiles, and serial killers could be considered as suffering from over-triggered animal instincts programmed in their genes.

Worst of all, animal interactions to kill offspring are triggered in too many of us for this or that unreasonable or berserk reason. For example, in the United States a father's rage toward his wife triggered him to turn their seven-year-old son into a screaming torch by throwing gasoline and a lighted match on him. In a small town a young mother rolled the family car into a lake with her two little boys strapped to the back seat with seat belts (she must have heard them cry out for her). In 2002 a mother drowned all her five children in the family's bathtub (she must have seen the desperate look in their eyes). In 1996 it was reported that in the U.S. more than six hundred children were murdered by their parents. These were cases in which murder was proven. National data indicates that such cases have increased in the twenty-first century. Psychologists know that stress caused by such factors as poverty, violence, and depression is usually the cause in situations where parents have killed their children. Similarly, environmental stress triggers some animals to kill their offspring.

In short, almost everything we feel, think, believe, and do, whether it is to hate, kill, love, worship gods, or create things is triggered from our species' multispecies potential. It is difficult for most of us to relate our interactions to inherited animal interactions because they are not like the interactions of any particular animal species. Our programmed interactions come from all kinds of animal interactions. In other words, the ugliness and the beauty of animal evolution is thrown wide open in our species.

Depending on how we exhibit our interactions, U.S. social scientists identify them as *instinctual* or *learned*. For example, a newborn baby's suckling is perceived as instinctual because the mother's cuddling quickly triggers her infant to search for her nipple and begin suckling. In contrast, although walking on two legs is triggered from our potential, babies take several months to "learn" to walk. In other words, we think of walking as something we learn to do because it takes the toddler some time to master. Similarly, most of us think of language as something learned, but whether it is through hand-finger or mouth-tongue movements, language is genetically programmed in our potential. It is instinctual. According to behavioral research, deaf babies' hand movement responses and hearing babies' babbling responses appear at the same age; both groups of babies form their first words by age one. Although language is innate to our species, we need an appropriate environment such as our parents' modeling and formal education to trigger correct usage (syntax, inflections, vocabulary, etc.). Linguist and sociopolitical scientist Dr. Noam Chomsky explains it this way: "Language is as innate in the infant as flight is in the eaglet and children do not so much learn language as develop spontaneously in response to a stimulus" (Ross, 1991, 146). As it is with babies' suckling, walking, and talking, all our interactions are triggered from our genetic potential by the environment (timespace, people, etc.).

The distinction between instinctual or learned interactions is the time it takes for them to be triggered from our genes. The partitioning of these inter- actions could be due to the U.S. culture's religious beliefs. The beliefs strongly influence most citizens to think that *only* animals have instincts.

In contrast, in European cultures and in many other cultures, ethologists consider all of our interactions as instincts triggered from our genes. No dis- tinction is made between those that occur instantly and those that take time to emerge. Timing is not a divisive criterion as it is for most U.S. social scientists.

A Free Will

A free will wraps up the animalness programmed in us. In the United States most of us believe that we have a free will to interact the way we want to with- out input from our genes and the environment. A free will, therefore, is some- thing common animals would agree we all have. According to Dr. Carl Sagan and Ann Druyan (Sagan and Druyan, 1992), an animal cannot become aware that it is genetically programmed to do whatever it decides to do. It cannot understand that what it does is genetically triggered. The creature simply has a "gut" feeling that it does whatever it wants to do. Similarly, freewill Homo sapient believers simply feel they have a free will to do whatever they do. They find it difficult or impossible to understand that what they do is limited to what can be triggered from their genetically programmed potential.

Where do freewill believers think their free will comes from? For most be- lievers, their idea of a free will is primarily based on religious beliefs, whether they are aware of it or not. It is in the nature of freewill believers to have beliefs void of logical reasoning or scientific basis. The idea of a free will in Christian- Judaic cultures might have come from the ancient Greeks who believed that the soul gave us direction. The word for soul in Latin is *anima*, the root word for "animate" and "animal." Thus, it seems natural that some of us instinctively feel we have an animal (*anima*) in us that guides us (Sagan and Druyan, 1992, 171).

Sociobiologist Dr. E. O. Wilson makes it quite plain that biological reasoning trashes the delusion of a free will. He explains: "If our genes are inherited and our environment is a train of physical events sent in motion before we're born, how can there be a truly independent agent within the brain? The agent itself is created by the interactions of genes and the environment." Wilson adds: "Our freedom is only a self-delusion (Wilson, 1984, 71)."

The Few Gifted

The second major factor of our transitional species' potential is its genetically "gifted" members' interactions. Depending on how the environment triggers their interactions, they are also identified either as instinctual or learned.

Gifted individuals emerge with a potential to interact with the environment at higher levels of awareness and understanding than the rest of us are able to. They introduce the rest of us to things and ideas that we would not experience without them. Through the ages, their interactions have increased and continue to increase the rate and degree of our species' interactive evolution. Most of us are aware of how the gifted ideas, inventions, discoveries, and creations of such individuals as the Buddha, Jesus, Confucius, Michelangelo, Galileo, Marx, Darwin, Newton, Bach, Tchaikovsky, Pavlov, Gandhi, Einstein, Picasso, J. Huxley, E. O. Wilson, and Chomsky expanded and continue to expand our species' interactions.

Instinctual giftedness

Instinctual giftedness is seen as occurring with limited reciprocity with the environment. It is usually detected in children. For example, a gifted child amazes us with computational skills that require guidance from university professors, not from elementary schoolteachers. Or, we're surprised by a child's ability to master the piano and compose complex music. Childhood giftedness is usually exhibited in mathematics, music, and other skills triggered mostly from the brain's right hemisphere. In other words, an instinctually gifted child comes up with complex interactions, skipping much of the "how to" of learning (as Amadeus Mozart did in composing music).

From what we know of ancient ancestors' interactions, it is logical to think that at the dawn of our species' emergence, all gifted individuals would have been considered *instinctually* gifted. At that time accumulated knowledge was nonexistent. Therefore, interactions such as tool making, use of fire, and communicating with drawings were triggered instinctively from our species' genetic potential. Also, some 50,000 years ago, a few individuals had ready-set instincts to plan and lead a group across fifty-four miles of open sea to discover the island continent of Australia. (Anthropologists marvel at this incredible feat.) We can assume that such interactions as navigating skills, craft-making skills, and creating specialized tools were triggered from gifted individuals' potential. In fact, our species' first stone tools with chiseled "waist" marks, indicating the ingenuity of handles, were found in Australia. Today's workers using hammers, axes, and shovels are unaware that the idea to get a handle on things emerged from a gifted ancestor's instincts some 50,000 years ago.

It can also be assumed that an ancient instinctually gifted ancestor's idea, discovery, or invention was restricted to the timespace of his group. This may explain why some of our gifted ancestors' interactions of 50,000 to even 20,000 years ago were not repeated elsewhere until tens of thousands of years later. The ocean trip to Australia was not repeated until tens of thousands of years after the first migration to the island continent. It is reasonable to think that not every isolated group around the world had a gifted individual to trigger the group's interactions beyond the commonality of our species' norm. Or, if there was a gifted person in the group, his peers might have considered his or her ideas too absurd or undoable. In such cases, a gifted individual might have been ignored, ostracized, or killed for being too weird.

To conceptualize and appreciate the potential of an instinctually gifted ancestor, we can imagine the task of having to think of designing and building sea crafts from scratch to make a 54-mile ocean trip to an unknown island. Or, imagine being able to think of and create abstract symbols to convey a language and numbers that would make sense to a lot of people for thousands of years. Or imagine being able to plan and organize the construction of pyramids. Even in today's world, in spite of accumulated knowledge and vast technology at hand, to do any of these things requires far more potential than what can be triggered from the common person. What gifted individuals did tens of thousands of years ago tells us that the environment can trigger some individuals among us to interact markedly beyond the level of interactions triggered from the rest of us.

Gifted individuals can be triggered with similar instinctual interactions worldwide. This explains why similar gifted ideas and discoveries were triggered in different parts of the world around the same periods. For example, about 40,000 years ago there were large migrations from northeastern Africa to Europe as well as from Siberia to the Americas. Gifted persons probably made these migrations possible. Some 17,000 years ago gifted individuals in different parts of the world were triggered to document some of their interactions and things about their environment on cave walls. Gifted individuals were triggered to instinctively construct pyramids in different parts of the world about the same era. Their purpose was also similar, to honor their gods. An individual's gifted interactions can be triggered as easily as a newborn's interactions are triggered to search for a nipple.

Learned giftedness

Learned giftedness is also genetically encoded, but it is not considered instinctual by most U.S. psychologists. It is seen as a phenomenon that requires more genetic-environment (GE) reciprocity (research, experiments, thinking, reading, and so forth). It requires more triggering of the person's genetic potential with the help of accumulated information. It sometimes takes a gifted individual many years to accomplish his or her theories, inventions, and works of art or literature.

When considering learned giftedness Galileo, Darwin, Marx, and Einstein come to mind. Such "learned" gifted individuals are triggered to discover new things, ideas, methods, and so on. They are highly motivated to study and analyze accumulated information and formulate new ideas. They seem to need to unite dangling parts into a tangible *new* whole. It is as one biographer wrote about Galileo's giftedness: "His ever-accumulating wisdom helped him regard certain ancient concepts in fresh ways" (Sorbel, 1999, 348).

We recall that the potential of dead entities' interactions is the foundation of animals and our cells' interactions. Just as dead entities' interactions are triggered in animals to apply the concept of condensation, geometric patterns, etc. in their interactions, they are triggered in us. How else could such gifted individuals as Galileo, Newton, Einstein, and Plank come up with their insights on the universe's dead matter?

> "My unquiet mind will not rest from mulling it [treatise on motion] over...because the latest thought to occur to me about some novelty makes me throw out much already found there."
>
> Galileo

Most of us cannot grasp the depth of complexity, or the significance of many of their concepts, ideas, or inventions. However, gifted individuals explore the sciences and create theories, write books, etc. to explain the complexities of existence that the bulk of us would not otherwise understand. Gifted individuals' ideas, discoveries, and creations enrich our environment via universities, libraries, and so on. Through such institutions gifted individuals' interactions (awareness, perceptions, conceptualizations, and so on) are transmitted from generation to generation.

Gifted individuals do not become geniuses by shocking peers with what they can do here and now, but by what their ideas, discoveries or inventions come to mean in the future. The genius of a gifted individual is confirmed by how the environment can trigger his individualized belief-reality to retrieve interactions from our species' genome that could not be retrieved by the rest of us. Their gifted interactions are manifested by their discoveries, inventions, art, literature and so on. Their gifted interactions are passed on through timespace for generations increasing our species' belief-reality.

Experiments have indicated that a gifted environment can even increase a chimpanzee's belief-reality potential. It seems that a gifted environment can trigger an ape's belief-reality to retrieve interactions from its species' genome that would not be ordinarily retrieved. Scientists playing the role of "gifted apes" can trigger chimpanzees to learn sign language and communicate with Homo sapiens. In these experiments scientists enriched the chimpanzees' environment with a variety of pictures and objects and rewards. In this enriched environment, the "gifted apes" (scientists) trigger the chimps to communicate feelings that they could not communicate, otherwise. We can speculate that if evolution had sprinkled gifted chimpanzees among the species, they would be protesting against experimentations on animals and against deforestation.

Our species' interactions would certainly not have evolved to the degree that they have if it weren't for gifted individuals. Our species would not have been awakened to move much beyond the fears, gods, and superstitions that were programmed in our species and manifested in our ancestors of thousands of years ago. Without the input of gifted individuals and enriched environments we would definitely be much more animal than we are today.

Humane Caring

The third factor of our transitional species' potential is Humane caring. This level of caring is unique to our species. It is an advanced level of caring for the welfare of others because it goes beyond the ultimate level of caring inherited from animal nature. Humane caring is not even part of our species' belief-reality that makes us interact as a species. Therefore, humane caring is not common to all members of our species. In other words, humane caring is triggered from our species' genome only in some of us. The majority of us interact as Homo sapiens without the interactions of humane caring.

The authors refer to individuals with this extraordinary potential as being *Human*, since no animal can be humane. At this stage of our species' evolution it is apparent that only a minority among us has the potential to be Human. Humane caring seems to be the major factor that is transitioning our species out of animal nature. No other trait is so telling of our species' transitional status than its humanness. (Being Human is discussed in Chapter 12.) It took Mother Nature billions of years to evolve humanness.

Without humanness, our species would be an animal species. However, because of its multispecies potential, it would still be the most advanced species of the animal kingdom.

To have an understanding of the kind of animal our species would be without humane caring let's imagine that a shortsighted scientist alters the genes of an ant species. The scientist creates an ant species with the combined interactive potential of all earth's ant species. The result is a super ant species with an incredible range of interactions. However, because of the nature of ants, the queens establish no-nonsense dictatorships with strong acts of allegiance and patriotism. But do the super ant queens unite into a worldwide queendom for the benefit of all members of the species? No. Although the species has an incredible range of interactions, its level of caring for the welfare of others is still that of an animal species.

Super queendoms are frequently at war with each other because they can only care about their own kind (their own colony). The welfare of other colonies even of the same species is of little or zero concern. Thus, the strongest super ant colony will take what it wants from weaker colonies through force and other means. A world order of social equality and cooperation is unthinkable to the super ant colonies. The super ants are not programmed for humane caring. If by some genetic quirk of nature, an ant emerged among them with the humane caring of Jesus they would kill that ant in the most painful way possible. Instinctively, they perceive humane caring as wrong and dangerous to *their* animalistic way of life.

Although the super ant species has an incredible range of interactions, most individual super ants feel it is their right to attack and kill others for slaves, best food sources, and so on. Because of their instinctual righteousness of my colony right or wrong mentality, they seem to lack compassion for other ants being killed or for the destruction of others' colonies. They are programmed to know that *their* queendom's competitive way of life of attacking and taking advantage of others is the way it has always been and always will be.

Although our species has the potential for humane caring, our cultures have much in common with the super ant species' queendoms. Our U.S. culture has much of the same animalistic interactions of the strongest imagined super ant colony. For hundreds of years its righteousness and competitive nature of the animal world has triggered it to take whatever it wants from weak or underdeveloped cultures. As individual members of our U.S. culture, most of us are culturally programmed to share its righteousness and lack of compassion for its oppression and killings of others. Yet, unlike an animal species, some of us feel compassion for those who are being oppressed and killed. A few of us even try to prevent our culture from taking animalistic actions. Again, this occurs because of our species' incredible range of caring interactions, from the caring levels of primitive animals to the caring level of *Humans*.

▪   ▪   ▪

In summation of our species' potential, not only does it seem to have the entirety of its animal ancestry programmed in its genetic potential, but it can also display this vast inheritance. This lessens the importance that our genetic makeup is as closely related to chimpanzees as horses are to zebras. Our transitional species is related to the whole of our animal ancestry. Therefore, we might look like and interact like certain animals, but our species is definitely not an animal species. Gifted interactions, particularly in scientific research, and humane caring create a continuum of advancing interactions that is characteristic of only our Homo sapient species. Humane caring, however, is mainly what is transitioning our species out of animal evolution. This startling transition is comparable to the transformation of dead interactions to living interactions via the cell.

With what we now know about the nature of our species, it is not surprising that some of us exhibit considerably more expanded caring for others than caring chimpanzees, and some of us exhibit less caring for others than horses do.

Our Belief-Reality

We are all programmed with interactions from our species' belief-reality, which give us the potential to interact (feel, think, behave, etc.) with the environment as Homo sapiens. However, we each have our own "individualized" belief-reality, which comes from our species' belief-reality. The development of our individualized belief-realty depends on our genetic potential and our environment (education, reading, travels, and other experiences). In other words, we can expand our individualized belief-reality. The more we can expand our individualized belief-reality the more potential we have to cope and interact with the environment (people, things, events, etc.).

On the other hand, gifted individuals can

All members of a species have a belief-reality. A belief-reality is a "ready-set way" of responding to and coping with the environment (See Chapter 2). All members of a species have in their belief-reality interactions that make them interact as members of their species.

activate interactions beyond our species' belief-reality. This is what separates the gifted from the rest of us. Beyond our species' belief-reality is our species' vast inheritance of billions of years of nonliving and living interactions. Their genetic potential enables them to interact with the environment to discover, create, and understand things that the rest of us cannot.

Our individualized belief-reality can make us perceive and interact with the environment differently from each other. Even identical twins interact differently because they still have their own individualized belief-realities. Although they are genetically programmed to respond the same to a stimulus, the environment can still trigger different interactions from their belief-realities. This is because each twin still has different environmental experiences. So, although identical twins' interactions are triggered from the same fundamental genetic potential, their individualized belief-reality enables them to interact differently.

As a result of different individualized belief-realities, some of us create beauty as well as indescribable ugliness, profound caring as well as sickening uncaring, and much in-between these extremes. Most of us have a belief-reality that enables us to interact better than a chimpanzee, and a few of us cannot interact any better than a horse. In other words, because of our vast differences among the infinite number of individualized belief-realties we, as a species, manifest the gifted interactions of a Galileo to the interactions of an individual with a severely limited intellect, as well as the caring of a Jesus to the lack of caring of a psychopath.

Language and beliefs (religion, philosophies, etc.) have managed to bring about degrees of togetherness and uniformity to form cultures and civilizations. Historically and globally, religions have influenced our individualized realities with ancient stagnant myths about the environment and our existence. By the mid 1900s, however, social-political changes began to indicate that religion's huge power base was being replaced by science. Science is based on what our ablest brains continuously find out about reality. Unlike religion's static and divisive influence on our individualized belief-realities on what is reality, scientists' continuum of research and discoveries is developing a unified perception of reality. No doubt this will take a long time because so much ignorance exists, and much of this ignorance is based on and maintained by religious beliefs. Consequently, science has the awesome task of taking our species out of a vast swamp of ignorance. Such a huge task might be accomplished by our next civilization.

Summary

It didn't take long for the environment to trigger our ancient Homo sapient ancestors to create weapons to kill for food, territory, and for sport. We can speculate this is why such wise ape (hominid) species as Neanderthals and Archaic sapiens became extinct some 30,000 years ago. After all, these wise apes were at a great disadvantage against a transitional species with a superior interactive potential. (These species might have been the first animals that our species made extinct.)

Our species' potential appears as a "Jack of all trades but master of none." Members of our species become soldiers, food gathers, merchants, builders, architects, scientists, and so on. (In contrast, most animals can be considered "masters of one" because of their species' narrow and static potential.) The environment continuously triggers our interactive potential.

Our species' potential enables us to overcome many of our shortcomings. For example, we did not emerge with the strength of elephants, the flight of eagles, the speed of cheetahs, or the long distance communication of whales. But, we have the potential to use dead matter to give us the strength of elephants, the flying power greatly exceeding that of eagles, the speed countless of times faster than that of cheetahs, and incredibly further long distance communication than that of whales. Gifted scientists have opened great possibilities for our species, including exploring the microcosm creating existence, deciphering the genomes of living entities, and exploring the vast macrocosm. Our species' potential is such that there seems to be no end to how much the environment can trigger from it. Its interactions have markedly advanced from some 55,000 years ago, and from two thousand years ago, and even from two hundred years ago. Even as a transitional species emerging out of animal evolution, our species' interactive potential makes it the most incredible creation of timespace.

Of all the vast interactions programmed in our genetic potential, most of us have sensed that caring is the most important of life. Although humane caring is far from being our species' common level of caring it is humane caring, not our advancements in technology, that is taking us out of animal nature. Therefore, having individuals with the genetic potential to care for others beyond the potential of animals is what separates our species from being an animal species. In the next chapter we will see the animalness that is impeding our species' progress out of animal nature.

5

Animal Beings

"Conservatives" by Another Name

Science classifies our Homo sapient species as an animal species because it evolved genetically from animal species, "more specifically from apes" (Mayr, 2001, 235). This is why our DNA is as close to that of chimpanzees as the DNA of horses is to zebras. Scientists have known this for a long time. Yet, *because* of our inherent animalness, it is not surprising that it is difficult to impossible for most of us to accept and understand the significance of our animalness. However, a few individuals have the potential to become aware of the animalness in us and to understand why our animalness profoundly affects our interactions. Scientists such as biochemist Aleksandr I. Oparin, ethologist Konrad Lorenz, and social biologist E.O. Wilson explain that our species' animal heritage is encoded in our genetic potential. Therefore, it's imperative to become aware that our animalness is hindering our species' Human evolution. For, although we are classified as an animal species, it is caring for the welfare of others beyond animal levels of caring that sets us apart from animals.

Most of our species' vast range of caring, however, is made up of animal levels of caring. Consequently, our animal heritage profoundly influences how much or how little we care for the welfare of others and the general environment. Although our species has the potential for humane caring, the bulk of us interact with the caring levels of animals. This means that in caring for the welfare of others we are limited to the caring levels of primitive animals to the caring levels of advanced animals.

Caring As Primitive Animals

Some of us interact with the limited caring of primitive animals. Like reptiles some of us are incapable of caring even for our offspring. Similar to snakes, turtles, and lizards some of us have our babies and "slither" away. We have mothers who abandon their newborns in trash bins, in deserted alleys, buildings, and so on. We have mothers and fathers who kill their children much like some animals kill their offspring. Some parents will shake an infant to death similarly to how an animal will grab its offspring from its scruff and shake it to death.

Like insects most of us react to our neighboring culture's sufferings similar to how ants of a colony feel about the plight of a neighboring ant colony. The ants of one colony are entirely incapable of manifesting compassion or even concern for a neighboring colony. This would be true even if the two colonies were among the last of the entire ant species. This would still be true even where cooperation between the two colonies was necessary for each other's survival. Due to their primitive nature, the ant colonies would likely war with each other, resulting in the reduced quality of life for both colonies and possibly extinction. How many of our cultures kill and mutilate each other's peoples and destroy each other's food and water sources, homes, hospitals, schools, historical buildings and so on rather than find ways to cooperate with each other?

Like the ants, most people of one culture are entirely incapable of manifesting compassion or even concern for neighboring cultures. Too many of us are simply too insect-like to identify with the suffering of others. We can live in a wealthy culture feeling good that we are not suffering the effects of poverty, disease, illiteracy, etc. suffered by our neighboring culture. Many of us feel the same way about members of a different gang, nationality, religion, race, and others that we don't identify with. The smaller the group of people that we can identify with, the more our caring is that of primitive animals.

Caring As Advanced Animals

Fortunately, due to the level of caring interactions inherited from the advanced animals, most of us can care for our offspring most of the time. Like apes we nurse our young, we cuddle and groom them, and we protect them from harm. Similar to elephants, we can adopt someone else's child and take care of him or her. Like "African wild dogs" we can care for the ill and the aged whom we know and identify with. Research shows that our species mostly exhibits the level of caring found in advanced animals, namely a level of caring for those perceived to be of "our kind."

As in animals, "our kind" is a strong measure for determining whom we associate with, identify with and care for. Therefore, some of us can dislike a certain group of people and yet be able to learn to identify with a member of that group. For example, some of us may be prejudiced against "Muslims," "Jews," "Mexicans," "white trash," or some other group that we don't identify with. However, if at our workplace we become friends with a "Muslim" we come to identify with him and can care about him. Perhaps we might even come to care about his family. Yet we might not ever care for the welfare of other Muslims. In other words, caring for our own kind is limited to caring for those we know and identify with.

Caring only for our kind also means that we care less or do not care for the welfare of people who we perceive as *not* of our kind. We can think that we care for the welfare of our village or for our U.S. nation, but we are unable to realize that we don't care for most citizens. Yet we don't want health services for everyone or advanced education for all students that want it. Due to our limiting animal identification with others, we can only think that services for the welfare of all citizens would raise our taxes. It is difficult to impossible for most of us to accept the fact that *not* caring for others whom we perceive as *not* being of our kind is triggered from the animalness in us.

No matter how unlike animals we see ourselves, caring for the welfare of others with the caring of animals keeps us being animals. Being genetically programmed with animals' limited caring makes it difficult for us to care for billions of others in need of food, health care, and shelter, even when they are members of our own culture. It is even difficult for us to care about the thousands of hungry, homeless people in our city. Yet we are easily triggered to care for the welfare of our cat and dog because we know them and we can identify with them. A dog owner or even a neighbor who knows the owner's dog will pay for an expensive veterinarian bill. Yet, these individuals will not donate to a fund for a child's medical bill, even if the child attends the same school as their children. They do not know the child and cannot identify with him because of their animalness.

Much like animals our identification with a group—a gang, a race or a religion—is a highly defining apparatus for those who we can care about. If we are Christian evangelists this defines whom we can care about. If we are U.S. citizens this defines whom we can care about. If we are Europeans (white) this defines whom we can care about. For example, our culture's use of the atomic bomb on Japan was palatable to most U.S. citizens because they did not identify with the Asian race of the Japanese. However, bombing Germany would *not* have been palatable to most U.S. citizens because they would identify with the German peoples' European race. In other words, with only an animal's advanced level of caring we can only identify with and care for those of our kind.

Our U.S. culture's constant demand to identify our race serves our animalness well. It is an institutionalized identification of our kind. It serves our advanced animal level of caring for those we perceive as of our kind.

Animal beings

At this stage of our species' evolution it appears that the majority of us can *only* care for others with the level of animals' limited caring. Therefore, the authors identify members of our species whom can *only* interact with the caring levels of animals as *Animal beings*.

The reality that most of us are Animal beings is difficult to accept for several reasons. Foremost, it is because most of us are Animal beings that we do not see ourselves as being animals. We are also culturally programmed through religion to separate ourselves from animals. And, we are culturally shaped with the false belief that we all are "Human." (The authors remind readers that "Human" is not used indiscriminately to mean all members of our Homo sapient species.)

Lastly, most of us are ignorant about evolution, life, and so on.

Human beings are a struggling minority among the majority of us Animal beings. Some of us, however, are able to conceptualize our animalness because we are members of a transitional species that is evolving out of animal nature. Some of us have the potential to become aware of and understand what scientists tell us about our animal heritage and how it profoundly affects our interactions.

Most members of our species are Animal beings with a range of caring levels of primitive animals to advanced animals. Animal beings therefore can react in the most heinous manner or compassionately. Their interactions are considered as acceptable or unacceptable by their cultures. Those who interact as primitive animals with little or no caring for others are usually identified as unacceptable. The authors call these individuals *unacceptable* Animal beings. Those who mostly interact within their culture's values, rules, and so on are seen as "normal" citizens. The authors call these individuals *acceptable* Animal beings. We will see how this last group can be the most dangerous to our species.

Unacceptable Animalness

Most unacceptable Animals beings interact with little or no conscience. For example, two U.S. teenage boys killed another teenager because they supposedly felt the need to experience killing someone, anyone. They chopped up his body, put the pieces into a plastic garbage bag, and put the bag in the trunk of the family car of one of the killers. Their killing, somewhat like a crocodile's matter-or-fact bloody killing of its prey, was easily triggered from the primitive animalness at the forefront of their belief-reality (their ready-set way to interact with the environment).

In another case, a seventeen-year-old boy from a small town in the state of Wisconsin killed a 37-year-old man. He shot him in the back of the head and stabbed him several times. The teenager, considered a normal good boy, boasted about his killing to some thirty classmates. He told them he had done it just to see if he could get away with it. The town's newspaper editor explained that none of the thirty schoolmates had reported the killing until questioned by police because in small towns "people protect their own kind." Fortunately, the killer had boasted about his killing to a girl from another town, and she informed the police (Newsweek, March 15, 2004). The animalness of the killer was easily identified, but not the animalness of the thirty schoolmates. The schoolmates didn't identify with the murdered man. He might have been of their community, but they did not know him. However, the killer was known to the schoolmates and therefore identified with him.

Animal beings addicted to killing (serial killers) interact without a conscience. In the state of Washington, the serial killer known as the Green River Killer admitted he could not remember how many women he had raped and killed over the years, or who they were. There was evidence that he had killed forty-eight or more women and had hidden the bodies, much like a dog hides bones. Yet, at the time of his arrest the serial killer was living a culturally acceptable life. This killer was married, had children, and held a good job. In other words, this Animal being was acceptable until the culture discovered he was a serial killer.

Once the primitive animalness of killers, pedophiles, psychopaths, and rapists is discovered, such Animal beings are easily identified as "animals" and "monsters."

Acceptable Animalness

Acceptable Animal beings' limited caring is widely accepted. They make up most of the population of their culture, and their limited caring is the norm.

The U.S. culture is the richest nation on the planet. Yet it is culturally accepted that Animal being politicians and their supporters have ensured that millions of its citizens remain unhealthy, ignorant, and impoverished. They have determined that health care, college education, and other basic essentials of an advanced culture should *not* be available to all citizens. So even in the richest and most powerful nation in the world Animal beings' denial of basic essentials to the most needy is acceptable. This is similar to the limited caring of lions and hyenas where the strongest and most vicious eat most of the kill. In other words, the culture's Animal beings' level of caring doesn't reach that of such animal species as the African wild dog where nourishment of the young is the pack's priority. It is clear that United States' voting citizens strongly support Animal being politicians. The culture's dominant acceptable animalness also clearly shows the consequence of our species' inherited animalness.

Globally, throughout history Animal being politicians and their supporters have caused the suffering and death of countless of families. Unlike unacceptable animal beings whose heinous acts kill only a few individuals, Animal being politicians can easily do worse, and with plenty of flag waving. With the help of their culture's military and mercenary soldiers, Animal being politicians kill thousands of men, women, and children for the accumulation oil, land, and other animalistic reasons.

Animal being politicians always have reasons to set off military interventions, from fighting foreign terrorists, to removing "unfriendly" political leaders trying to free their nation from capitalism's exploitation. Most of these reasons come under the umbrella of "in defense of national interests" or for "freedom." These reasons have been repeated for generations to the point that their validity is not questioned. The consistent result is the deaths and mutilations of thousands of young soldiers and civilians. Yet few of these Animal beings politicians are identified as killers, and fewer are punished for the deaths and misery that they cause. Most of them are allowed to continue as political leaders primarily because their cultures support their animalness. As Animal beings, we cannot identify with the suffering of foreigners caused by our Animal being leaders and the military. After all, they are thousands of miles away and they are not of "our kind."

From the many murderous Animal being political leaders in recent history, Hitler's and Pol Pot's genocidal sprees come to mind. Although these political leaders murdered many thousands of men, women, and children, they shared the same limited level of caring with Animal beings that were only able to murder a few. Hitler and Pol Pot were no less caring than a serial killer who killed half a dozen children.

Hitler, however, had a highly organized and disciplined culture supporting his freedom to fully express his animalness. His leadership is a classic example of a culture that fully accepted and supported his animalness, complete with flag waving and patriotic garbage. (It was letting Hitler be Hitler.) Give any Animal being political leader the liberty to fully express his limited caring for those not of his kind, and things tend to get very bloody. Other examples include: Cambodia under Pol Pot, Chile under Pinochet, Russia under Stalin, Cuba under Batista, Japan under Hirohito, and so on. The success of Animal being leaders depends on the support of millions of Animal being citizens. There are always plenty of patriotic Animals with a "my country right or wrong" mentality, ready to support a "Hitler," "Pinochet," or some other vicious Animal leader.

Fortunately, most Animal being political leaders do not turn into a Hitler because their cultures (or other cultures) restrain their animalness. For example, although Animal being politicians run the United States, its laws and institutions restrain them from fully expressing their animalness. Therefore, Animal being Presidents Andrew Jackson, Woodrow Wilson, Richard Nixon, Ronald Reagan, George Bush, Sr., George Bush, Jr., and Vice President Dick Cheney didn't have the freedom to fully express their animalness. Still, when these Animal beings were in power, the culture showed how uncaring it could be with its own citizens, not to mention how uncaring it could be for the global environment. In essence, when such politicians are in power our culture's identification with others, even with its own kind, shrinks.

Some intellectuals are now advocating the need to hold scientists accountable for not resisting, in whatever way they can, the production of weapons of mass destruction (WMD). This is because WMD energize political Animal beings' aggressiveness. They want to expend this aggressiveness by using or wanting to use such weapons against other cultures. Albert Einstein was aware of the dangers of having enormous destructive power in the hands of our Animal being leaders when he stated: "The unleashed power of the atom has changed everything, save our mode of thinking, and thus drift toward unparallel catastrophe." In other words, we are drifting toward a catastrophe because "our mode of thinking" is primarily that of animals.

Animal Beings: Alias Conservatives

It would have been an insurmountable task to identify most of our political leaders as interacting with the limited caring of animals, if it had not been done hundreds of years ago in political circles.

Up to the French Revolution of 1787, European Animal being politicians were in complete control of their cultures. It was the apex of a world of Kings, Queens, Czars, Shahs, and so on. These dictatorship regimes had been getting along with wealthy individuals (capitalists) for hundreds of years. However, the time came when the French monarchy began having problems with its common people. They wanted to be heard and they wanted some equality. This led to the French Revolution (1787–1789). The French Revolution changed the culture by extending caring from only its royalty and wealthy few to include caring for working families and the poor. The revolution succeeded in throwing out the culture's monarchy, but it did not remove the insectival instinct of having the interests of an "elite" few above the common people's essential needs.

The Revolution also brought about political identifications, which are still used today. Animal being politicians who were known for their limited social caring were identified as "right-wingers" and "conservatives." The Revolution set the stage for identifying and separating the culture's *right-wingers* (conservatives) from the culture's social caring politicians, the *left-wingers* (liberals). This came about because "right wing" and "left wing" referred to the seating arrangements in the French Legislative Assembly of 1791. The royalist Feuillants who supported the wealthy old aristocratic and religious interests sat on the right side of the chamber. The liberal Montagnards who supported the new government's actions on behalf of workers and the poor sat on the left side of the chamber. Thus, the *left-wing* represented common people's interests, and the *right-wing* represented the interests of royalty and the wealthy few. The French Revolution and labeling politicians as either *conservative* or *liberal* had a lasting influence on politics in Western Europe and in the United States.

Not surprisingly, the French Revolution's attempt of installing some equality for the welfare of the culture's common people triggered fear in European and United States Animal being politicians. Their fear was similar to the fear dawn brings to the proverbial bloodsucking vampire. These politicians attacked the French Revolution's goal as destructive to the their idea of having a "natural hierarchical order" of the wealthy few in power. Their animalness toward democracy and equality for their own citizens triggered them to respond vehemently against the French Revolution. They interpreted the social caring movement toward a democratic equalitarian culture as being unnatural. This triggered United States' right-wingers to embrace English philosopher Edmund Burke's ideas in his book, *Reflections on the Revolution in France* (1790). Burke rebuked the French Revolution and defined the differences between the right-wing's and left-wing's ideologies. He did not see the right-wingers' (conservatives) limited caring as being bad, but he did see left-wingers' (liberals) social caring as dangerous. Edmund Burke explained: "A perfect democracy... is the most shameless thing in the world." By 1800, western European cultures and the United States were identifying political Animal beings with the non-offensive label of "conservatives." The label was reserved for politicians and other cultural leaders whose interactions focused on conserving the culture's animalness.

Going with the cultural flow we shall use *Conservatives,* with a capital "C," as another name for Animal beings. The good Englishman William Shakespeare would have agreed that a spade by any other name is still a spade. He would have also agreed that calling Animal beings "Conservatives" was not to the point, but would have added, "'tis enough, 'tis will do." As he implied in his play, *Romeo and Juliet,* a rose by any other name is still a rose. In our case, an Animal by any other name is still an Animal. As Shakespeare suggested, it is not the name "rose" that matters as does the color, texture, shape, and fragrance of the flower. Likewise, it is not the name "Conservative" that matters, as do the feelings, thoughts, and behaviors of the Animal.

It was inevitable that some members of our species would evolve to identify the discrepancy of caring among our cultures' political leaders. Now, however, it does not mean that all *Conservatives* interact with *only* the caring of animals and that all *liberals* care for the welfare of others beyond Conservatives' caring. Nevertheless, in our U.S. culture these labels are extensively used to identify politicians and other social leaders' viewpoints in caring for the welfare of citizens. This is why people who interact similarly to former Vice President Dick Cheney are easily identified as "Conservatives," and those who interact similarly to Dr. Martin Luther King Jr. are easily identified as "liberals."

Focus is on our U.S. culture's Conservative political leaders because their interactions negatively affect the welfare of people globally (more so than the interactions any other nation's Conservatives).

Our Founders' Conservatism

Our culture's Conservative Founding Fathers installed a republic, which does not represent or treat citizens equally. Their perception of their kind was so limited that the Founders didn't even identify all people of the European (white) race as of their kind. European men who were not wealthy enough to own property were not of the Founders' kind and neither were all women. A wife was her husband's property. She did not have legal ownership of her children, property, earnings, or of any inheritance acquired before or during marriage. In writing the Declaration of Independence and the Constitution in the 1700s the Founders solidified their belief in inequality by focusing on securing comfort and wealth for *their* kind.

In the Declaration of Independence Thomas Jefferson underscored "all men are created equal," which became a favorite cultural phrase. (A beautiful phrase, but we should not forget reality.) At the time, "all men" only meant wealthy men of the European race, and George Washington made a special effort to make it known that "all men" included Jews (males). In August 1790 he sent a letter to the Hebrew Congregation in Newport, Rhode Island accepting them as equals. Washington, the top representative of the culture, included the Jews because he identified with the Judaic belief of being of god's chosen few.

Today's Conservatism

The culture's Conservatives have perpetuated the lie that the culture has a long history of democracy. The lie overrides the truth about our culture's history in spite of what honest historians and sociologists tell us. Historian Howard Zinn explains that although we have been taught that our nation is civilized and humane, too often its actions have been uncivilized and inhumane. Social-political philosopher Dr. Mortimer Adler states: "The notion that this country was founded as a democracy, of course, is sheer rot. It was anything but that: It was an oligarchy of the most severe kind" (Kidder, 1987, 6). (An oligarchy is a form of government in which the ruling power belongs to a few, and in most cases they are the culture's wealthy few.) Social-political scientist Michael Parenti tells us that the Founders saw democracy as "the worst of all political evils" (Parenti, 2008, 43). This is why, in forming the Constitution, U.S. Supreme Court Judge Samuel Chase reasoned that if all citizens were given the right to vote, the country would "sink into a mobocracy" (Gottfried and Fleming, 1988, 53). In short, our culture was founded on a platform of inequality.

The culture's Conservative electoral and judicial systems often support Conservative politicians' efforts to maintain inequality. It took many years of peaceful and violent protests by the common people for the culture to evolve to the level of indirect democracy it now has. It took nearly two hundred years for most U.S. citizens to gain the right to vote, a major criterion of a democracy. People of the American race (bronze or red), people of the African race (black), and all women had to struggle for their right to vote. From the time our Conservative Founders wrote the Constitution in 1789, women did not get the right to vote until 1920 with the adoption of the 19th Amendment. Although the 15th Amendment of 1870 was suppose to allow all men to vote, Africans were violently barred from voting and even killed. People of the American race generally did not even bother attempting to vote. Democracy has not come easy for the United States, in spite of politicians' systemic lies that it has been a cradle of democracy. The Voting Rights Act of 1965 had to be readopted and strengthened in 1970, 1975, and 1982 in order for the 15th Amendment to work for non-European (non-white) citizens.

Although all citizens now have the right to vote, electors of the Electoral College, not the millions of voting citizens, ultimately decide who our president will be. University of Texas law professor Sanford Levinson explains that the Electoral process "is an undemocratic and perverse part of the American [United States] system of government that ill serves the United States" (Levinson, 2006, 82). Levinson goes on to explain that the Electoral College has elected candidates as presidents who did not get the majority of the peoples' votes. The last time this happened was in the 2000 presidential election. Al Gore received more votes from the people than Bush did, but the electors from the Electoral College made Bush the president. Legal disputes over the results ended up in the U.S. Supreme Court. The Court made it clear that the Constitution gave the Electoral College the right to determine the winner. It is therefore a semi-lie that the people elect the president. According to U.S. historian Howard Zinn, "The fact that the Supreme Court refused to allow any reconsideration of the election meant that it was determined to see that its favorite [Conservative] candidate, Bush, would be President" (Zinn, 2003, 677). These interactions are pointed out because they manifest acceptable animalness at the highest echelons of our culture. Yet it has worked well for over 200 years for several major reasons. Most of us are acceptable Animal beings and we identify and support our culture's animalness. Most importantly, there have been enough liberal trends to impede rampant animalness.

As for our culture's legal bastion, it was the Founders' intention to establish the Supreme Court (1789) as an "undemocratic institution" to maintain the culture's Conservatism. Although, the Court prevents politicians' runaway animalness, as it did Bush's lack of caring for the environment, it was built into the culture's Conservative nature. Therefore, by design it is a Conservative institution. Legal journalist Jeffrey Toobin explains: "The justices were not elected; they were not accountable to the public in any meaningful way; their life tenure gave them no reason to cater to the will of the people" (Toobin, 2007, 2). In fact, Supreme Court judges cannot democratically select their leader, the chief justice. The president appoints him. Conservative George W. Bush appointed young Conservative John Roberts as chief justice in 2005 for life. To this day, nine individuals interpret Constitutional verbiage and the nation's laws for as long as they want, even when they get too old or too ill to function adequately. Of course there is a positive side to their life appointment. The justices are insulated from lobbyists and they don't have to cater to a president's whims. They function as a gang of nine legal dictators.

Through the years, certain events have caused the culture to install some degrees of social caring and equality for its citizens. For example, the great economic depression of the 1930s brought about the election of the nation's first liberal president, Franklin Delano Roosevelt. The depression triggered the new president to install social caring programs. His "New Deal" social caring programs relieved the country from turmoil and much of the citizens' suffering.

Then after World War II (WWII), in 1946, the GI Bill was installed. It made it possible for millions of war veterans from working class families to attend universities. Some became liberal social scientists, intellectuals, lawyers, and judges who began interpreting the Constitution with more social caring than our Founders had intended. This enabled the U.S. Supreme Court, for a short period, to go against the culture's inequality. In 1954, in *Brown v. the Board of Education*, the Court outlawed racial segregation in schools. Yet, in the 1960s President L. B. Johnson had to use federal military troops to enforce African (black) children's constitutional right to attend schools together with European (white) children. The Court's liberal trend also increased women's rights by doing away with laws against abortions (*Wade v. Roe*, 1973). In short, the Court began interpreting the Constitution to support "common" citizens' rights.

However, by 1986 Conservative President Ronald Reagan's attorney general, Edwin Meese III, provided a framework for a Conservative attack on the Supreme Court's liberal trend with what he called a "jurisprudence of original intention." This meant restricting decisions to only what our Founding Fathers meant. In essence, this meant reversing liberal social caring actions that the Court had previously made. Conservative federal Judge Robert Bork stated, "The framers' intentions with respect to freedoms are the sole legitimate premise from which constitutional analysis may proceed." In other words, according to Reagan, Meese, and Bork, the proper thing was to get the culture back on our Founding Fathers' Conservative track. This conflicted with liberal Supreme Court justices such as William Brennan who stated in 1985: "The genius of the Constitution rests not in any static meaning it might have had in a world that is dead and gone, but in the adaptability of its great principles to cope with current problems and current needs" (Toobin, 2007, 14). For Animal being justices and politicians static ideology is okay, and the "old framer's" Conservative world is not dead and gone, but here and now.

By 1986 the Reagan regime was relishing its selection of judges who were bringing the Supreme Court back to its original Conservative nature. Toobin pointed out, "They [members of the Reagan regime] didn't need better arguments; they just needed new justices" (Toobin, 2007, 17). By 2007 a series of Conservative presidents had selected enough Conservative judges to be in

control of the Court. It is Conservatives' duty, whether they are judges, senators…or the president, to conserve the culture's Conservative nature as close
as possible to our Founders' intentions.

In 2010 the Court swayed the culture toward the Founders' intentions of
having the wealthy in power. The U.S. Supreme Court, by a 5-4 vote, over-
turned a 20-year-old ruling that said corporations could be prohibited from
using money from their general treasuries to pay for their own political campaign ads. The decision, written by Justice Anthony Kennedy, removes limits
on independent expenditures that are not coordinated with candidates' campaigns. The Court's decision strengthens corporate power (the wealthy few)
and the culture's animalness.

Liberal President Barack Obama in his State of Union speech rebuked the
Court for its decision:

> "With all due deference to separation of powers, last week the
> Supreme Court reversed a century of law that I believe will open
> the floodgates for special interests—including foreign corpora-
> tions—to spend without limit in our elections. I don't think
> American [U.S.] elections should be bankrolled by America's
> [United States'] most powerful interests, or worse, by foreign
> entities. They should be decided by the American [U.S.] people
> and that is why I'm urging Democrats and Republicans to pass a
> bill that helps to right this wrong" (State of Union, 1/27/2010).

In 2008 a majority of voting citizens went against our Founders' intentions
of having "their own kind" in power, and Barack Obama was elected president.
(History will point out that President Obama's inauguration speech showed
that he did not know how much of a deviation he was from our Founding
Fathers' beliefs.) In the 2008 presidential election enough United States citizens sensed that a liberal African (black) man was better than the continu-
ing deterioration of the nation under the values and ideals of a Conservative
European (white) presidential candidate. The last time that the United States
culture sensed such a thing, a liberal European (white) man, Franklin Delano
Roosevelt (FDR), was elected president in 1933.

Most U.S. citizens are ignorant about their culture's animalness. Likewise, they are ignorant that liberal politicians try to reduce the culture's animalness. Because of their animalness, most citizens have difficulty identifying with liberal politicians' efforts to install social caring programs and equality benefiting all citizens. This is why the Founding Fathers' Conservative nature has been maintained for over 200 years, and continues…

Conservative Hierarchy of Social Caring

Social theorists such as Dr. Robert Nesbit and Dr. Michael Parenti bring out political Conservatives' lack of social caring. Nesbit points to their opposition to special social entitlements, affirmative programs for equality, and proposals for reducing the culture's huge financial inequalities. For example, the Conservative regimes of Reagan–Bush Sr. and Bush Jr.–Cheney maintained the culture's financial inequality—more for the wealthy few and less for working families. Dr. Michael Parenti explains that during the Conservative Reagan–Bush regime the gap between the rich and the workers increased. Workers' labor union membership, benefits, and wages all declined. Yet, there was more wealth and less taxation for the wealthy few. About a decade later, the culture's grossly unequal financial distribution continued under the Conservative Bush Jr.–Cheney regime. During this period corporate executives were making about 400 times more money than their workers were, even when their corporations were financially failing. By 2007 it was reported that corporate executives made far more in one day than a typical working professional couple made in a year. These regimes are model examples of how Conservatives maintain the culture's financial inequality. These regimes should not be considered as being intentionally animalistic. They merely interacted with the limited caring of animals genetically programmed in our species.

This is why when an Animal being is president there is less health care for workers and their families. Marian W. Edelman of the Children's Defense Fund pointed this out: "It's obscene that our political leaders are not debating how we get health care to every one of the 10 million children who don't have it, but how to take away health care from millions more" (Edelman, 1996, 40). There is no public outrage over the lack of health care for children because it is a normal occurrence in our wealthy animalistic nation. In 2005 there were 46.6 million people without health insurance coverage, up from 45.3 million people in 2004. In 2009 there were over 47 million people without health insurance, yet Conservative politicians were still opposing any efforts for a "universal" health care system for all members of the culture. Most Conservatives are incapable of identifying with the physical and mental health needs of children of working class families. They cannot associate these children's interactions with the future welfare of the culture. Due to their limited identification of their kind, even of their own culture, Conservative politicians cannot identify all children's health as important for the development of productive citizens for the nation's future.

It is natural for the culture's Conservative political leaders to oppose long-term caring solutions for citizens' in need. They feel that people in need should depend on private charitable organizations that grovel to workers to regurgitate money and on wealthy individuals' short-term charitable whims. This kind of temporary help is in line with their animal nature, their lack of identification with those not of their kind. Some decades ago while visiting the U.S., noted international Swedish economist Gunnar Myrdal exclaimed that of all the rich nations this country "is least generous in giving economic security to its old people, its children, its sick people" (Maddocks, 1989, 10). Such lack of caring for the health of workers and their children is within the culture's range of accepted animalness.

Most Conservative politicians become adept at masking their limited caring for the general welfare of the culture's citizens. A favored way of masking their limited caring is with religion. They quickly become righteous over a popular issue that they can relate to religious morality. For example, some decades ago well-financed Conservative religious think tanks took up abortion as a good political issue to righteously oppose. Conservative pro-life organizations were soon screaming about how they cared for unborn fetuses. Conservatives choked with grief and shed tears as they talked about how a pregnant woman should not have the right to end the life of her fetus. Their verbal attacks against women favoring pro-choice escalated to bombing abortion clinics and killing some of the clinics' physicians and health care workers.

Conservatives dearly enjoy barking that they are pro-life. Yet once babies of needy citizens are born, they oppose allocating money to social programs for childcare.

Conservative President George W. Bush righteously opposed programs for the welfare of children. Although his educational program's theme was "no child left behind," he "proposed cutting funds for childcare, after-school and summer-school programs, assistance to abused and neglected children, and treatment for substance abuse" (Parenti, 2008, 101). Conservatives easily verbalize that they care for all citizens. Yet they hamper or block help for children and the needy.

Animal instincts of having a hierarchical system of inequality are not limited to only Animal being politicians and some wealthy individuals. Most workers' are also Animal beings with the instincts to identify and respect the top status of the wealthy few. The culture therefore easily conditions workers to go along with proposals giving more power and wealth to the wealthy. This makes it easy for the culture's Conservative political system to install programs favoring the welfare of the wealthy few and to minimize programs for common working citizens. For example, in 2009–2010 President Obama proposed health care reforms to benefit most citizens. What was startling to political scientist Dr. David Runciman was U.S. citizens' backlash to the reforms. He thought it striking that the people who most disliked the whole idea of healthcare reform were the ones it would most benefit "Why do people vote against their own interests?" (BBC News 3/21/2010, Internet) In short, the bulk of Animal beings accept their culture's hierarchical system of inequality, even when they're at the trash level of the system.

Our species' animalness has a rich history in our cultures. One has only to review biblical stories on the treatment of "others" and the teachings of historically famous doctors of philosophy to see why institutionalized inequality and lack of caring for others has been transmitted through the years. (The word doctor comes from Latin meaning *teacher* or *to teach*. The first doctorate was not of law, medicine, or education, it was the doctor of philosophy–Ph.D.). Some 3,000 years ago Aristotle, Socrates, and Plato taught that limited caring for the common people was proper. These ancient philosophers identified financial and social status hierarchies, the basis of inequality, as correct. It was logical for them to think common people would forever need to kiss the hand or "whatever" of royalty and the wealthy, since almost all people of that era were slaves or peons. The strong theme of the times was "Each man must perform functions proper to his station and his nature" (Parenti, 1994, 119). In other words, the masses or common people did not have the right to be treated with the same level of respect and caring that was enjoyed by the few of royalty and wealth.

Noted Conservative political writers such as Thomas Carlyle have kept this theme alive. Carlyle wrote: "It must be recognized that man has his superiors, a hierarchy above him, one which extends up degree by degree to God himself" (Nesbit, 1986, 53). Political Animal beings have always championed the concept that those at the top, because of wealth or royalty, need only bow to god.

Uncaring for the Global Environment

Animal beings' caring is limited to their own timespace. Therefore, it is difficult for Conservative politicians to actually care for the future of the nation and impossible to care for the welfare of the global environment. Of course, they verbalize otherwise.

One of the biggest problems addressed by major cultures in the early 2000s was global warming and its effects: intense droughts, floods, rising sea levels, famine, and disease. At that time the Conservative leadership of the most powerful culture could not care about the global environment. The Bush–Cheney regime blocked efforts to deal with the danger threatening our species and all other life forms. Although the culture was the largest carbon dioxide polluter, this Animal being duo played down the threat and opposed policies curbing global pollution. This even caused the Conservative U.S. Supreme Court in 2007 to step in and restrain the Bush–Cheney regime's level of animalness. The Court ordered the Environmental Protection Agency (EPA) to do what it was supposed to do, protect the nation's environment for the health and safety of its people. (The disagreement between the Bush–Cheney regime and the Court shows animal nature's broad range of limited caring.)

Throughout the Bush–Cheney era, the U.S. culture refused to join the

Kyoto Protocol, which is a global community effort on curbing carbon emissions into the environment. In October 2005 Russia, Japan, and other cultures, which had been holding back, ratified the Kyoto Protocol. The United Nations reported that the Kyoto Protocol would have failed without Russia's participation because it needed to be ratified by fifty-five nations that emitted the bulk of the pollution in order to pass. Although, the U.S. was the largest emitter, the Protocol passed without the United States signing it. So the U.S. culture was free to continue polluting the global environment. The Bush–Cheney regime claimed that it would have harmed the U.S. economy, which is the world's wealthiest. So why should nations such as China and India that desperately need to increase the health of their economy be expected to sign the Protocol?

The Bush–Cheney regime's lack of caring for the nation's environment should have been identified as treason. But no one yelled treason because U.S. citizenry is conditioned to perceive Conservative leadership's lack of caring for the environment as normal. It is sickening and pathetic that billions depend on the most powerful Conservative culture to be the leader in caring for the future welfare of our species.

In Favor of Weapons of Mass Destruction

Under Conservative leadership, our U.S. culture is most dangerous and most threatening to the global environment.

U.S. Animal being leaders are forever waving the flag, barking out the word "freedom" and producing all kinds of weapons for national defense. Conservative leaderships' interactions have indicated to the world that not only would it not give up any of its arsenal, but it would also continue to expand its weapons of mass destruction (WMD). In 1970 the Nuclear Non-Proliferation Treaty was signed by 183 non-nuclear nations. In the treaty, non-nuclear nations agreed *not* to seek the possession of nuclear weapons. (Israel, however, soon had nuclear weapons with the help of the United States.) In exchange for their agreement, the five nuclear weapon nations—the United States, Britain, Russia, France, and China—were to get rid of their nuclear bombs. As time passed, the U.S. decided not to get rid of its nuclear bombs. Instead, the U.S. went on to develop nuclear strategic man held missiles, torpedoes, land mines, and other small sized nuclear weapons. The other nuclear weapon nations, including Israel, also decided not to get rid of their nuclear weapons. The United States, however, did not worry about other nations' nuclear weapons. The U.S. knew these nations would not be able to keep up with the nuclear delivery systems of its well-financed military industrial complex. (The U.S. has nuclear delivery weapons on ships, submarines, and airplanes all over the globe. It also has access to land bases in Anglo-European nations such as the U.K., Australia, New Zealand, and Canada).

In 2002 the Bush–Cheney Conservative regime introduced its own nuclear doctrine, the "Nuclear Posture Review" (NPR). The intent of NPR was to keep nuclear weapons as major components of U.S. military might. It was reported that by 2020 the Bush–Cheney regime foresaw land-based nuclear missiles with the power to incinerate an entire city, within an hour, anywhere in the world. This administration intended for nuclear arsenal to remain an integral part of the U.S. military far into the future. In his self-righteous nature and because of the culture's weapon superiority Bush said in August of 2002: "We owe it to our children to free the world from weapons of mass destruction in the hands of those who hate freedom" (*Tikkun*, July/August 2006, 27). The kind of "freedom" Bush was referring to did not mean freedom to travel without passports, freedom from hunger, freedom from military threats, and so on. (The "freedom" Bush referred to is that of free enterprise or capitalism, the topic of a later chapter.)

U.S. weaponry superiority has caused Animal being politicians to think and behave very bravely (especially since they don't have to go into battle). This is why in 2005 the Cheney-Bush regime did not hesitate to announce that the U.S. would not rule out making preemptive strikes (strike without warning) against perceived unfriendly nations. When the dictatorship nation of North Korea developed a nuclear bomb in 2006, it immediately verbalized the same animalistic threat to the Bush–Cheney regime. The Bush–Cheney regime's aggressiveness, with access to WMD, triggered a heightened level of animalness in other cultures. This can be compared to how vicious dogs barking on one side of a fenced property will incite dogs on the other side to retaliate with their vicious barking. The U.S. keeps triggering global primitive animalism in other cultures' Conservatives. Why would Conservatives of other cultures trust the United States military to go on expanding its weaponry without trying to keep up in whatever way possible? This is why the more presidential terms Conservatives have, the more our species' animalness is triggered, globally. Furthermore, the effects of their animalness remain beyond their administration's term in power.

U.S. political leaders have access to the highest financed and most advanced military power. This includes its hundreds of military bases all over the world and the support of many dictators, permitting the use of their nations' airports and naval bases. Consequently, when Animal beings are in control, which happens frequently, the U.S. can become very aggressive. What the U.S. does or does not do, via its Conservative political leaders, affects the stability and instability of nations worldwide.

Support of Animalistic Brutality

The U.S. supports the School of the Americas (SOA), a major U.S. military training center at Fort Benning, Georgia. A major part of the school's mission is to train military Animal beings of Spanish speaking nations to be experts in oppression, torture, and killing. The *School of the Americas Watch*, an organization that reports on the SOA, has documented massacres connected to SOA training such as the ones that occurred in Columbia, El Salvador, Peru, and Chile, from the 1960s to the present. In other words, the U.S. supports military brutality via the SOA.

For decades, the SOA facility has trained Hispano Conservative (right wing) military personnel to control Spanish speaking American nations with intimidation and assassinations. As of 2001, more than 60,000 military officers from Spanish speaking American nations had received the best of training at the expense of U.S. taxpayers. In 1996 the Pentagon released some of the school's training manuals on torture and execution. Graduate military officers of the school include a list of many of the most notorious Animal beings of North and South American cultures. In 2001 the school changed its name to the Western Hemisphere Institute for Security Cooperation (WHISC) in a move to change its image, but its mission remained the same.

Although there are hundreds of documented cases of torture and killings by former students trained at the school, as of December 2008 the United States Congress was still funding the terrorist training school. The Bush–Cheney regime's refusal to ban torture has made more people aware of WHISC.

In fact, the Bush's regime devised a policy called "extraordinary rendition." It allowed CIA agents to kidnap individuals of any nation thought to be enemy combatants and secretly fly them to secret sites in various foreign countries where they could be tortured or killed. The Conservative regime completely ignored the legal and human rights of these individuals. Yet, because of his limited caring and awareness, Bush righteously felt that he did more for human rights than any other U.S. president. He called himself a "compassionate conservative." Yet during the Bush–Cheney regime, Amnesty International condemned the U.S. culture as being a world leader in violating human rights. It was reported that: "Bush has chosen to demand the legal right to torture anyone he wishes" (Branfman, March/April 2006, 34). (Vice President Cheney was the supporting spirit for torturing. He and the CIA orchestrated to the public the torturing issue to one method, "water boarding." This form of torture is unquestionably unpleasant, but nothing in comparison to the methods available to Cheney's torturing boys. Yet the media made it seem that it was the worst form of torture used. Therefore, torturing individuals with such things as electric shock, noise shock, injections of all kind of drugs causing severe thirst, itch, pain, hot to cold head temperatures, and drug addiction were not mentioned.)

In short, it is in the nature of our species' most advanced culture to use its wealth and other resources to maintain its coercive power over others with the latest weapons, large military force, and trained terrorists (domestic and foreign mercenaries). The U.S. spends billions of dollars on war equipment and military personnel rather than on its citizens' health care and education. In 2006 the culture spent $800 billion on weaponry and military personnel (Parenti, 2008, 78). Yet there is no large public movement for change because of the overall Conservative nature of our culture.

The U.S. demands for itself what is natural to the mentality of a top dog. For as far as Animal beings are concerned, if their nation is not top dog, another nation would be. And yes, another Conservative culture as top dog would interact similarly. From Conservatives' animalistic viewpoint, this is the way it has always been and will always be for our species. They are dead certain about this. In the mentality of Animal beings a democratic equalitarian civilization cannot exist. The closer our caring is to that of primitive animals, the more we foam at the mouth when someone mentions a global caring democracy. Our Animal being leaders see any attempt to develop an equalitarian global civilization as utopian and unnatural. Their limited caring is incompatible with democracy and social equality.

A "Unifying Explanation" of Conservatives

Dr. Jack Glaser an associate professor from The University of California at Berkeley and other professors conducted a study on political Conservatives (posted on *World Net Daily* on the Internet, 23 July 2003). It was the first to synthesize a huge amount of data to put out a "Unifying explanation" for Conservatism. The study identified Conservatives' dominant traits of dogmatism, intolerance of ambiguity, fear, and aggression as being at the core of their opposition to equality and resistance to change. Their need for cognitive closure, uncertainty avoidance, and terror management was also linked to their Conservative nature. The researchers referred to these traits as Conservatives' marked psychological motivations. These traits were a dominant part in the personality of Adolph Hitler, and U.S. Presidents Ronald Reagan and George W. Bush. The research also found that in time of crisis, Conservative tendencies appeal more to U.S. citizens than liberal tendencies do.

The study concluded that Conservatives were "less complex," implying that they did not need to go through complex thought processes to justify their interactions. For example, the study quoted one of George W. Bush's typical remarks that he made to an assembly of world leaders in Italy in 2001. Bush told world leaders: "I know what I believe, and I believe what I believe is right." His statement also shows that in his simplistic world he believes that he has been blessed to know what is right and what is evil. Similarly, common animals have little or no doubt in what they do and think. (The study, published in the American Psychological Association's *Psychological*

Bulletin, was conducted by Associate Professor Jack Glaser and visiting Professor Frank Sulloway of UC Berkeley, Associate Professor John Jost of Stanford University's Graduate School of Business, and Professor Arie Kruglanski of the University of Maryland at College Park.)

It can be said that Conservatives run most cultures because our species is mostly composed of Animal beings. However, of the developed cultures, the U.S. clearly has the most animalistic history toward other cultures, and its Conservatives can be the most dangerous because of the nation's wealth, aggressiveness, and global military superiority.

Summary

Writing about some of our cultures' contemptible practices is to identify the animalness of our species. Becoming aware of and identifying the animalness of our species, however, is not a case of belittling our species. It is an evolutionary matter of becoming aware of what we are, members of a transitional species (evolving out of animal nature) with most of us interacting with *only* the limited caring found in animals. In spite of our limited caring for others, at this stage of our species' evolution, we Animal beings are normal members of our Homo sapient species.

Animal beings are the dominant members of our cultures, and we have seen that their caring interactions range from the acceptable to unacceptable. We have seen how acceptable Animal beings minimize financial distribution, education, health care, and so on for the people of their culture because it's in their instincts to conserve our species' animalness. Their common sense is to solve conflicts with other cultures by intimidation, torture, assassinations, and wars. Thus, they are likely to trigger the use of nuclear weapons, either from their own military complex or from other cultures.

In summation, if Animal beings of advanced cultures continue to lead us further into the twenty-first century, an imminent catastrophe is awaiting us. In other words, the greatest danger to our species lies within our species.

Part III:

Our Animalness: Cultured & Civilized

"A culture has no existence apart from the behavior [interactions] of the individuals who maintain its practices."

DR. B.F. SKINNER

6

Being Cultured

It is a universal commonality for a collectivity of entities to create a greater entity. In our species, a collectivity of individuals' ongoing interactions creates the entity of a culture. This collectivity forms a "most complicated system." Ethologist Dr. Konrad Lorenz explains: "The working structure of the instinctive and culturally acquired patterns of behavior which make up the social life of man seems to be one of the most complicated systems we know on this earth" (Lorenz, 1966, xiii). The social life, or culture, that Lorenz speaks of is complicated because our species' potential is created by a vast genetic heritage of nonliving and living interactions. Our cultures are the greatest manifestation of our species' potential

In trying to understand the complexity of the cultural process, most of us seem to be programmed to ignore our animal heritage. Yet it is at the foundation of our interactions. Therefore, most have only a shallow understanding of the complexity involved. However, even the most cursory of examinations reveals how our animal heritage profoundly influences our cultures' interactions. For example, in the U.S. our culture's aggression, lack of social caring, and greed are triggered from our inherited animalness. These interactions cause conflicts within the culture as well as with other cultures. Yet the culture

continues to program its citizens with these dysfunctional interactions generation after generation.

For better or worse, we are genetically and culturally programmed. We
are genetically programmed with our species' inherited potential, and we are
programmed with the values, beliefs, etc. of our cultural environment. The
culture "shapes" our interactions to mold us into *citizens* who uphold and
pass on its dominant interactions. This brings us to identify a culture's "belief-
language" core.

Belief-Language Core

Every culture tends to have both a dominant language and belief structure. The
authors call this combination a "belief-language" core. The core of the culture
has much to do with shaping its members' interactions (feelings, thoughts,
behaviors, etc.). This is because people with the same beliefs and language
(verbal and nonverbal) develop similar perceptions, values, goals, and so forth.
Members of a culture develop loyalty to the culture's socio-political system,
goals, and traditions. A belief-language core not only bonds people to their
culture but also creates the nature of the culture—its persona and character.

Beliefs

Of all our beliefs, whether they are of Darwin's evolution or Marx's revolution, none are as authoritarian and influential as god beliefs. Since there is
nothing to substantiate, prove or disprove, god beliefs have lasted for thousands of years. No matter the scope or depth of their ignorance, god beliefs
provide many with the feeling that they know what *it's* all about. No matter
how dense one may be, god beliefs are easier to digest than beliefs based on
Darwin's or Marx's theories or on science in general. This reinforces god belief
permanence.

People are influenced by god beliefs whether they are damn sure there is
a god or damn sure there isn't one. For example, in our culture many parents
have the skin of their son's penis trimmed. This trimming is called circumcision. Parents subject their sons to this religious tinkering because they are culturally programmed to believe it is a necessary medical procedure. However,

most people of the culture (including some physicians) do not know that circumcision is a Jewish holy ritual that originated in northeast Africa thousands of years ago. It began as a ritual for branding males belonging to the Jews' "god Judaic."

Since our culture's Christian belief is bonded to Judaism, the ancient Judaic ritual of circumcision became a standard surgical procedure in maternity wards. Consequently, whether they know it or not, many U.S. males walk around like certified Jews with a penis *à la* Judaic. Thus, in many parts of the world non-Jewish U.S. males in shower rooms are perceived as Jews. Jews know the reason for this and are quietly happy about it. Hence, whether you are religious or not, god beliefs can affect you whether you know it or not.

> It has benefited Jews not to name their god because when only the term god is used, it is not Jesus or any other god; it's the Jew's god. Hence, to equalize gods, the authors refer to the Jews' god as god Judaic.

God beliefs influence our interactions (feelings, perceptions, reasoning, etc.) much more than most of us are aware. In the 1980s, a national study found that about 80 percent of the U.S. population believed in divine miracles and 50 percent of the population believed the world was created only about two thousand years ago. In other words, as far as half the U.S. population is concerned, the early Egyptians, Chinese, Mayans, Incas, Jews, Romans, and Germanic tribes (Vandals, Vikings, etc.) never existed. In 2005, the Beliefnet Poll found that 79 percent of the people polled said they were spiritual, 67 percent indicated that when we die our "soul" goes to heaven or hell, and 80 percent believed their god created the universe. Knowing these facts about our U.S. culture sheds light on why our citizens seek advice from professional mystics and indulge in all kinds of scams and fantasies more so than citizens of other advanced cultures.

Some of our Species' Major Religions

Belief System	Believers (estimate)	Where	When (estimate)	Founder	Scripture	Deity
Buddhism	325 m	Asia	600 BC	Buddha	Tipitaka	pan
Judaism	45 m	Afro-Asia	1000 BC	Abraham	Old Testament	god
Christianity	1960m	Europe	30 AD	Jesus	New Testament	god
Islam	1130 m	Afro-Asia	600 AD	Muhammad	Koran	god
Hinduism	793 m	India	1000 BC	(unknown)	Vedas, esp. Upanishads	poly

Language

Language is the carrier and organizer of our interactions (thoughts, beliefs, behaviors, etc.). It is also a major variable in expanding our interactions. According to linguist Dr. A. N. Sokolove, "It is through language that most thoughts are formulated, and it is language that makes it possible to analyze, synthesize, abstract, and generalize. More than this it is primarily through language that we become aware of thoughts of others—and they of ours" (Lefrancois, 1959, 254). Dr. Konrad Lorenz explains that language "opened unprecedented possibilities not only for spreading and sharing knowledge…but also for transmitting it from one generation to the next. Knowledge became heritable" (Lorenz, 1981, 342).

Revisiting our culture's capitalistic traits of aggression, limited social caring, and greed, we can see how language made such traits heritable. The culture uses systemic lying to sell products and services of all kinds because such lying serves capitalism's greed. Systemic semi-lying via the mass media (which are for-profit enterprises) invigorates capitalism's freedom of speech to say and sell almost anything to make a profit. This is the essence of the Constitutional right of "freedom of speech." Capitalism's greed is embedded in the culture's values, goals, and beliefs. It is not surprising that workers will parade, scream, riot, and even kill to preserve capitalism in their culture. Most are ignorant that capitalism's lack of social caring and greed are genetically inherited animal traits that are certainly not for the benefit of workers. As a result, workers will continue to work and fight for such inherited capitalist traits because they are programmed to perceive the traits as necessities of life.

**Four of the Twelve Language Branches Creating
the Indo-European Family of Languages**

The Latin branch: French, Spanish, Italian, Portuguese, Romanian, Moldavian.

The Celtic branch: Irish Gaelic, Scottish Gaelic, Breton.

The Germanic branch: German, English, Flemish, Icelandic, Austrian, Dutch, Danish, Swedish, Norwegian, Faroese, Yiddish.

The Slavic branch: Russian, Serbian, Ukrainian, Czech, Byelorussian, Bulgarian, Polish, Macedonian, Slovak, Sorbian, Bosnian, Croatian.

Spanish and Portuguese are the dominant languages of South America. Spanish and English are the dominant languages of North America. These are not American languages; they are of the Indo-European Family of Languages covering an area from India to Ireland.

The Cultural Environment

As we have seen, the belief-language core creates and maintains the cultural environment. This is easily done because the core is triggering and shaping genetically programmed interactions from within us. As explained in Chapter 1, the environment can activate or deactivate our genes.

We cannot escape from our culture's environmental influence. Too often, professionals dealing with people's interactions ignore the influence our cultural environment has on our genetics. For example, some U.S. psychological studies on children's criminal activities assumed that genetic factors were entirely responsible. One such study indicated that a significant number of children whose parents had been convicted of crimes also became involved in crime. The study pointed out that this was true even when the children had been separated from their criminal parents at an early age. The study concluded that the children's genetic heritage was the reason for their criminal activities. Ignored was the fact that the children had remained in the same cultural environment that had triggered their parents' criminal activities. Consequently, the same environment triggered criminal activities from the children's genes inherited from the parents. It would therefore be incorrect to conclude that the children's criminal activities were triggered solely from their genetic heritage without considering that the cultural environment triggered and shaped their criminal activities.

On the positive side, the cultural environment's institutions of museums, libraries, and universities can trigger and expand our individual potential. The cultural environment triggers all kinds of creations from us—the works of artists, authors, scientists, and intellectuals.

It is easy for members of any culture to identify and comment upon the flaws of other cultures and their peoples. For example, one could write about cultures that use religion to exploit the young to kill in the name of their god, where men go unpunished for sexually abusing women, where women are tortured for various reasons, the plight of India's untouchables, and so on. Since it is their own culture, the authors focus on the U.S. cultural environment and on what its belief-language core triggers. Furthermore, as the world's most influential and militarily powerful culture, the interactions of the U.S. affect the global environment.

Summary

We have seen that the belief-language core is the major variable creating a cultural environment and shaping our interactions. With this realization we can understand why cultures with a similar core, such as the Anglo (English) cultures of England, United States, Australia, Canada, and New Zealand, share similar values and goals. On the other hand, cultures whose belief-language cores are markedly different tend to have conflicts. In the following chapter, which may be seen as a second part of the current chapter, we look at the emergence of the belief-language core that united a conglomerate of cultures to form our present great civilization.

7

Our Judaic-Germanic Civilization

Each civilization marks a significant
timespace of our species' evolution.

As our species gradually progresses out of animal nature, its interactions (feelings, beliefs, behaviors, etc.) evolve beyond the dominant interactions that brought about each of our great civilizations. In other words, a civilization's demise is inevitable because our ongoing interactive evolution eventually brings in a more advanced civilization. Our present great civilization began some two thousand years ago with the demise of the Latin-Roman Civilization. Larger than previous civilizations, there is a group of core cultures at its nucleus and many other cultures attached to its *Judaic-Germanic* (belief-language) core.

A figurine of Abraham, the founder of Judaism, could serve as an icon representing the belief-language core of our Judaic-Germanic civilization. It would be solid gold, with blue diamonds for eyes, and stamped "Judaic-Germanic" underneath. "Judaic" would refer to the belief roots, from which the civilization's dominant Christian belief emerged. Jewish historian Abba Eban explained: "More than one writer has remarked that Christianity began as a Jewish sect" (Eban, 1984, 104). (According to the Jews, Abraham created Judaism. Like

Judaism, Christianity and Islam are defined as Abrahamic god beliefs.) Christianity began as Catholicism some two thousand years ago. Then about 400 hundred years ago, Protestantism emerged from Catholicism in the early 1600s. The Protestant belief was initiated by the German priest Martin Luther (1483–1546), and was reinforced by French theologian John Calvin (1509–1564). By the 1600s Protestantism was on its way to becoming the dominant Christian belief of our civilization's core. "Germanic" would refer to the Germanic family of languages, from which English emerged to become the dominant language of the civilization. All contemporary cultures with an English-Protestant core evolved from, and maintain, the civilization's nucleus.

The civilization's English-Protestant core-cultures include the United Kingdom (U.K.), United States (U.S.), Canada, New Zealand, and Australia. The dominant language of Israel is Hebrew, an Afro-Asian Arabic language, but its embodiment of Judaism gives it a special status in the civilization's nucleus. (The nation of Israel was created in 1948 by being carved out of Islamic-Arabic land in Afro-Asia. The top cultures of the civilization, the U.S. and the U.K., created this miracle for the Jews.) Aside from the English-Protestant cultures and Israel, the civilization also includes the rest of the Germanic linguistic cultures such as Germany, Austria, Netherlands (Dutch), and Switzerland.

Dozens of non-Germanic cultures form the fringes of the civilization. These cultures are united with the civilization's foundation via Christianity (Catholicism). Such cultures include Ireland and the Latin cultures of France, Spain, Italy, Portugal, and Romania. Catholicism also bonds some Eastern European cultures such as Greece and Poland to the civilization. Even further out in the fringes we find the Catholic Latin cultures of North and South America.

Emergence of the Judaic-Germanic core

Although the creation of our civilization evolved from infinite events, there is one historical event that stands out as symbolic of the merger of Judaic beliefs and Germanic languages. In 850, a group of Jews instinctively used the German language and their Hebrew language to create the semi-Germanic language of Yiddish. We say instinctively because the Jewish group was not in Germany, but in Poland, a Slavic linguistic culture. (Latin was the dominant language of Europe at that time.) In other words, it was nearly 1,200 years ago that a Jewish group sensed that a Germanic language would best benefit the future of Judaism. They were right. Jews' Yiddish language and Judaic beliefs established them as a semi-Germanic ethnic group. This historical Judaic group's god beliefs, with their hybrid language of Yiddish, most likely initiated the civilization's belief-language core.

It is difficult to say which component (belief or language) has been more influential to the civilization's potential. However, Jewish historians promoting the importance of the Judaic component are by far the most vocal and righteous. Perhaps they have reason to be, but we shall first examine the Germanic component.

The Germanic Component

The civilization's Germanic linguistic roots go back over two thousand years to the Goths, Barbarians, Vikings, Vandals, and other Germanic tribes. These Germanic tribes, which Latin Romans called "White heads," were proud warloving tribes. Even their gods, as one called Odoz, were symbols of aggression, battle, and bloody orgies. These tribes were aggressive and brutal. In fact, some of their tribal names such as *Vandals*, *Vikings*, and *Barbarians* became English terms synonymous with gory animalism.

These aggressive Germanic tribes swarmed out of the cold areas of northern Europe, where they had been content killing and stealing from each other for hundreds of years. After the year 300, they expanded their attacks to the south of Western Europe where the civilized Latin people of the era lived. By the winter of 476, under the leadership of a tribal chief named Odoacer, a group of Germanic tribes went south to lick clean what was left of Rome. As the power of Rome disintegrated, Germanic tribes looted and raped most Western European cultures whenever they felt the urge to do so. Eventually, Latin remnants of the once great fighting legions pulled together one last time and herded the Germanic tribes out of the areas that are now Portugal, Spain, Italy, and France. Over the years, Germanic tribes formed into northern European cultures such as Sweden, Germany, Netherlands, Luxembourg, Switzerland, and Austria.

The islands that now make up the U.K. were regularly looted and eventually conquered by sea-warring Vikings and Vandals. As a result, England evolved as a Germanic linguistic culture. (The Irish, having not been conquered by Germanic tribes, did not develop into a Germanic ethnicity.) Naturally, these tribes created much of the genetic and ethnic ancestry of the U.K.'s Anglo-Saxon people. These Germanic descendants inherited their tribal ancestors' love for seafaring warships and the business of looting treasures from others. They have continued to impose their aggression globally. They have taken art treasures, lands, and other natural resources from cultures all over the globe. Today, England's museums have the world's most impressive collection of treasures that belong to other cultures. (The U.S. is second in this category.) Germanic ethnicities' aggression and love of weaponry permeate the nature of our great civilization.

The Judaic Component

Judaism has a history of some three thousand years. Most importantly, it was the first god belief documented for Africans and Europeans. Jewish scribes created documents to prove, beyond a reasonable doubt, that Jews were the chosen people of god Judaic. They sealed their group's status in holy books in an era when only a few individuals could read and write. Jewish scribes read their holy books to Jews and non-Jews alike to pass on the word of god Judaic. The Jews' Hebrew holy books were translated into many of the Indo-European languages of the era. For over 1000 years Judaic beliefs were transmitted from generation to generation, culture to culture, to become the belief foundation of our great civilization.

As the centuries passed, no other god story in Afro-Asia and Europe came up with the potential to confront Judaic beliefs, which were accepted as the word of everyone's god in many cultures. The idea of one powerful god over all others was patented by and for the Jews. (This is why Jesus could not be a god on his own in the Christian's story. The Jesus story had to be related to the god Judaic story by making Jesus the son-of-god Judaic).

Judaism Sprouts in Europe

The "Jewish dispersion" or migration from northeastern Africa was not so much of a *dispersion* as it was a beeline to the prospering cultures of Western Europe. By this time Jews were already experts at moneymaking schemes.

Their Judaic god beliefs indoctrinated the expertise of moneymaking: "One who wishes to acquire wisdom should study the way money works, for there is no greater area of Torah-study than this. It is like an ever-flowing stream" (Jewish Talmud, Bava Batra 175b). Jews' migration to European cultures presented them with the opportunity to increase their profits with their moneymaking expertise to a far greater extent than had been possible back in their homeland.

Throughout their migration into different European cultures, Jewish groups carried their own belief-language core. This enabled Jews to easily communicate and bond with each other in their businesses no matter what host cultures they moved into. They were able to create "a network of trust and confidence, of kinship and affinity, with Jewish bankers and merchants in the various countries of the Jewish dispersion" (Eban, 1984, 88). The Jewish network (dispersion) facilitated Jews to expand into international trade by trading with each other from the many cultures they were in. Even before the 700s, Jewish jewelers, shippers, cloth-makers, moneylenders, and slave traders had connections from northeast Africa to Holland, Germany, Belgium, England, Italy, Spain, and France. Jews dealt in the slavery business long before slaves were taken from western Africa and sold in the English colonies of North America, the Caribbean, and Brazil. Jews had been selling Slavic people from Eastern Europe to Christians and other Jews in Western Europe. In fact, the English word for "slave" is derived from the German word *Slav* or *Slavic*.

The expansion of the Jewish network in Europe invigorated Jews' moneymaking expertise in the prime cultures of Western Europe. Since Jews traded mainly with each other, they controlled international trade and prices. Jewish groups' strong ethnic bonds and financial network of bankers and merchants eventually brought about the international banking and commerce centers of Europe. The Jewish network was an exceptional benefit to Germanic cultures such as England, the Netherlands, and Belgium. Belgium became the diamond control center of the world and remains so to the present (hosting the De Beers family of companies). The network linked Jewish commerce from one end of the Mediterranean to the other. (Jews also mated with each other to keep material wealth within families. This practice eventually led to genetic health problems.)

As Jews wandered in and out of European host cultures as a minority ethnic group, they were envied and disliked for their financial schemes. One such scheme was based on the idea that if one had more money than one could spend, then one could make more money by lending it to others with interest. This scheme perplexed and enraged the ignorant working class, the borrowers. It inspired the good Englishman William Shakespeare to portray Jews as merciless economic controllers. In his play, *The Merchant of Venus*, Shylock, a successful money-lending Jew, took his case to court because he wanted to extract a pound of flesh from the man who could not repay the money he had borrowed with interest. Portia, the defense lawyer, got the slouch off by convincing the court that mercy was of a higher order and more important than money. The lender lost his money, and the debtor kept all his fat. Shakespeare was aware of Judaic freedom and the consequences of workers as borrowers. He tried to enlighten working people on the control lenders had over borrowers. According to the Old Jewish Testament, "the borrower is servant to the lender" (Eban, 1984, 163). Thus, charging interest on borrowed money could have the borrower forever paying off his debt to the lender. Traditionally, Jews have been the lenders. Their idea of charging interest on monies loaned continues to make capitalist bankers wealthy and workers forever paying off accumulating interest fees.

There were times when common people became annoyed with the "chosen few of god," with tricks for acquiring wealth here, there, and everywhere. Laws were made to restrain Jews' moneymaking freedom. However, when Jews encountered these laws, they found they could buy their freedom to practice their god–given rights. The price for their freedom to pursue wealth was a share of their profits to the host culture's leadership. For example, King Charlemagne (800–814) of Germany did well with Jews, and Jews did well with the "good" king. This king protected Jews' moneymaking freedom in exchange for what they could do to increase his wealth. In France in the year

845, a collection of laws to protect the French working class from Jews taking too many liberties was submitted to King Charles I, but the King refused to ratify the laws. The Jews also had a financial arrangement with French King Philip II of the late 1100s. In spite of this king's lifelong dislike for Judaic practices, he still protected Jewish moneylenders' practices in return for a share of their profits. A great deal of these kings' wealth depended on Jews' freedom to practice their moneymaking schemes.

Throughout history, Christianity has come to the aide of Jews. As far back as 598, the Catholic pope of the period began announcing legal protection for Jews and their synagogues. Although papal protection through the centuries has not been faultless, Jewish groups could call for papal protection even when kings hindered their freedom. Catholic popes have been performing sacred miracles for Jews for over 1,500 years.

Through the centuries, Jews have identified their expertise "in the pursuit of happiness" with surnames indicating wealth or prestige in various European languages. In English, such surnames as Jewels, Silver, Pearl, Gold, Golden, Diamond, Ruby, Rich, Richer, Wonder, Wiseman, Freeman, Free, Freedom, Paris, Berlin, Spain, England, Alexander, and so on are used. Such clichés as "time is money," "ban taxation," "free enterprise," "free market," "diamonds are a girl's best friend," "god's people," and the "Promised Land" represent cherished Judaic beliefs.

Jew's Search for the Promised Land

Jews' recorded religious history has been vital in maintaining their ethnic identity and practices. The Old Testament (Hebrew Bible) is a compilation of stories about Judaic tribes' beliefs, practices, and promises. It includes tales about what god Judaic said that gave Jews their semi-godly status and what goodies were in store for them. For example, before any Jew left Africa, god Judaic promised "his" people that they would have their own land in order that they would not have to live as squatters on other peoples' lands. In addition to their pursuit of material wealth, Jews were forever looking for the Promised Land to become a reality. (Historically, Jews' search for the Promised Land, and their pursuit of freedom to obtain wealth, has brought Jewish people both huge benefits and deadly repercussions.)

The reality of the Promised Land was first perceived around 711. God Judaic kept his promise and, *dios mio* (my god), it was in southern Spain! The land was a dreamland—a sunny, beautiful area on the Mediterranean Coast of Western Europe. The Promised Land miracle began to unfold as North African military forces of the Islamic religion crossed the Mediterranean Sea and invaded southern Spain and Portugal. The Jews in Spain saw the Arab invasion as god-sent and gleefully welcomed the Muslims to their Christian host culture. In fact, according to Jewish historian Abba Eban, "The Jews not only welcomed them, but fought along side them and administered the cities they conquered" (Eban, 1984, 141). In other words, it was a classic charitable case of *mi casa es su casa* (my house is your house). With this generous hospitality and assistance provided to Muslims in taking over most of Christian Spain began an unspeakable period of ecstasy for Jews. Freedom bells rang wildly from 711 to about 1285. The Jews dearly enjoyed the Promised Land in southern Spain for over five hundred years. Jewish historians refer to this sacred period as "The Golden Age." Such a glorious period reinforced the idea of being "the chosen" of everyone's god. Historian Abba Eban marvels at such a period of unrestrained freedom and writes: "The degree of autonomous and uninterrupted cultural activity of Jews in Spain arouses wonder" (Eban, 1984, 148). However, like too much of a good thing, the "autonomous and uninterrupted" Jewish period of *mi casa es su casa* for Muslims had to end. European Christian military forces drove the Muslims out of Spain and back to North Africa, jailing some of the collaborating Jews in the process.

The prosperous Jewish community was shocked that the sacred orgy was over. The Jews had believed that the Promised Land was a thing of forever. Yet forever was too long, even for god Judaic. (At any rate, god Judaic is not beholden to give Jews another go at the Promised Land for that length of time.) In his defense, he did keep his promise by giving them as much freedom in sunny Spain as he morally could.

Soon after the *mi casa es su casa* Jewish orgy ended, the devilish and despicable Spanish Christian Inquisition raised its ugly head to seek out Jews. As a consequence to the Jews' Golden Age, Christians created the Inquisition to find out who among them were Jews. The Christian Inquisition was not as beastly as might have been expected. Even so, it was harsh to Jewish sensitivity. The Inquisition's harsh punishment for high treason, for having given comfort and aid to the enemy, was for Jews to leave Spain or become Christians. Most Jews thought this punishment too severe. This was not a mythical "let my people go" situation. Feeling forced to leave, most Jews had to convert their real estate and businesses into jewelry, gold, silver, diamonds, and cash, wealth they could carry out of Spain.

Most of them migrated to England, Holland, and Belgium. Jews leaving the country labeled the Jews who stayed *Marranos* ("swine" in Spanish). The Marranos were left with the freedom to take liberties on departing fellow Jews. They found themselves in the excellent position of buying exiting Jews' properties at reduced prices. For the Marranos, converting to Christianity basically meant concealing the Star of David and hanging a cross around their neck. For centuries Jewish leaders have described the Spanish Christian Inquisition as being the worst period for Jews.

After the Christian Inquisition, however, there were other hard times for Jews. Over three hundred years later, Jews' financial schemes and successes triggered deadly consequences in Poland. In the 1600s there was a popular Polish proverb among the masses: "What the peasant earns, the noble spends and the Jew profits by" (Eban, 1984, 215). Such a proverb indicates that it did not take much for a zealot Polish leader such as Bogdan Chmielnicki to trigger a massacre of Jews in 1648 and 1649. Again, a cry for "let my people go" was not needed. Jews were free to leave Poland.

Less than three hundred years later, Jews thought they had another go at the Promised Land. This time it was in Germany. However, by 1938 Judaic freedom triggered the beast in the German culture. On November 7, 1938 the Nazi party began its deadly attacks against German Jews. This outright, violent attack became known as *Kristallnacht*, meaning "the night of broken glass." Jews' businesses and synagogues were vandalized and destroyed. Ignorant about its own civilization's foundation, the German (alias Nazi) culture believed that it was possible to do away with all that was Jewish. It is a complex, nasty, sick story, but the highlights are that Adolph Hitler, as leader of millions of Barbarians and Vikings, viewed Judaism as a thing to weed out once and for all. Millions of Jews, Gypsies, and others who were considered as an infectious disease to the health of the German people were systematically murdered. After the torturous and murderous ordeal under Nazi Germany, few if any Jews still believe the Spanish Christian Inquisition was the worst of times for Jews.

The German culture's warped leadership did not realize that, even if it were possible to remove all Jews from earth, there would remain countless millions of individuals throughout the civilization who adore the essence of what Judaic freedom stands for. Hitler and his millions of followers were unable to see the indispensable part that Jews and Judaism play in the civilization. It was ironic that by trying to destroy the existence of Jews, the German culture was out to destroy itself and the civilization of which it is a part.

After World War II, Adolph Eichmann, one of Hitler's organizers of the Jews' genocide, escaped to America. Peter Malkin, a Jew and noted Nazi hunter, captured Eichmann in Argentina. Eichmann had been living with his wife and their young son in a modest neighborhood for fifteen years. In a conversation with his captor Eichmann stated, *"Ich liebe Kinder"* (I love children). On hearing Eichmann's professed love of children, Malkin responded: "My sister's boy…he was just your son's age. Also blond and blue-eyes just like your son. And you killed him." After a pause, Eichmann, a clean, organized and highly cultured German, answered: "But he was Jewish, wasn't he?" (Malkin, 1990, 214) The boy was of Eichmann's German ethnicity and European race, but still outside of what Eichmann perceived to be "his kind." Although most German Jews were of the European race, Hitler and his Nazi tribe saw Jews as a small, foreign ethnic group, a group not of their kind.

Malkin had described his nephew to Eichmann because it is well known that being a blond blue-eyed European is the essence of "our kind" for Germanic cultures and especially for Nazism's Aryan sentiments. What is not well known is that Jews have a longer history of zealously prescribing blond blue-eyed Europeans as the look to have. So as far as Malkin was concerned, Eichmann killed a child of his own kind. However, Eichmann could not identify the boy as being of his kind—"But he was Jewish, wasn't he?" Eichmann's

German culture had programmed its citizenry to hate Jews by constantly repeating that Jews were a people to distrust and to get rid of. In other words, our species' limited animal caring for others was easily triggered in the German culture to identify Jews as people to eradicate. Yet, the majority of German Jews were of the same European race as Hitler and his gang of millions. It was as a news commentator of the French Vichy government said, "If Jews had blue skins...things would be easy, but since they don't, we have to find other ways to recognize them" (Buruma, 1995, 44). Jews were forced to identify themselves with a yellow star sewn to their clothing. Without the yellow star, most Jews would be mistaken as Germans of the European race, which in fact most were.

Catholicism *Judaized* Europe

How did Judaism, a closed religious cult with an ethnocentric god syndrome, come to conquer the beliefs of the European masses? Their belief that god created them as his chosen people made it absurd for Jews to go around trying to convert common people to Judaism. Besides, why would anyone want to join them since they were generally disliked? So how did the beliefs of a religious cult with an ethnocentric god manage to become the core belief of our great civilization?

There are a few outstanding reasons why Judaism became the core belief. To begin with, there is the simple commonality in nature that some things survive while other similar things die out. A second reason is that it was the first god belief ever documented in the Afro-European area. Just being written and read by someone was a miracle for most people of the times. A third reason is that most members of our species innately need a god, and having the word of a god written down was a ready-made packaged god belief to hand out. A fourth reason is that the survival of Judaic beliefs depended on the Jews, and Jews were not about to let anyone forget that they were god's chosen people. They made damn sure that this wonderful "truth" survived. Lastly, although Catholicism focused on Jesus, it secured Judaism to the foundation of a great civilization. This is because Judaic stories such as Abraham's conversations with god Judaic, the Jews as the chosen of god, and Jesus as the son of god Judaic were used as a foundation for Catholicism. In other words, when Catholicism emerged in Rome nearly two thousand years ago, it was Judaism in a digestible form for Latin European cultures.

Catholics, the only Christians in the early period of Christianity, stopped everyone they met to tell them the story of Jesus, the most caring of beings. At that time Latin Roman laws forbade the spread of Catholicism, and Catholics suffered deadly consequences in their crusade to establish Jesus as god. Unlike Jews who were able to pay authorities for protection by sharing their profits with them, Catholics could not make such business deals. Catholics did not seek freedom and liberties to become wealthy; they sought converts for god Jesus. Catholics faced the suicidal task of confronting Roman law and beliefs. Jews were not about to put their lives on the line to confront Roman law and beliefs. In contrast, Catholics did put their lives on the line for Jesus' godly status. Countless men, women, and children gave their lives for the cause of converting others to believe in Jesus. They did not know that believing in Jesus meant accepting Judaic scriptures.

Catholics' persistence in the face of death paid off. Priests persuaded the last Latin Roman Emperor, Constantine the Great, to convert to Catholicism just before death in 350. This changed Catholicism from an outlawed religion to the official religion of all cultures of the dying Latin Roman Civilization. Once Rome was no longer the capital of Roman emperors backed by the military might of Roman legions, it became the Holy City (or the Holy Roman Empire). Rome became the papal center of Christianity's conquering beliefs. Catholics now had the power to insist that everyone be Christianized.

Catholicism had focused on Jesus so much that the Jews' Old Testament had lost much of its status and meaning for Catholics. This triggered Catholics to aggressively target Jews for conversion to believe in Jesus. They believed that Jews needed to be updated and saved from hell, but Jews could not accept Jesus as god.

Jews' resistance to the Christian revolution left memorable tragedies in Judaic history. One of these is the bloody story about Rachel, a devoted Jewish Ashkenazim of Germany. Rachel chose to kill her four children rather than allow them to be baptized as Christians. She ordered her children to come to her so that she could kill them. Isaac, the oldest son and her two daughters, Bella and Matron, came obediently. On seeing the bloody scene, Aaron, the youngest child, ran away crying and hid. After killing Isaac, Bella, and Matron, Rachel shouted for Aaron and then went to search for him. She found little Aaron hiding under a chest, dragged him out by his feet, and butchered him (Eban, 1984, 159). The story reveals the strong Jewish sentiment of what it means to be a Jew.

Throughout the centuries, the empowering idea of being ordained god's chosen people made it possible for Jews to survive hardships that would have been impossible without such a belief. The permeating feeling of being god's chosen people has given Jews an encompassing, empowering, and godly self-image. (A psychologist would identify such a godly self-image as the most empowering attribute any group could have in a species drenched with the instincts to believe in gods.)

Most of Jesus' followers were former Jews and they incorporated much of Judaism's Old Testament into the New Testament. The Jesus story in Christianity's New Testament was made as a sequel to the Old Testament. A "good" Christian, therefore, has to believe that god Judaic bestowed Jews' semi-sacred status upon them and that he is the father of Jesus. Thus, each Christian serves as one more confirmation to the validity of Jewish holiness. It is as a Jewish friend whispered to one of the authors: "The beauty of it is that all Christians also believe that we Jews are god's chosen people." Jewish writers simply explain, "We [Jews] remain a people in history because we remain, in some obscure yet certain way, god's treasured folk" (Borowitz, 1989, 53). It is written in the Old Testament, a universally recognized holy book, that Jews are a semi-sacred breed created by and for god Judaic. Therefore, the Christian movement had to uphold Jews' god-given status and maintain that Jesus was a son of the one and only god Judaic of the Jews' Old Testament. Thus, when the European masses accepted Jesus, they accepted Judaic beliefs.

Although most Jews consider Christianity a Judaic sect, it has significant differences from Judaism. To begin with, only Abraham heard god Judaic's voice. Much later a few other elite of the chosen few claimed to have also heard it. In contrast, god Jesus appeared in the flesh among the common people. He was heard, seen, touched, and loved by his followers. While Catholicism was for establishing love and social equality for everyone, including Jews and nonbelievers, Judaism emphasized caring for the chosen few, inequality, and the freedom to pursue wealth. Jesus' caring-for-all belief was in step with our species' caring evolution. Catholicism took the lead in caring for the welfare of others.

Catholicism's nature permitted its Judaic foundation to be introduced to the general masses. This was something that Judaism could never do due to its belief that only Jews are the chosen people of god. Without Catholicism (Christianity), the European masses would have eventually booted the *Hapirus* ("dusty ones" in Hebrew) and their Judaic ideas out of the windmills of their minds. Judaic beliefs and practices would never have become part of the civilization's foundation. Yet when Europeans became Christians they unknowingly became Judaized.

Judaism at the Core

With Judaic beliefs at the foundation of the civilization, the essence of being civilized is to believe that people of the civilization's dominant core cultures are the "chosen group" and that the essence of life is the *freedom* to pursue material wealth. In capitalist cultures such as the United States, this kind of *freedom* is capitalism, free enterprise, free market, and free trade. *Freedom* is now the code word for capitalism. According to the noted early 1900s German economist-sociologist Werner Sombart, "The social attitudes and economic practices associated with Judaism had been the primary source of the spirit of capitalism" (Green, 1959, viii).

Historian Thomas Cahill, having a profound knowledge of the Judaican way, sums up the essence of Judaism at the core of our civilization. He blurts out that the Jews are "it." He maintains that their expertise in Judaic beliefs makes them the most civilized members of the civilization, and therefore the most influential. By saying "it," Cahill suggests that Judaic beliefs show up in the things *we* care about, the underlying values that make us tick, click, and slick. Without Judaic beliefs influencing us, *we* would see things differently, hear about things differently, and feel differently about things (Cahill, 1998, 3).

In other words, without Judaic beliefs our mindset for feelings, thoughts, and behaviors would interpret experiences differently and come up with different conclusions. For example, if Judaic freedom's unrestrained pursuit of wealth were not at the core of our civilization, *we* would have different morals and would set different goals for our lives. Our focus would not be on inequality, greed, and on hoarding as much material wealth as possible at the expense of other peoples and their environment. Indeed, how *we* would care for the welfare of people and the environment would be quite different. By *we*, Cahill means all of us who keep our great civilization alive by practicing and passing on Judaic beliefs generation after generation.

As a civilized people, we are either Jews or *unlabeled* Jews. Jews need no further description other than being the "chosen few" of god Judaic. Who the *unlabeled* Jews are takes a bit more explanation. Unlabeled Jews are the bulk of us that are affiliated with Judaism through the influence of its beliefs and practices. It does not matter if we are unaware or disagree that we are unlabeled Jews. The major difference between Jews and unlabeled Jews is that Jews are identified as Jews while unlabeled Jews are not. Otherwise, both groups have much in common. As Jews or unlabeled Jews we support and practice our civilization's Judaic freedom. This is what makes us civilized. This is why Jewish historians can be most vocal and righteous in promoting the importance of Judaism being at the core of our civilization.

A Religion—Not a Race

It can be assumed that the nomadic Hebrew tribes that initiated Judaism were light-complexioned Africans from the areas of northeastern Africa. (Due to European racism this area became known by the ridiculous names of "Middle East" or "Near East" in an effort to associate it with Asia rather than with Africa.) Today Jews may be of any race or combination thereof, just as people of other religions are. Regardless whether some Jews have African racial traits, the United States officially identifies all Jews and Arabs as of the European race, whites.

The erroneous belief that Jews form a racial group is based on their historical self-acclaimed specialness. Jewish historian Abba Eban ridiculed the Germans' (Nazis') belief that Jews were a racial group. Yet, he wrote: "Judaism is a Jewish religion, those who were born Jews are Jewish people. But what constitutes the Jewish race?" (Eban, 1984, 297) In spite of ridiculing the Nazis' belief that Jews constitute a race, Eban throws in the belief that "Jews are born Jews." This suggests a genetic factor and perpetuates the errant idea that Jews form a race. Jews do not form a race, just as Protestants, Buddhists and Catholics do not form a race. In other words, just as Protestants are not born Protestants, Jews are not born Jews. Judaism, Protestantism, Buddhism, and so forth are beliefs that are learned. One learns to become a Jew, a Protestant, a Buddhist, a Muslim, and so on. It is misleading to say that "those who are born Jews are the Jewish people."

The idea that "Jews are born Jews" is based on the Judaic belief that only those born from Jewesses are Jews. (Any converts to Judaism are considered "pseudo-Jews.") Famous individuals who otherwise claim they are not Jews are still considered Jews by the Jewish community because they are suspected of having a Jewess in their ancestry. This is why the Jewish community identifies such individuals as Sigmund Freud, Albert Einstein, and Jesus as Jews. Judaic beliefs perpetuate a mythical Jewish race.

Protestants—the New Jews

In the 1600s Protestantism emerged from Catholicism and became the dominant religion of Anglo cultures. Protestantism, although a Christian faith, rejected the essence of Christianity and incorporated much more from the Jews' Old Testament than from the New Testament. The emergence of Protestantism changed Christianity's dominant focus from the nature of god Jesus to the nature of god Judaic. This was the transformation of millions of Christians from favoring Jesus' level of caring-for-all to favoring god Judaic's self-caring beliefs and practices for a chosen few.

Protestantism facilitated the expansion of Judaic freedom for a chosen few to include a Christian belief of Judaic freedom for all. Judaic freedom was no longer only for Jews, but also for unlabeled Jews. In other words, Protestantism enabled Christians to become part of the chosen people of god Judaic and still be able to call themselves Christians. However, Protestantism stopped Catholicism's Jesus caring evolution by converting billions of Christians over the years to Judaic beliefs and practices.

Protestants believe that the Judaican way is the essence of being good Christians. The acquisition of material wealth is not taken lightly in Judaism. It is demanded by sacred commands in the Jews' Old Testament. This is why such historians as Max Weber explained that Protestants' goals and values pivot from "a motivation for making a profit by equating material success with personal salvation and a sign of God's blessing" (Robbins, 2002, 338). Yet, early Protestants were ignorant of where the motivation for equating material success with god's blessing originated. Some Protestant authors even began to write books indicating that such beliefs had originated with Protestantism. By the 1600s the Catholic Church began to identify Protestants as *Novus Iūdaeus* (the New Jews).

By the 1700s Protestantism was expanding its influence throughout the civilization's core cultures. These cultures began shaping their laboring masses with Protestantism's Judaic beliefs: People were programmed to identify the accumulation of wealth as something sacred and divine. They were programmed to see economic prosperity as evidence of being chosen by god and that not all of us are chosen by god to enjoy economic prosperity. These prominent Judaic beliefs were no longer only those of Jews, but of countless of millions of Protestants. In essence, Protestantism demanded that Judaism be accepted by the civilization.

The Protestant cultures of England and the United States became the best breeding grounds for Judaic freedom. It's not surprising that the god beliefs of these cultures influence their righteousness to aggressively take other cultures' wealth. It is in their nature to take what they feel they are blessed to have. Some Protestant ministers explain that we, in our U.S. culture, have a "prosperity theology..." A theology marketed globally by evangelists via telecommunications. The beliefs and practices of pursuing wealth without restraints, which had previously instilled hatred toward Jews for centuries, were now dearly welcomed in Protestant cultures under the label of capitalism (free enterprise, free market, free trade, etc.).

Karl Marx (1818–1883), historical expert on social evolution, explained that the Jews' constant need to accumulate wealth, while paying little concern for the working people, triggered animosity. He saw their need for the acquisition of wealth as part of the essence of being Jewish. Historian Julian Huxley (1887–1975) also maintained that throughout history the dislike for Jews has been based on economic reasons. It seems that noted intellectuals as Marx and Huxley concluded that the practice of Judaic freedom triggered the Jews' persecution and dislike. Unfortunately, contempt for Judaic freedom triggered and continues to trigger the bestiality and tragedies that innocents such as Anne Frank and countless others have suffered. ("Despite everything, I believe that people are really good at heart." Anne Frank's dairy.)

It is important to note that the dislike for Judaic practices has been focused on Jews. Unlabeled Jews who love and practice Judaic freedom are not attacked because they are not perceived as Jews. This lets the multitude of unlabeled Jews off the hook. They can go on practicing Judaic freedom without restraint and without being persecuted or disliked. Many unlabeled Jews actually join the attacks on Jews.

Migration to North America

Since Judaic beliefs had conquered Europe, it was natural for England to have exported Judaic freedom to most of the world at the zenith of the civilization. Anglo-Protestant pilgrims came to North America with their beloved Judaic beliefs and practices.

Jewish historian Abba Eban explains that our Founding Fathers "were steeped in the ideas and cadences of the Hebrew Bible, and the first English colonists, the Puritans, had modeled their society on the theocracy of Israel in biblical times" (Eban, 1984, 268). In fact, in 1776 Thomas Jefferson, the third president and favorite Founder of today's U.S. liberals, wanted to flaunt the nation's Judaic-Germanic foundation on a seal for the new culture. He suggested that one side should show "the children of Israel in the wilderness, led by a cloud by day and a pillar of fire by night. On the other side Hengist and Horsa, the Saxon chiefs [of Germanic tribes] from whom we claim the honor of being descended, and whose political principles and form of government we have assumed" (Wolfram, 1997, 10). Benjamin Franklin, another favorite Founding Father, enjoyed quoting the Jewish Bible: "Seest thou a man diligent in business? He shall stand before kings" (Prov. 22:29). Franklin's loved quotation, "Time is money," is as contemporary today as it was when he glee-fully sang it in the 1700s. According to Jewish historians, the message in the U.S. Constitution is sheer Judaism in action. In other words, our Founders molded the foundation of our culture from old Judaic beliefs and practices.

Since the 1700s, for most Jews the Promised Land has never been any-where but in the culture that is now the center of our civilization. More than half of the estimated Jewish population lives in the United States. The largest Jewish community in the world lives in New York City. It is such a huge cen-ter for Jews that some New Yorkers affectionately refer to the city as "Hymie Town." It is no wonder that Jews have reached the height of their potential in the United States. Although their numbers are a minority, Jews righteously say, write, sing and dance it, that they are in the top financial, judicial, and business echelons of the civilization's center...more so than any other group.

The world now identifies the U.S. culture as the soul and protector of Ju-daic freedom. The U.S. also serves as the protector of the Jews' nation of Israel. This is obvious by the amount of money and weapons the U.S. government gives Israel. According to John J. Mearsheimer and Stephen M. Walt's research for their book, *The Israel Lobby and U.S. Foreign Policy*, as of 2005 the U.S. has given Israel nearly $154 billion. This money came from U.S. taxpayers of course. "Israel now receives an average of $3 billion in direct foreign assistance each year" (Mearsheimer and Walt, 2007, 26). To put this favoritism into per-spective, this foreign aid amounts to a direct subsidy of more than 500 dollars to each Jew living in Israel. (However, in 2010 BBC Internet News, 3/21/2010, reported that financial aid is not distributed equally among all Jewish citizens. About 1.2 million citizens are Israeli Arab descendents, about a fifth of Israel's population. They own 3.5 percent of Israel and have higher poverty levels than "Jewish Israelis.") Compare this favoritism to what the U.S. gives poor nations such as Pakistan, which gets about $5 per person, and Haiti, which gets $27 per person (Ibid). In addition to the billions of dollars our nation gives to Israel, it also gives its leadership up-to-date scientific breakthroughs and secret global information obtained via space satellites. Other U.S gratuities include special financial loans (for which the U.S. usually waives repayment for various reasons) and ready-made war equipment (including nuclear weapons). This is why the small Jewish nation of Israel is militarily superior to the whole might of its Arab neighbors and why it is not afraid to take them all on at the same time. Most world leaders have awakened to the reality that Israel remains an aggressive force because of military support from the U.K. and the U.S.

In appreciation for its ardent U.S. support, it seems that Israel has served as a terrorist state for the United States. Israel's appreciation for U.S. aide was unexpectedly disclosed. A 42-page document "outlines a massive international terrorist network run by the United States... One of the main players is Israel: they've helped the United States penetrate black Africa and they've helped support the genocide in Guatemala" (Chomsky, 2002, 5). The assassinations and revolutions in Nicaragua, Chile, Angola, and Afghanistan were also part of the Israel–U.S. terrorist activities. Most of these bloody terrorist activities happened under the Reagan–Bush administration. Knowing about these activities explains why, after the Reagan–Bush period, some "innocent" Jewish centers were bombed in South America. The 42-page document surfaced during U.S. Colonel Oliver North's trial and the Iran–Contra Hearings of 1989. (Later in the 2000s under the Bush–Cheney regime, the U.S. terrorist network got worse.)

The United States has evolved as the center of our great Judaic-Germanic civilization. Major happenings in the U.S. serve as a bellwether for the status of our civilization. For example, in the early 2000s the nation began suffering severe economic problems inherent to the constant pursuit of wealth via the nature of Judaic freedom. In addition, cultures outside the civilization began voicing displeasure with the global greed and inequality instituted by the civilization's capitalist core cultures. Such displeasure is not new, but now some large, fast evolving cultures are identifying the need for a responsible global system that is not for the prosperity of a chosen few cultures.

The destiny of our civilization is that it will be replaced by a new civilization with a different belief-language core, and therefore new beliefs and practices. For just as the Latin civilization followed the Egyptian civilization with Rome, and our Judaic-Germanic civilization followed the Roman civilization, our civilization will be followed by a new civilization. This is natural for a species that is not an animal species, but a transitional species whose interactions (beliefs, practices, etc.) are continuously evolving. (It is also natural for us to feel that we are different and that our beliefs and practices will stay on as before, somehow.) However, the decline of our civilization poses grave dangers because the weaponry available to our Animal being leaders can bring about a deadly global catastrophe. The danger to our species is most likely to come from our U.S. nation or a fellow nation such as Israel; for there are too many of us Animal beings that will do our "god's will."

Summary

In so many words, the Old Testament lets us know that a Jew is a near god persona. In the world of god beliefs there is no greater sacred position than that of Jews. This is like the near-Jesus position of the Catholic pope. The big difference is that man selects the pope, whereas god Judaic selects the Jews. In other words, Jews are the chosen people of god Judaic simply because they are Jews.

Today most Jews would agree that Christianity (specifically Protestantism) has made it possible for them to survive in Africa, Europe, and in the United States. It is also because of Christianity that the state of Israel came into being and is maintained. In the world of god beliefs, Christianity exists because of Judaism, but in the world of reality, Jews exist because of Christians.

The Judaic-Germanic configuration created a dynamic foundation for the greatest civilization to date. Although the Germanic and Judaic ethnic groups that started the language and belief components were thousands of miles apart, they had important interactive patterns in common. Both groups were able to acquire much of the material wealth of the cultures they encountered, but with a different mode of operation. While Germanic tribes looted material wealth by the might of their battle axes, Judaic tribes looted by what was to become known as capitalism, free enterprise, or simply as "freedom." In the merger, Germanic aggression came to be empowered by god Judaic. This combination evolved our civilization's nature, its spirit, and its *chutzpah*.

8

Our Five Major Races

Identification with our racial kind

Splitting our species into five racial groups began when people of the European (white) race were motivated to separate "their kind" from people of the African (black) race. Consequently, race became a significant identification for people in our Judaic-Germanic civilization. Depending on your race, you are either identified as being of the civilization's "own kind" or as non-European ("non-white"). As a non-European, you are identified as belonging to a "minority" group. This label identifies you as a member of any of the other four racial groups and separates you from the civilization's kind.

One's racial identity is especially important for the civilization's core Anglo-Protestant cultures of Australia, New Zealand, Canada, and the U.S because these cultures occupy lands of peoples who are not of the European (white) race. Instinctively, they have felt that people of the native race should not exist. The U.S. and Australia, for example, took ownership of the *American* and *Australian* labels. The American and Australian racial identifications therefore do not exist in these cultures. The result creates a ridiculous cultural environment. In the U.S. people of the American race are called "indians," "Mexicans" and "Hispanic" (Hispano). In Australia people of the Australian race are called "aborigines" or "bush people." Consequently, ignorance about race as well as racism is ongoing in these cultures. (Racism is the topic of a later chapter.)

The intent therefore is to explain what race is and is not. A brief overview of the origination of racial groups is also presented.

What Race Is

In simplest terms, race is biologically determined; it is a genetic identity. Racial traits such as blood type, eyes with or without an epicanthic fold, thin or thick lips, curly or straight hair, dark or fair complexion, small or large jaws, small or large buttocks, flat or round foreheads, and other features are genetic traits. Most any of these traits can be found in all five races because we are of the same species. However, environmental isolation and inbreeding for thousands of years produced different dominant genetic traits in certain groups of Homo sapiens around the world. A group of individuals sharing similar environmental factors and genetic traits determined a group's racial appearance. In other words, a race is the outcome of many generations of sexually transmitted traits within a group.

The evolution of genetic traits began as our species settled in Africa and Asia and wandered out of these areas to settle in other continental areas of the globe. The isolation and inbreeding of these groups in different environments, for tens of thousands of years, created different physiological features that came to be identified as racial traits. A population with similar genetic traits was identified as a "race."

Anthropologists can say our Homo sapient species is of one race, or of many races. This is because there are physiological differences even among people of the same race. Most anthropologists, however, agree that there are five major populations native to six of the seven continents. These populations' genetic traits identify them as our species' five races. These are the African (black) race, the Asian (yellow) race, the Australian (brown) race, the European (white) race, and the American (bronze) race of South and North America.

Although most of us identify with one of the five major races, most of us are a mixture of two or more of the five major races. DNA research shows that it is difficult to be of one race after some 65,000 years of Homo sapient existence and migrations all over the world. Perhaps only some individuals in isolated areas of Africa and Asia might still be of one race.

What Race Is Not

For many people a race is any group of people whom they choose to call a race. They ignorantly think that nationalities, ethnicities, religions, or even surnames are racial identities. These are not racial terms.

Nationality is a legal political identification of your citizenship of the nation in which you were born or became a naturalized citizen. Ethnicity is related to a group's culture, language, religion, and so on. For example, if you are a citizen of the United States ("Unitedstaten"), you are probably Protestant, speak English, have an English (Anglo) or some other Germanic surname, and enjoy eating hot dogs and watching baseball. If you are a citizen of Mexico, you are probably Catholic, speak Spanish, have a Spanish (*Hispano*) surname, and enjoy eating tacos and watching football (soccer). In other words, your nationality or ethnicity is characterized by such attributes as beliefs, language, surnames, religion, traditions, favored foods, and so on. These characteristics are *not* biological traits; they are learned interactions.

Once we understand that ethnicity has to do with one's cultural environment and that race is genetically inherited, we can understand that people of the same nationality can be of different races and vice versa. For example, let's take four ethnicities of North America. Canadians and Unitedstatens are dominantly of the European (white) race. Yet, there are some Canadians and Unitedstatens who are of other races. Likewise, Mexicans and Guatemalans are dominantly of the American (bronze) race, yet there are some Mexicans and Guatemalans of other races. In other words, Canadian, Unitedstaten, Mexican, and Guatemalan identify one's ethnicity or nationality, not one's race.

People can change their nationality by legally immigrating to another nation and changing their citizenship, but their race will remain the same. In other words, our race, whether it is African, Asian, Australian, European, or American, remains the same whether we change our nationality from Unitedstaten to Canadian, Unitedstaten to Mexican, or Mexican to Unitedstaten, or Japanese to Canadian, and so on.

Splitting Our Species Into Races

Hundreds of years ago, Europeans' awareness of their geographical proximity to Africans triggered them to become concerned about the possibility of scientists identifying them as related to the African race. In the 1700s, noted German anthropologist J. F. Blumenbach took on the task of identifying Europeans and Africans to be separate groups of peoples, racially. He identified the *European race* and the *African race* in a credible and scholarly manner.

Although Blumenbach's identification of races was primarily on the basis of his analysis of skulls, he categorized our species into five races: African, Asian, Malaysian, European, and American. In the mid 1900s, however, anthropologists replaced the Malaysian with the Australian race. They determined that the Malaysian group was a mixture of the African and Asian races. As for the Australian race, DNA data not only identified the native people of Australia as a race, but also as forming the third oldest race. Anthropological data suggests that about 65,000 years ago Homo sapiens evolved in Africa and in Asian. The Australian race evolved from the African race about 50,000 years ago. The European and American races evolved about 35,000 to 40,000 years ago.

The African Race

Africans have more mutations in their mitochondria genes than people of any other race, which indicates that the African stock evolved directly from our wise ape (hominid) ancestry. This is why African genes' long evolution created the greatest diversity of racial traits. In central Africa, peoples' physiques range from the racehorse jockey physique of the Pygmies to the basketball player's physique of the Watusis. Western Africans' complexions range from a dark brown to black. They have wide flat noses, thick lips, large buttocks, and kinky dark brown hair. Northeastern Africans tend to have a fair complexion, narrow nose, thin lips, and small buttocks. Eye colors include brown, hazel, blue and green; hair color and texture range from light brown wavy hair to straight black hair. This diversity of genetic traits in the African race is widely unknown or ignored, especially by Germanic cultures. The U.S. culture stereotypes the appearance of Africans as that of Western Africans since people from that area were brought to North America as slaves.

The Asian Race

Similar to the African race, the Asian race's longevity and the isolation created a wide range of racial traits. In one area of Asia we find people with round chubby faces, large lips, flat or wide noses, stocky stature, and eyes with a pronounced epicanthic fold. In other areas, we find people with narrow faces, narrow noses, thin lips, tall and slim stature, and eyes without the pronounced epicanthic fold. In some areas of China and Japan we also find Asians with fair (white) complexions. In fact, some Asians have fairer complexions than many people identified as Europeans (whites). Most people are unaware of the vast diversity of genetic traits in the Asian race because of the stereotypical racial image Europeans have created of Asians.

The Australian Race

In the mid 1900s, anthropologists identified the Australian race as the third oldest race. The people who began the evolution of the Australian race some 50,000 years ago are famous for their incredible fifty-four mile ocean trip to discover and settle Australia. The long oceanic trip preserved the genetic purity of the Australian race on the island continent for a long time. There is no evidence of later groups having made the open sea trip to Australia until Europeans began to migrate there in the 1800s. This indicates that a great deal of inbreeding took place on the island continent for a long time. As a result, it is likely that today's appearance of the Australian race most resembles our species' earliest appearance of some 65,000 years ago.

The European Race

In his research, Blumenbach had difficulty deciding where African racial traits ended and European racial traits began. He had difficulty because anthropological data now indicates that groups of people with European racial traits began to evolve in northeast Africa tens of thousands of years ago. This is why the oldest mummified remains of people with European features are not found in Europe, but in northeast Africa. Anthropologists speculate that people from northeast Africa began to migrate north toward Europe (Syria, Iraq, Turkey, etc.) about 30,000 years ago. It is believed that these people were lighter-complexioned Africans than were those who had migrated south toward Australia some 20,000 to 25,000 years earlier.

Nevertheless, Blumenbach succeeded in separating the European race from the African race. He identified peoples of northeast Africa (Saudi Arabia, Egypt, Israel, Palestine, Jordan, Syria, etc.) as being of the European race. Blumenbach also referred to the European race as "Caucasian" because he had admired the complexions and physiques of people from the Caucasus Mountains of Russia that he had visited during his research.

The oldest trace of our species in Europe is a 25,000-year-old skull found in the mountain range between Spain and France (about a two-day walk from the Mediterranean Sea). It was found in the Cro-Magnon caves and was named Cro-Magnon Man. School children in the United States are taught that the Cro-Magnon skull was of a "white" man. However, it is logical to conclude that the man's complexion was tan because very pale skin and very dark skin are believed to be relatively new evolutionary genetic traits.

The oldest and best-preserved corpse ever discovered in Europe is of a man found buried in ice for some 5,300 years. The corpse, referred to as "the Iceman," is evidence that early Europeans were not pale people. This priceless discovery of European genetic roots was found in 1991 entombed in a glacier, high in the Otztaler Alps between Austria and Italy. The Iceman was described as being thin with limbs like sticks..."His ribs protruded against his skin, taut and brown, like tanned rawhide" (*National Geographic Magazine* David Roberts, June 1993, 67). An artist's reconstruction portrait of the Iceman depicted him with a light brown complexion, a somewhat flattened nose, not overly thick lips, brown eyes, brown wavy hair, and a sparse beard. The artist's drawing resembled an individual of the Australian race. The Iceman's appearance angered some German citizens because he had the "wrong" complexion. It was not of a pale European, but of a man with a genetically built-in tan.

Germanic animosity toward the discovery of the tan-complexioned Iceman in the midst of Western Europe was not surprising. For example, a Munich television journalist refutes the discovery of the Iceman in his book, *The Otztal Fraud*. The journalist wrote: "The dead man comes from a distant, strange country, not from the Val di Senales or from the Otztal. Hence he does not come from a glacier. He was deposited there" (Spindler, 1994, 262). In so many words, the frozen corpse was called a fake, and Dr. Konrad Spindler and other Austrian scientists involved in the discovery are accused of treason.

Although the Iceman did not have the preferred European racial traits, genetic research published in the American Journal of Physical Anthropology confirms that his roots lay in Central Europe. Other evidence suggests his lifelong travels were confined to a 60-kilometre (37-mile) range southeast of where his body was found. The probability is that all Europeans and perhaps all Homo sapiens had tanned complexions as recently as ten to fifteen thousand years ago.

Austrian archaeologists describe the Iceman as being well dressed for the period. He was slender, about 40 years old, and ill with arthritis and intestinal parasites. They determined that he was murdered, dying from a gash in his left subclavian artery. It is believed that an assailant shot him from behind with a flint arrowhead that went through the Iceman's left shoulder blade. Scientists have concluded that he died in early spring because traces of yellow pollen from hornbeam blossoms that bloom in spring were found in his body (*National Geographic Magazine* July, 2007).

In the United States, efforts were made to change the public's perception of the Iceman's appearance. An artist in Washington, D.C., made a bust of the Iceman with a pale face and European features for the U.S. government. This new portrayal of the Iceman was televised for the U.S. public in the summer of 2000. To be aware of Germanic Europeans' intense focus on being "white," is to understand their desire for the 5,300 year-old corpse to have only European genetic roots.

The American Race

Some 30,000 to 40,000 years ago when northern and northeastern Africans were discovering the "New World" of Europe, northeastern Siberian Asians were discovering the "New World" of America (South and North America). Just as Europeans have Africans' migrations to thank for their racial existence, Americans have Asians' migrations to thank for their racial existence.

An international linguistic team from the United States and Russia identified three different families of American languages. These three languages seem to have been created over the course of three migrations into the American continents (Greenberg and Ruhlen, 1992, 97). The first migration of some 32,000 years ago is believed to have created the oldest family of American languages. The linguistic team identified American languages spoken from the southern part of what is now the United States and throughout South America as belonging to the oldest family of American languages. Such tribes as the Pueblo, Moxica (Mohican), Apache, Olmec, Chimu, Moche, Zapotec, Mexica, Aztec, Toltec, Inca, and Maya speak these languages. Genetic data taken from South American populations supports the linguistic data that our ancestors began to settle in the area about 30,000 years ago (Cavalli-Sforza 1991, 108). The second oldest family of American languages was found in various groups in the northern areas of what is now the United States and in Canada. The newcomers, the Aleuts (Eskimos) of Alaska speak the newest American languages. The three families of American languages are associated with the three major Asian migrations into the American continents.

Forty-thousand-year-old Homo sapient remains found on a route toward Alaska in northeastern Siberia are considered to be traces of the first Asian migrations to North America. Current research indicates that some groups traveled in rafts or boats from Siberia across the Bering Straits and south along the Pacific Coast. Traces of some of these early ancestors are found in Canada. Anthropologists from Canada's University of Toronto believe that some bone fragments were tools belonging to migrating groups entering North America as early as 40,000 years ago. However, anthropologist Richard Moorland admits that although the bones were broken in a certain way that had not occurred before 40,000 years ago, something else was the cause. He does agree that a handful of stone tools, including one dated to be 25,000 years old, found in the Bluefish Caves of Canada, indicate the presence of Homo sapiens (Lewin, 1988, 160).

At a site in Venezuela, the remains of a mastodon were found with a 13,000-year-old broken spear inside its pelvic cavity (Lewin, 1988). In Brazil, French scientists uncovered a cave with evidence that different tool-making groups had repeatedly occupied it. They dated the earliest occupation to have occurred about 32,000 years ago. A rock of a 17,000 year-old sheltered hearth with traces of red painted lines was also discovered. (Cave drawings of that same time period were also found in African and European caves.)

The American race, similar to the Australian race, was isolated for a long period of time. It remained isolated until America was invaded by people of the European and African races about 500 hundred years ago.

Some aspects need to be understood in order for the American race to have meaning for the reader. Geographically, all of us who live in the Western Hemisphere can claim to be Americans, regardless of our nationality and race. However, racism makes a mockery of the word American as it is used by the culture that was engrossed in the genocide of the American people. Having failed to rid itself of the Americans, the U.S. culture identifies them as "indians." Indians are citizens of India. (When "indian" is used to refer to a person of the American race, the authors write it with a lower case "i" to remind the reader that racism is responsible for this term.)

Other racial groups endure similar insults by Germanic cultures. In South Africa the Dutch Europeans were the "Afrikaans," and people of the African race were the "blacks," for as long as the Netherlands (Dutch) had control of the nation. In Australia Anglo Europeans took the whole continent and became the Australians. The Australian and American races are erased because Anglo Europeans do not want the American and Australian peoples to identify racially with the lands they (the Europeans) are occupying. This is primarily why Anglo cultures prefer to accept the existence of only the African, Asian, and European races.

Summary

Our species is separated into five major races based on different physiological traits. These traits evolved tens of thousands of years ago as our species migrated to and settled in the different continents. The isolation and longevity of groups in different areas evolved physiological changes that are now identified as racial traits. These traits are used to identify our species' five races.

The identification of races appears to have been instigated by Europeans wanting to separate themselves from the African race. One's race became the most important identification in the civilization. In the following chapter we will examine the effects of our culture's historical racism.

Part IV:

Animal Beings
Threaten the Survival
of Our Species

The Buzzard never says it is to blame
The panther wouldn't know what scruples mean;
...A jackal doesn't understand remorse...

On this third planet of the sun among the signs of
bestiality a clear conscience is Number One.

WISLAWA SZYMBORSKA, 1995

9

Racism

"There is not a country in world history in which racism has been more important, for so long a time, as the United States"

(ZINN, 2003, 23).

Racism is an exhibition of our animal nature, manifested in the way we treat others not of our kind. For example, in their studies of different ant species, Drs. Bert Hölldobler and E. O. Wilson found that, "At one extreme, intruders are accepted but offered less food. At the other extreme the residents attack ... with extreme violence" (1990, 197). In other words, ants of one species (resident ants) react to other ants not of their kind with interactions that range from limited caring to violence. Because such animal instincts are encoded in our genes, some of us are triggered to interact negatively toward others not of our race, not of our kind. This is racism.

Racism is commonly triggered in Germanic cultures, especially in Anglo (English speaking) cultures. Most Unitedstatens of the European race practice racism in various degrees against Unitedstatens of other racial groups who are referred to as minorities.

Since this chapter is devoted to racism, American, European, Australian,

Asian, and African will be used mainly to refer to our species' five races, unless otherwise noted. The authors call attention to this because of the widespread misconception of our species' five races. For example, most people erroneously think of an American as being a U.S. citizen of the European (white) race. This makes it difficult to think of an American as a person of the American race, the native race of the American hemisphere.

The Chosen Race

To understand why Jews are empowered by being the chosen of god Judaic is to understand why Europeans are empowered by being the chosen race of god Judaic. Simply being European (white) instills a sense of superiority over all others in some inexplicable, yet real way. This is true regardless of one's personal appearance, intellect, or economical status. Such beliefs might seem absurd to nonbelievers, but for believers it means a "hell of a lot." This powerful belief endures because it is simple enough for even the densest of Europeans (whites) to grasp and pass on.

People of the European race form the dominant group of our Judaic-Germanic civilization. This factor combined with the civilization's Judaic belief foundation might have triggered Europeans' perceived racial superiority. There is reason to speculate that this perception began when Anglo Europeans began to adopt Judaic beliefs via Protestantism in the 1600s. They adopted the Jews' priceless belief of being the "chosen of god Judaic" and came to believe that Europeans were the "chosen race of god Judaic." As a result Jews' priceless belief was extended to people of the European race.

Anglo European Protestants began to reinforce their "chosen race" beliefs during the 1600s. When they began to invade and to occupy non-European peoples' lands. These invasions included huge land areas from Africa to India, Australia, and North America.

U.S. Anglo-European Racism

The Protestant Anglo-European Founding Fathers of the United States established a socio-political system harboring Conservative ideologies of inequality and racism. They viewed Africans as property. Americans were viewed as detestable "indians" to kill. (This was not unusual, since the trend of the times was unrestrained animalness, more so than it is now.) From that time to the present, racism against non-Europeans has worked as an orchestrated cultural conspiracy. This means racism against non-Europeans is intrinsic to the culture. This means that the culture's belief-language core triggers European citizens to perpetuate racism in various forms and degrees. They are programmed to express racism against non-European citizens similar to how ants are programmed to react to other ants not of their colony. Consequently, if you are not of the culture's kind, of the European race, you suffer from racism in a multitude of ways whether you are aware of it or not. In other words, racism is not a temporary occurrence, but a permanent cultural trait.

However, the culture prefers to see racism as not being culturally induced, but as emerging independently from individuals' nature. Yet the racist nature of the cultural environment is what triggers racism from individuals. While efforts are made to suppress individuals' racism, the culture's racist nature endures mostly unscathed. It endures because the culture itself reinforces racism.

The culture's racism against Africans is widely known. Racism against Asians is less well known. Racism against Americans is least known, even though it involved genocide. Racism against Americans continues to affect a growing population of Americans who are not identified as "indians." Therefore, after noting racism against Unitedstatens of the African and Asian races, the focus is on racism against Unitedstatens of the American race.

> The terms "American" and "Americans" refer to people of the native race of the American hemisphere as explained in Chapter 8. Unless otherwise noted, the terms will be used with this meaning.

Racism Against Africans

Immigrant Anglo Europeans came to the northeastern coast of North America in the 1600s with their African slaves. They brought Africans with them to North America as commodities to sell and buy. Europeans' enslavement of African people continued for over 250 years until the 13th Amendment of the United States Constitution abolished it.

As slaves, Africans lived under their European owners' whims and were indoctrinated to interact submissively in the Anglo-Protestant culture. Racist slaveholders imposed their Protestant beliefs and English language on their slaves by splitting up those who spoke the same language. They also sold family members to different buyers. By breaking up African families, the Europeans destroyed the Africans' social relationships and identifications with their cultures. African slaves were forced to acquire their slave owners' language and god beliefs.

In spite of their historically suppressed conditions as slaves, semi-slaves, and oppressed citizens, their Anglo-Protestant acculturation helped them develop a strong racial identification. This eventually helped them develop skills to become a stable force against the racist culture they were forced to join. However, it wasn't until the late 1950s that significant numbers of Africans began to rebel against their racist culture. It took peaceful marches and violent interactions to get the culture to make some changes. Their efforts yielded improved conditions for themselves as well as for other non-European citizens and for European women. European women began to reach corporate executive and political positions, which had been reserved for European men. Unitedstatens of the African race have been at the forefront of social change to reduce the effects of racism.

Only a few examples are necessary to become aware of the breadth of racism Africans have endured and continue to endure. As late as the mid 1940s, the United States government officially promoted racism. President Woodrow Wilson ordered the segregation of Africans, a mandate that outlasted his presidency (1913–1921). Not surprisingly, during his administration, lynching Africans became popular again. After Wilson, no other president felt motivated to remove the segregation of Africans until World War II. Wilson's mandated segregation, which lasted over two decades, was terminated in order to enhance efficiency among U.S. military fighting units, not because racism had lessened against Africans.

In the 1940s, at the time that Nazi physicians were performing experiments on Jewish German citizens, U.S. physicians were experimenting with the health of U.S. Africans. U.S. Public Health Service physicians observed and kept records on 400 male citizens of the African race with syphilis in Macon County, Alabama. This was the Tuskegee Syphilis Study, which ran from 1932 to the 1970s. For some forty years medical personnel tracked these patients' health to see what would happen to them when syphilis was left untreated. For decades, patients were not even treated for pain. When their wives contracted the disease, they were simply added to the group being studied. The same was true when their children were born with syphilis. In the study, physicians lied to their patients about their illness. Some were told they had bad blood. This racist deception continued long after penicillin was known to cure the disease. According to the final report of the Tuskegee Syphilis Study, the study was "the longest non-therapeutic experiment on human beings in medical history" (*Final Report of the Tuskegee Syphilis Study Legacy Committee,* Internet, 5/20/1996). In this classic case of U.S. racism, physicians and other medical personnel of a government agency were no less animalistic than Nazi physicians who experimented on Jews and Gypsies during World War II.

The nature of racism in the U.S. culture is such that it leaves lasting scars on individuals even when they reach the apex of their life's goals. Danny Glover, a gifted and successful actor, said about living in the United States: "Every day of my life I walk with the idea I am black, no matter how successful I am" (*AARP,* May/June 2004). Expressing similar negative feelings, author James Baldwin said: "To be a Negro in this country and to be relatively conscious is to be in a rage almost all the time."

Historically, Unitedstaten Anglo Europeans' racism against Africans has been primarily due to their appearance, which Europeans readily identify as not being of their kind. Yet, their racism seems to be combined with conflicting feelings of a close relationship with Africans. This is probably because for over 200 years Europeans and Africans lived and worked closely together. During this long period there were many Afro-Euro (African-European mixture) generations created, even by the wealthy and the elite white political figures of the nation. Africans not only served the Europeans in accumulating wealth with their labor, but as soldiers of the U.S. Calvary, they helped Europeans massacre Americans and occupy their land. Science may someday determine that it was because of genetics that Europeans felt an instinctive need to bring Africans to join them in confronting the foreign-looking people of the American race. (Europeans' animosity for Africans was incomparable to their animosity for Americans. Africans were people to exploit, but Americans were people to kill.)

The Anglo European and African relationship in North America was not something new. Africans' presence in England can be traced back to Septimius Severus, a North African Libyan, who ruled England as Roman Emperor between 193-211 AD. Another example of Africans in ancient Britain is the case of the Roman military garrison on Hadrian's Wall in Cumbria. Also a 4th century (500 AD) inscription indicates that the Roman auxiliary unit, Numerus Maurorum Aurelianorum, was stationed at Aballava, modern day Burgh-by-Sands. There is a gap in the recording of African presence in England for nearly 400 years. According to historians, the African presence in England was not publicized until the start of the 16th century. Thereafter the information was found only in universities.

Racism Against Asians

Racism against Asians began soon after the United States took over most of Mexico in 1848, which expanded the U.S. nation all the way to the Pacific Coast. Three years later, in 1851, the U.S. culture again resorted to the exploitation of imported workers. Chinese men were imported as contracted slaves to build the railroad network needed to take California's riches to New York City. Three years after the Chinese arrival, in 1854, Anglo Europeans passed a law preventing Asians from testifying in court. This left them without legal protection and at the mercy of employers. The saying, "He doesn't have a China man's chance," evolved from this era in California because of outright legalized racism against Asians. The law also made it difficult for them to establish small businesses. In 1882, thirty-four years after taking California from Mexico, the U.S. Congress passed the Chinese Exclusion Act, prohibiting the immigration of Asians to the United States. The act barred Asian men from sending for their wives and children and created a scarcity of Asian women. Therefore, a Eurasian (European-Asian genetic mixture) population blossomed as European women began to have children with Asian men. The situation triggered the 1910 California law prohibiting marriages between Europeans and Asians.

Three decades later, in 1942, because of war with Japan, a large population of Unitedstaten Asians of the Japanese ethnicity suffered a generous serving of racism. This racism was mandated by an Executive Order from President Franklin D. Roosevelt. Some 120,000 men, women, and children were arrested and imprisoned in concentration camps for the duration of World War II. Their crime was being of Japanese ethnic ancestry. Our Founding Fathers' glorified Constitution (Bill of Rights) did not exist for these U.S. citizens. Few in the nation questioned the constitutionality of this legal racist act. Most people shared the sentiments of Lieutenant General John L. DeWitt, the man in charge of the arrests. He is noted to have said, "A Jap is a Jap." The families were given just enough time to get ready and take only what they could carry. Some lost their homes and others lost their rich farmlands in the San Joaquin Valley of California. They were moved out of California to concentration camps set up in desert areas. This racism enabled Anglo Europeans to buy the ousted citizens' lands and businesses for a fraction of their true value. All this was a result of U.S. racism against its own citizens of the Asian race.

An Asian of Japanese ethnicity recounted to the authors about his family's forced exodus from California. His mother, baby sister, and he, at three years of age, had been placed in the Santa Anita racetrack stables for three months before being sent to a concentration camp. His mother recalled the unsanitary conditions and the stench. His father, a U.S. citizen, had been imprisoned because he knew how to speak and write Japanese. He was ultimately sent to a concentration camp.

Although the U.S. was at war with Germany as well as with Japan, such racist actions were not taken against Unitedstatens of German descent. While Asian U.S. citizens of Japanese descent were being imprisoned, European U.S. citizens of German descent were not harassed. In fact, Nazi troopers were flown from Europe to the United States. Unbelievably, these Nazi prisoners were flown not only across the Atlantic Ocean, but also across the North

American continent to California. Millions of taxpayers' dollars were spent flying thousands of Nazi troopers to "rehabilitation camps." These camps, unlike those for the Asians, were situated in the most beautiful California farmlands of the vast San Joaquin Valley. This was the same beautiful area where most of the Asian families had been evicted. Once in California, the Nazi troopers were taken on outings in uncovered military trucks so they could enjoy the scenery of the San Joaquin Valley and the beautiful Sierra Nevada range while cruising along scenic Highway 99. (No Japanese prisoners were flown from Asia to the United States.)

In spite of the culture's racism against its Asian citizens of Japanese descent, many sons of families in concentration camps agreed to form a U.S. military unit that was sent to the front lines to fight the Germans in Europe. These young men, loyal patriots in the mold of "my country right or wrong," risked their lives for Old Glory, while their families had been stripped from the security and comfort of their homes and land, only to be imprisoned in desolate areas. Those who refused the draft were punished. Most U.S. citizens, including some Asians, did not see all this racism against U.S. Asians and favoritism toward Nazi troopers as acts to condemn. There were no public demonstrations because the bulk of the U.S. culture perceived the murderous Nazi troopers as of their kind, whereas working Asian U.S families were not.

Unknown to most U.S. citizens is that some 2,300 Asian families of Japanese descent were also taken from their homes and farms from other American nations and brought to concentration camps in the United States. It did not matter to our racist culture that these Asians were citizens of Spanish speaking American nations.

Racism Against Americans

The following is an overview of the culture's racism against Americans, beginning with the culture's genocide of large populations of the American race. For some three hundred years, Anglo Europeans systematically massacred Americans and stole from them the land that now makes up the United States. In addition, the invading Europeans removed the existence of the American race by taking the label of "Americans" for their own identity and calling Americans "indians." By taking Americans' identity as their own, Anglo Europeans made Americans a "raceless" people (a "non-people"). In the end, Unitedstaten Europeans accomplished what they had tried to do through genocide. After the genocide, racism against people of the American race called "indians" has continued. In addition, there is racism against a larger American population of Unitedstatens who are not identified as "indians."

U.S. Genocide of Americans

Unitedstaten Europeans were the first to attempt a Germanic culture's "final solution" to eradicate a people. This went on from the 1600s to the early 1900s. The white Anglo-Saxon Protestants (WASPs) did not want to coexist with Americans, and they did not want their labor because they had African slaves. What the WASPs wanted was to make Americans disappear so that they could occupy their lands.

Anglo Europeans' greed for property was a foreign idea to Americans. Land was communal for Americans. It was never the American way to make the pursuit of material wealth the essence of life. In other words, the American way has never been the Judaican way.

Upon landing on the eastern coast of North America Protestant Anglo European immigrants perceived Americans as non-people to remove from a new Promised Land. Protestant god beliefs sanctioned Europeans' animal-ness in their pursuit of property. After all, Americans were not mentioned in the Jews' Old Testament or in the Christians' New Testament. Africans, Europeans and Afro-Euros (African and European mixture) are people of the Jewish and Christian holy Bibles. Therefore, Protestants who were immersed with Judaic beliefs were quick to assure themselves that their god was giving them another go at the Promised Land—this time in North America. So it was okay with god Judaic to kill Americans for the Promised Land.

The deadly European smallpox disease reinforced Anglo Europeans' beliefs that god was on their side. Epidemics of smallpox in some areas of North America and the Caribbean killed off entire American populations. (By the late 1700s Americans ceased to exist in the Caribbean islands and were replaced by Africans.) As whole villages of American families died, John Winthrop, governor of the Massachusetts Bay Colony, called the plague "miraculous." In 1634 he wrote to a friend in England that god [Judaic] did not care for the Americans—"...for 300 miles space the greatest part of them are swept away by the smallpox...so as God hath thereby cleared our title to this place..." (Loewen, 1995, 72). The deadly smallpox plague gave the Europeans the idea of how best to kill entire American villages. By the late 1700s U.S. troops began using smallpox as a biological weapon. They spread the disease to larger populations of Americans by giving them blankets with smallpox pus and scabs. As they were dying, Americans must have felt that their "gods" had abandoned them when they saw Europeans and Africans survive the disease. Protestant Europeans thanked their god (god Judaic) for killing Americans with the disease. Americans were not immune to smallpox as Europeans and Africans were.

The fact that Americans lived off the land and would not go away kept triggering racial hatred from Protestant European immigrants. When George Washington became the nation's president, the genocide of Americans became systematic. Washington, the culture's top racist leader who had taken much land for himself, called the Americans "red savages" and compared them to wolves: "both being beasts of prey, though they differ in shape" (Parenti, 1994, 127). Military expenditures to murder Americans and take their lands "absorbed eighty-percent of the entire federal budget during George Washington's administration and dogged his successors for a century as a major issue and expense" (Loewen, 1995, 108). U.S. military budgets continued to fund expeditions to destroy Americans' villages, to poison their water and food sources, and to hunt down fleeing American families. Freedom in the pursuit of property was the European motive for mass murder.

During President Jefferson's administration, "in the pursuit of happiness," Anglo squatters were encouraged to settle in Americans' lands further west of where the U.S. border then extended. This was reason enough to clear off American families from their lands. Whole villages of men, women, and children were massacred. At this time, the vast area west of what was the United States belonged to Spain, which was *Nueva España* (New Spain).

In its "pursuit of happiness" the young nation began to take Spanish land by military invasions and shrewd schemes. On one occasion the United States took land from Spain under the pretext that it had bought it. The U.S. claimed to have purchased a huge area west of the Mississippi River under the lie that the land had been purchased from France (the Louisiana Purchase of 1803). This land belonged to Spain, not to France. According to U.S. historians, President Thomas Jefferson had doubts about the "constitutionality of the purchase." Nevertheless, he took it. This area doubled the size of the U.S. and provided access to what is now the Gulf of Mexico. It triggered further greed from the United States as it decided to look into taking Nueva España's land bordering Canada, all the way to the Pacific Ocean. The U.S. sent an excursion, the Lewis and Clark expedition (1804-1806), with the intention of accessing a route into Nueva España's northwest area to the Pacific Ocean. At the time, the military favored a northwest invasion route because that area was less inhabited. The southwest route to the Pacific Ocean though Texas, New Mexico, Nevada, Arizona, and California was more populated. There were many villages, towns, and cities with *Hispano* (Spanish) Europeans, Americans, and Amer-Euros (American and European mixture) in the southwest.

A cunning tactic used to take lands from Americans, besides killing them, was to encourage tribal leaders to identify their tribes as "nations." This gave the U.S. government some semblance of legal rights in taking ownership of land belonging to an American tribe's "nation" after a battle. The military could also give leaders of "indian nations" the option to sign a peace treaty rather than have their whole village massacred. The intent of treaties was for tribes to move further west, or to unwanted land areas under the false promise that they would then be left alone. According to U.S. historians, the United States broke every treaty it made with Americans.

U.S. military incursions increased soon after Spain granted independence to Nueva España in 1810. Nueva Espana was renamed "Mexico." All tribal communities of the American race of the vast area including Amer-Euros and Hispano Europeans were now "Mexicans." Most of these communities were in California. Therefore, from 1810 on, the U.S. military was attacking and killing Mexican communities. (Prior to 1810, the Mexican ethnicity did not exist.) The United States had a great advantage over the newly formed Mexican nation, which was still in the process of organizing its government far south in Mexico

City. Mexico's military forces barely existed. The old Spanish forts that existed in heavily populated areas such as in California were drastically under funded and under-manned. There were no viable fortifications to stop Anglo European military incursions and the massacre of whole Mexican communities.

One of the bloodiest massacres suffered by Mexican tribes occurred in 1811. Under the leadership of William H. Harrison, military forces attacked the Shawnees, a bloody orgy that U.S. history schoolbooks like to call the "Battle of Tippecanoe." After the massacre, the U.S. took the land where the tribe had lived for thousands of years so that Anglo European immigrants could enjoy it. Following the massacre of the Shawnees, there was a series of military massacres, which are called the "indian wars" of 1812 in U.S. history textbooks.

During the 1830s, Conservative President Andrew Jackson and his Conservative successor, Martin Van Buren, continued the violent removal of Americans from their lands on both sides of the Mississippi River. Jackson hated Americans, just as Washington had. In his part of the "final solution," Jackson encouraged European immigrants to move onto Americans' lands as squatters. Jackson would threaten Americans to give their land to the squatters or be killed. Without weapons to match Anglo Europeans' firepower, Americans were constantly defeated. Jackson's animalness triggered him to use other cruel tactics to remove Americans from their lands. Large groups of American families were forced onto old, large barges to relocate them west of the Mississippi River. The unworthy barges sank and hundreds of American men, women, and children drowned. Americans were also forced to abandon their villages in the dead of winter without food and appropriate clothing. Bodies of American men, women, and children would be found all along the path of their exodus, having died from the cold, disease, and starvation. Such killing strategies came under "The Indian Removal Bill," which was President Jackson's legacy. Jackson's animalness eventually removed the culture's "indian problem" past the Mississippi River.

During this time, illegal Anglo European immigrants were making huge land claims deep into Mexico. This vast area included what are now the states of Montana, Colorado, and Oklahoma. The U.S. military continued to illegally establish forts inside Mexico to protect Anglo European squatters. The troops massacred entire villages and towns of American populations. The racist nation was determined to be successful with its "final solution" to the "indian" problem. To maintain its occupation of Mexican land, the United States had announcements in Western Europe enticing Germanic Europeans to come to North America for free land. As a result, hordes of Europeans came through the port of New York and began heading west into Mexico. Illegal land squatters that had already settled west of the Mississippi River were urging their politicians to expand U.S. borders further into Mexico and some were urging the takeover of Mexico. These illegal immigrants wanted to make their Mexican held lands legal under U.S. law. The U.S. westward invasion into Mexico went on without a declaration of war.

By the 1840s U.S. military forces had reached *Nuevo Mexico* (New Mexico) and *Texas*. In these areas there were growing Mexican communities of Hispano Europeans, Spanish speaking Americans, and Amer-Euros. (Spanish had been the dominant language in these areas for centuries.) In these areas the U.S. military began to identify Spanish speaking Americans and those without tribal identities as Mexicans. Therefore, people called Mexicans also became the military's object of hate and people to get rid of. The U.S. culture's racist hatred against Americans perceived as Mexicans became just as strong as that against Americans perceived as "indians."

In 1845, a militia of Anglo squatters did not wait for U.S. military support and took over some land in Texas. A Mexican militia confronted them at *El Alamo* (Spanish for the poplar tree). The Anglo militia's families were spared, but the men were executed. (Unlike Anglo Europeans, the Mexican militia did not kill the women and children.) This confrontation gave the U.S. military reason to support the squatters' illegal rights to the Texan land. The under-armed and under-manned Mexican militia of the area, composed mostly of members from the Yaqui tribe, was no match for U.S. troops' firepower. To justify taking Texas, the U.S. propagandized how the Anglo squatters had lost their battle at the Alamo.

After taking the large land area of Texas from Mexico with such ease, the U.S. military felt confident in taking the southwest route to the Pacific Coast instead of taking the northwest route that Lewis and Clark had surveyed.

The U.S. culture, however felt it had to give its invasion and occupation of most of Mexico some semblance of legality. Therefore, after taking Texas, an area larger than the nation of France, the United States declared war on Mexico in 1846.

Back in the east coast, Unitedstatens had been programmed for the declaration of war on Mexico with the idea of "Manifest Destiny," which first appeared in print on July 4, 1845, in New York City. It explicitly set the mood for citizens to feel that their Anglo-Protestant nation was endowed by god Judaic to take from others what it wanted. With its holy endowed Manifest Destiny, the WASP culture did not need much prompting to continue its invasion of Mexico.

When war was declared, a few notable U.S. intellectuals opposed the war against Mexico. Abraham Lincoln and Henry David Thoreau were among those few. Thoreau, philosopher and writer from Massachusetts, protested the war by refusing to pay the Massachusetts poll tax, which was used to support the war. For this he was put in jail for one night—his friends paid his tax (without asking Thoreau). Writer Ralph Waldo Emerson was also against the war, but thought it useless to protest. So when he visited Thoreau in jail, it is reported that he asked him, "What are you doing in there?" Thoreau replied, "What are you doing out there?" (Zinn, 2003, 156.)

The so-called "war" with Mexico lasted two years. The lack of transportation and communications of the period made it difficult for the U.S. to claim victory sooner. The war was an undeclared, one-sided invasion. The total land area taken from Mexico was about the size of Western Europe, including the U.K., Norway and Finland. This vast area had some of the richest farmlands in the world, rich deposits of gold, oil, and priceless forests and beaches. The takeover of most of Mexico meant murdering countless Americans, Amer-Euros, and some Hispano Europeans all the way to California's Pacific Coast and north to the Canadian border. It was in California where the highest Mexican military and political officials were killed and where large urban Hispano populations suffered atrocities.

The U.S. gave Mexico a peace treaty to sign in 1848. This gave the massacring orgy the semblance that a war had occurred between the two neighboring nations. Also, once the U.S. culture had taken what it wanted, it wanted perpetual peace with its southern neighbor.

The United States took over so much land so easily and quickly that the Anglo culture has yet to adjust to the added land. Even today, what was the Midwest before the U.S. took over most of Mexico is still called the Midwest, although the actual mid-west of the nation is now over a thousand miles west of that area.

After 1848, when most of Mexico became the United States, the genocide of Americans did not stop. Stories of "wild indians" and "Mexican bandits" raping and killing Anglo Europeans were propagandized to justify the continued genocide. Of the hundreds of times that whole American communities were murdered, here are a couple of examples: On January 29, 1863, under the command of Colonel Patrick E. Conner, the United States Calvary rode into the Shoshone village in Idaho and executed the entire population. Infants and toddlers were thrown into the icy waters of the river. The village leader was tortured and finally killed with a bayonet rammed through his ear. In another recorded massacre, in 1890, the U.S. Army invaded an American community at Wounded Knee, South Dakota and killed that entire population. Such atrocities were still part of the U.S. culture's solution to its "indian problem." The motive was to make Americans' land accessible to Germanic European hordes (English, Dutch, Germans, Austrians, etc.) coming through New York City in the pursuit of happiness, liberty, and freedom.

The genocide of Americans was so systemically executed that Adolph Hitler, on reading United States history, is said to have admired how Protestant Anglo Europeans had eradicated much of the American race in the area that is now the United States. He admired the concentration camps that the U.S. culture called "indian reservations" and praised the "'extermination—by starvation and uneven combat' as the model for his extermination of Jews and Gypsies" (Loewen, 1995, 118). Adolph Hitler no doubt easily identified with the U.S. culture's nature, that Americans were killed simply because they were of the American race.

The genocide of Americans by the Anglo European Protestant culture lasted from the 1600s to the early 1900s. No one has angrily cried out, "never again, we must never forget!" There is no monument for this holocaust, neither by the racist Unitedstaten culture nor by the subdued and stunned Mexican culture. The United States' genocide ended with hundreds of thousands of Americans massacred. Some of these Americans were called "Mexicans," but most were called "indians."

■   ■   ■

It is important to know about Hispano Europeans and Americans' coexistence. Under Hispano Europeans, beginning in the 1500s, Americans were not people to eradicate. When Spain gave independence to New Spain, the American population participated with the minority Spanish European population to rename and run the new nation of "Mexico." New Spain's people—Americans, Europeans and Amer-Euros (American-European mixture)—all became Mexicans. The new nation of Mexico did not change its social-political nature, which was the merger of the Spanish European culture with American tribal cultures. The merger became the Mexican culture. The Mexican culture, unlike the United States culture, was not about killing Americans. It was about coexistence. Americans and Hispano Europeans (whites) had been coexisting for some three hundred years.

The Mexican flag indicates the culture's identification with the American race. According to an American tribal legend, a wandering American tribe (before the Aztec era) is told by their god to settle where they would see an eagle grasping a snake. The tribe eventually saw an eagle perched on a large cactus grasping a snake. Their settlement, which they named Tenochtitlan, became Mexico City. This is why the Mexican flag depicts an eagle perched on a cactus grasping a snake. In addition, "Mexico" was derived from *Mexica* (also spelled *Mejica*), the name of an American tribe. Mexico had its first full-blooded American president, Benito Juarez, in 1858. He was the first American to lead a country in the Western Hemisphere. Following President Juarez, almost all presidents of Mexico have been Amer-Euros.

In the 1600s, while Anglo (English speaking) Europeans began murdering Americans, Hispano (Spanish speaking) Europeans had been integrating Americans into their communities, since the 1500s. While Anglo-Protestant

Europeans treated Americans as people to kill, Hispano Catholic Europeans treated Americans as potential converts to Catholicism. While Anglo Europeans were poisoning Americans' water wells and stealing their lands, Hispano Europeans passed laws to protect Americans' land and water rights. Under the Spanish *encomienda* (labor system) *encomenderos* (Spanish overseers) were in charge of Americans' education and conversion to Christianity in return for their labor.

By the time the United States confiscated most of Mexico, 55% of Mexico, not including Texas (*Treaty of Guadalupe,* Wikipedia, 2010), American and Amer-Euro labor, under the guidance of the Catholic Church, had already established towns and cities throughout the vast area. This was especially true in California where such Spanish-named cities as San Diego, San Juan Capistrano, Los Angeles, Santa Barbara, Santa Cruz, Monterey, San Jose, Santa Clara, San Francisco, and Sacramento had been built. This was in addition to the famous Spanish Catholic Missions throughout California. Americans and Amer-Euros had also created most of the music, folklore, and customs of the area. The unique Mexican culture emerged from the coexistence of Hispano Europeans and Americans.

The U.S. occupation of Mexico, however, destroyed much of this historical cultural heritage. Although the Spanish Catholic Missions were not destroyed, Anglo Europeans intentionally destroyed buildings, gravesites, American artifacts, and historical documents. Land titles, thousands of letters, books, and records of hundreds of years of the Spanish-speaking story of California were destroyed. The few documents in Spanish that remain are not easily accessible, although they are located in the Bancroft Library at the University of California at Berkeley. What Hispano Europeans and Americans had started in San Diego in 1542, ended 306 years later in 1848 when an Anglo racist culture took over California. By the 1850s Hispano Californians "had been dispossessed of their land, reduced to abject poverty, and had become politically disempowered" (Mora-Torres, 2005, 6). It wasn't until 2002 that a plaque was placed in Sacramento, the state capital of California, to commemorate the state's long Hispano history. Lieutenant Governor of California Cruz Bustamante helped make the commemoration possible.

If it hadn't been for the existence of the Mexican nation representing

Americans who feel and know of this bloody history will forever keep alive the memory of such men with the Spanish names of Murrieta, Pacheco, Geronimo, and those with the English names of Sitting Bull and Crazy Horse.

hundreds of different tribes and the integration of many tribes into the Mexican nation, the genocide of Americans would be even less documented and remembered. The recognition of the Mexican nation meant recognizing that these Americans had a nation. This forced the U.S. racist culture to leave a historical document, a treaty of the genocide, the *Treaty of Guadalupe*. The treaty is for the benefit of the United States. For the nation exists in occupied territory taken by an animalistic bloody invasion.

Europeans become the "Americans"

The U.S. culture's racist conspiracy against the American race did not stop with genocide. The Europeans made the racial identity of the American people of South and North America disappear by taking the term "American" for their own identity. Obliterating the Americans' racial identity began around 1815. J. W. Loewen explains that, "Until 1815 the word *Americans* had generally been used to refer to Native Americans; after 1815 it meant European Americans [Unitedstatens]" (Loewen, 1995, 117).

Geographically speaking, all people living in North and South America are Americans. Nevertheless, it is the racist nature of the U.S. culture to take the name of "America" for itself and "American" mainly for its Anglo European citizens, disregarding people of the American race. For example, a U.S. Anglo European journalist stated in his article for *National Geographic Traveler* that of all the tourists in a hotel in Argentina, he and his family were the only "Americans" in the hotel. Even such an informed journalist-traveler could not escape from his culturally programmed racism. He could not see that, geographically speaking, the *Argentinos* running the hotel were South Americans and that he and his family were North Americans.

The United States has called itself "America" for so long that its citizens and most people of other nations no longer think of "America" as the Western

Hemisphere of South and North America. People have been programmed to think of the United States as "America," and to think of Anglo European (white) Unitedstatens as the "Americans." For example, in an article about Albanians wanting to take land from the Serbs in order to create their own independent country in 2005, a Serb exclaimed to a U.S. reporter: "If Mexicans wanted to create a country from part of America, how would you feel?" (*Christian Science Monitor*, 2/5/06) Due to the U.S. culture's undisputed racist propaganda that it is America, the Serb did not know that Mexico is part of North America. More importantly, he did not know that most of the United States was created from land taken from Mexico. The culture's racist global propaganda machine has perpetuated lies about what America is and who the Americans are for so long, without opposition, that the lies are now truths for most of the world.

Few individuals overcome the U.S. lie about what America is. One such individual was a successful vocalist and composer from a Spanish speaking American nation. When a U.S. reporter asked her, "Now that you've been here [in the U.S.], for a few months, do you now feel you are Americanized?" The celebrity was intelligent enough to respond, "Yes I have been Anglicized." She explained that she had changed her Hispano (Spanish) musical routine to suit Anglo (English speaking) audiences. Such knowledge, however, is rare because the world is satiated with the U.S. lie that European Unitedstatens are the Americans.

All people living in North and South American cultures can be called Americans regardless of their nationality and race. Similarly, all people living in Europe can geographically call themselves Europeans regardless of their nationality and race. However, it is common knowledge that in terms of race Europeans (whites) are the native people of the European continent. Yet, it is *not* common knowledge that in terms of race Americans (bronze) are the native people of America (South and North America).

The fact that people of the American race lost their racial identity is made evident by the U.S. government. The government took control of the American label by controlling which people can be identified as "indians." The label "American indian" is used to identify the "indian" as a citizen of the United States. In addition, "American indians" are only legally recognized as such if they are registered as members of a U.S. "indian" tribe and have been assigned *control numbers.* For a newborn to be registered as an "American indian," at least one of the baby's biological parents has to be registered with a control number. In this manner the U.S. government limits the population of people of the American race basically to those living on "indian" reservations.

Programmed racism has cost U.S. Americans their racial identification. It has kept them stagnated with tribal identities. One may question how this has harmed Americans. Simply put, this deprives them of a genetic identification and identification with their American homeland (the American hemisphere). Without a racial identity and without the intimate identification with their American continents, Americans' self-image, self-concept, social development, and feelings of belonging to a greater whole are severely impaired. Unitedstaten Reverend Jesse Jackson once explained that being called black or negro is baseless, but being called African has a base of racial integrity. Similarly, being called "indian" is baseless, but being called American has a base of racial integrity.

Although the culture identifies people of the American race as "indians," it does not identify them as people of the "Indian race," because there is no such race. Nor can the culture identify them as being of the African, Asian, Australian, or European races. Consequently, most people perceive Americans as "indians," a raceless people. Early in U.S. history, Anglo European artists sketched Americans with African racial traits. And, as recently as 2008, televised documentaries about life in American communities in the Caribbean, before Colon's (Columbus's) arrival, people with African racial traits were used to portray Americans. It seems that some U.S. Europeans are triggered to give the "indians" a race.

The culture programs children early in their education with the racist notion of Americans as "indians." During the Thanksgiving Day celebration, one of the culture's most popular holidays, most teachers take the opportunity to teach children that to be an indian you need only stick a feather in your hair, stoop, and stomp around in a circle while making whooping monotone sounds. Children are taught that Anglo-Protestant Pilgrims fed "indians" a thanksgiving dinner. However, such a dinner never happened. Students are not told that it is a standardized U.S. cultural-serving lie. They are not told that the holiday came about when President Lincoln proclaimed the national "Thanksgiving Day" to muster up patriotism during the U.S. Civil War. The

Pilgrims had nothing to do with it. Teachers, however, have transmitted these racist lies about Americans and the Pilgrims for generations.

Young students are rarely taught that it was the Americans that initiated feasts to feed early European Pilgrims, and that Americans taught the Pilgrims how to survive in their foreign environment. Americans took in the European intruders and taught them to plant corn, hunt animals, and build shelters. Nor are children told the truth about how the Protestant Pilgrims and other European immigrants reciprocated. Nor are they told that Americans referred to Anglo Europeans as being "forked-tongued" in English, and "saxones" in Spanish. Both terms implied Anglo Europeans were not trust-worthy. Anglo Europeans retaliated by coining the phrase "indian giver," meaning someone who gives you something and then wants it back. The Anglo European slogan, "The only good indian is a dead indian," popular up to the 1940s, emerged early in U.S. history under the culture's belief that it was the culture's destiny to remove Americans from North America.

The U.S. culture has consistently held a demeaning image of the American. Up through the late 1950s, theater audiences joyfully applauded film scenes depicting the U.S. Cavalry massacring "indians." In the same era, *The Lone Ranger* was a popular radio and film series for children. The Lone Ranger was a European with two revolvers and a white horse named Silver. He was idolized as the Lone Ranger, but he had an "indian" named *Tonto* who appeared when the Lone Ranger needed him. It seems the WASP who named the "indian" character Tonto, thought that any "indian" loyal to an Anglo European had to be dimwitted. (Tonto means "dimwitted" in Spanish.)

Our culture's racism has programmed most of us to think of "indians" as a defeated people of the past. For generations, a painting of an American on horseback, in which both the warrior and horse look exhausted, has been a popular image symbolizing Americans' agony of defeat. The U.S. culture also likes to give the image of Americans as a diminishing people, like museum pieces of the past. Befitting this image, an American named Ishi, found living alone in an area in northern California in 1911, spent the last five years of his life living at the Anthropology Museum of the University of California at Berkeley. Anglo Europeans enjoyed focusing on Ishi as being the last of the

Yahi tribe of California, which had been massacred in the Three Knolls Massacre of 1866. No doubt Ishi's situation was remindful of the culture's favorite saying: "the last of the Mohicans."

The U.S. Fabricated "Hispanic Race"

The U.S. culture's racist conspiracy against the American race was forced to fabricate a racial identification to account for the large and growing populations of Americans and Amer-Euros that could not be identified as "indians."

The main reason for fabricating the racial label goes back to the fact that the racist culture has never wanted the American race to exist. The culture partially solved this problem with the genocide of many Americans. Then by taking the Americans' racial identify for its own kind, the culture reduced Americans to "indians." Most of these Americans were put into reservations and were given English surnames. Most descendants continue to live on reservations as "indians" with control numbers.

However, the U.S. culture's racist conspiracy has had to deal with the large and growing populations of Americans and Amer-Euros with Spanish surnames. The culture could not reduce these Americans to "indians." Nor did it want to racially identify them as Americans.

Let's regress to explain the history of the Spanish surnamed American population. Hundreds of years before the U.S. occupation of most of Mexico, Americans (bronze) and Hispano Europeans (whites) were already creating the biracial Amer-Euro population. Amer-Euro population's complexion varied from dark bronze to white. Most had Spanish surnames and Spanish was their primary language. Through the years, this American population with Spanish surnames has been growing. The growth of this population includes Spanish surnamed Americans coming north to the U.S. from what is left of the Mexican nation.

The large and increasing numbers of Americans and Amer-Euros with Spanish surnames created a dilemma for the U.S. racist nation. They could not be called "indians." The racist culture was forced to use ethnic and linguistic labels to identify these Spanish surnamed people of the American race. At first, "Mexican" was used as a racial term to identify Americans with Spanish surnames. When Unitedstatens with Spanish surnames complained about being identified as foreigners, it was changed to "Mexican American," with the understanding "American" meant U.S. citizen. The immigration of Americans with Spanish surnames from other Spanish speaking nations triggered a new racial label, "Latin" ("*Latino*"). Latin as a racial identification has been used off and on since the 1930s. However, Latin includes other languages besides Spanish (French, Italian, Portuguese, and Romanian). The culture then came up with another linguistic label for this large and growing population, "Hispanic" (Hispano in Spanish). Treating "Hispanic" as a race has been most appropriate because it includes only people with recognizable Spanish surnames.

Of course, it does not matter to our U.S. racist culture that people with Spanish surnames can be of any race, just as English surnamed people can also be of any race. In the U.S., there are Spanish surnamed people of the African race and Afro-Euros (African and European mixture) who are primarily from Puerto Rico, the Dominican Republic, and Cuba. Most of these people live in the eastern states. There are Spanish surnamed people of the Asian race who come mainly from the Philippines and live mostly on the Pacific Coast. There are also Spanish surnamed people of the European race who come from Spain, Argentina, Mexico, Cuba, and other Spanish speaking nations. Most, however, are native to the U.S. or Mexico and are of the American race or Amer-Euros.

The fact that Spanish surnamed people are of different races, just as English surnamed people are, does not stop the U.S. culture from treating Spanish surnamed people as being of one so-called "Hispanic race." However, for the racist culture it serves its purpose: Denying the existence of the American race.

Racism is so imbedded in the U.S. culture that no one questions medical information assuming that a certain disease is prevalent in Hispanics (Spanish surnamed population). For example, in some health studies physicians have claimed that a certain disease (let's call it disease X) is prevalent in the U.S. culture's Hispanic population. This occurs because the Hispanic population is perceived as a race. It would be just as ridiculous for a study to claim that disease Y was prevalent in the culture's Anglo population (English surnamed population).

The assumption that disease X is prevalent in the Hispanic population would be logical if all members were of same race and lived in the same environment. Similarly, the assumption that disease Y is prevalent in the Anglo population would also make sense if all members were of the same race and lived in the same environment. However, in reality all members of the Hispanic population are not of the same race, nor do they live in the same environment. The same applies to the Anglo population. In other words, it is illogical to assume that a certain disease is prevalent in a population because the people have Spanish surnames. However, because of the culture's racism, medical information on a fabricated race based on Spanish surnames is not questioned.

Why not fabricate a race from all English surnamed people? The racist culture would never fabricate such a race because it would include Americans in reservations and the bulk of its African population. On the other hand, identifying Americans as Hispanics and as "indians" masks the existence of the American race. Consequently, Americans with Spanish or English surnames remain raceless. The English surnamed American population disappears under the "indian" label, just as the vast Spanish surnamed American population disappears under "Hispanic," "Mexican," and "Latin" labels.

Mr. Loreto Caballero, Spanish speaking American, was born December 24, 1874.

Caballero's daughter Mary Louise was an Amer-Euro.

Paul S. Amador, Amer-Euro field worker in the San Joaquin Valley of California during the great economic depression.
Photo by Ben S. Amador

Spanish speaking Amer-Euro families at a work camp in the San Joaquin Valley of California during the great economic depression. Such groups have been celebrating the 16th of September (Independence from Spain) in California since 1811. California as well of most of Mexico was made part of the United States in 1848.

Photo by Ben S. Amador, September 16, 1935.

The genetic racial mixture that produced the large Amer-Euro (bronze and white) population in the mainland of North America began soon after 1492. By the 1530s, Spanish ships began sailing around South America and into what they named El Oceano Pacifico. The first Spanish ships explored the Pacific Coast from the tip of Argentina to a little beyond Vancouver, Canada. The Spaniards claimed this vast area for Spain. The Hispano European sailors enjoyed staying with Americans in a village at a California bay they named San Diego in 1542. We can assume that the birth of the Amer-Euro population in California began in 1542.

Most American nations' populations are mostly of a mixture of the American (bronze) and European (white) races. In American nations, as in Mexico, Peru, Ecuador and Bolivia, people of the American race make up most of these cultures' populations. In Mexico there is some awareness of the native race of America, but it is not named. What is mentioned is *"de la raza"* (being of the race). Mexico celebrates a national holiday called *Dia de la raza* (Day of the race). This holiday is celebrated in the United States as Christopher Columbus Day. (*Cristobal Colon* would not have answered to the ugly translation of his name. It is similar to translating George Washington's name to Jorge Uachinton.) To most Mexicans la raza (the race) certainly does not mean an "indian" race because for most Spanish speakers being called "indio" is comparable to being called "nigger."

There is a Mexican story about what it means to be *indio*. While touring in Mexico, a U.S. professor of anthropology, interested in the dress customs of various areas of Mexico, spotted a group of young Americans in Guadalajara and recognized their fashion of dress. After introducing herself to the group, in Spanish, she proudly announced, "I recognize you. You are indians from the state of Zacatecas." The group was silent for a moment. Then a young man burst out angrily: "Indians, you say! Can't you see we have shoes?" Before making a fast departure, the anthropologist apologized for being so stupid not to have seen the obvious. In Spanish speaking cultures "indio" means a poor, timid, and uneducated person.

More Labels for Non-Europeans

Racism is so intrinsic in the U.S. culture that it created all kinds of labels to identify its non-European citizens. Non-Europeans are identified either by their race or ancestral ethnicity with "American" tagged on to denote their Unitedstaten citizenship. As such, non-European U.S. citizens are identified as Mexican American, Japanese American, Chinese American, and so on. "American" is also tagged on to racial identifications such as African American and Asian American. Of course there is no need for people of the European race to be identified as European Americans. Neither is there need for such labels as English American, Canadian American, and Australian American because U.S. citizens of these ethnic backgrounds are mainly of the European race. For the same reason, there is no need for linguistic labels such as Anglo American or English American or Germanic American.

Racist labeling also applies to geographical maps of the Western Hemisphere. Many maps used in schools teach children that Spanish-speaking nations of North and South America make up "Latin America." Yet, the English-speaking nations of North America are not taught as making up "Germanic America." There are maps showing children that only the United States and Canada make up North America. The other nations of the North American continent, Mexico to the Panama Canal, are labeled as "Central America." The fact is that there is no such thing as a Central American continent.

Summary

Racism against American and African peoples has been ongoing since Anglo European Protestant Pilgrims landed on the shores of North America. To the present, in the U.S. most people of the American race who are called "indians" are kept much as the bush people of Australia…they are people that do not exist in the mainstream of the Anglo European culture. On the other hand, it has been easier for Americans with Spanish surnames to be culturally mainstreamed for several reasons: They comprise a large and growing population. They do not identify with tribal labels or identify themselves as "indians." Therefore, they have been able to develop a better self-image of themselves than their genetic peers who are perceived as "indians."

In addition to the genocide of Americans, U.S. racism has caused the destruction of much of the cultural heritage of Americans. The destruction ranges from obliterating the identification of the American race to the destruction of the cultural advancements of Americans in Texas, New Mexico, Arizona, and especially California. Anglo Europeans' instinctual destruction of Americans' history in California seems to have been to destroy evidence of the long bicultural relationship of Americans and Hispano Europeans.

Anglo European racism was triggered by the civilization's Judaic belief core, via Protestantism. Through the centuries, Anglo Europeans' Protestant beliefs and weapon superiority have reinforced their aggression toward others not of their kind. Therefore, those who think that racism can be removed from the U.S. culture are ignorant about what is intrinsic to the culture. To remove racism would call for removing our Founders' Conservative nature, which has been maintained for hundreds of years. It is as Karl Marx stated: "The ruling ideas of any age are the ideas of the ruling class." One cannot expect racism to be removed when the task has to be negotiated within the interactive core that developed and nourished racism. The culture's racism and all its ramifications—abuse, violence, inequality, etc., against non-Europeans—continue to be triggered and maintained by the founding nature of the culture.

For U.S. racists, no amount of discussion is going to convince them that their interactions (feelings, thoughts, etc.) against others not of their kind are wrong. This is because racism is reinforced by our culture in many ways and forms. The instincts underlying racism are in our species' animal heritage, and it is in the nature of our culture to trigger and maintain them.

10

Judaic Freedom

*"One who wishes to acquire wisdom should study
the way money works, for there is no greater area of
Torah-study than this. It is like an ever-flowing stream"*

(THE JEWS' TALMUD, BAVA BATRA 175B).

Judaic freedom is the pursuit of material wealth, and this pursuit demands freedom from the restraints of caring for the general welfare of people and the environment. Conservatives, especially politicians, glorify Judaic freedom with one word, "Freedom." In other words, "Freedom" is their code word for capitalism, Judaic freedom, free enterprise, free market, and money-power. (From this chapter on, Freedom with a capital "F" denotes capitalism).

Since it is their own culture, the authors focus on "Freedom" in the United States. In addition, the U.S. is the stronghold of Freedom, and it protects it with the greatest military that "an ever-flowing stream" of money can buy. Freedom keeps the United States perpetually in the pursuit of wealth (happiness). The culture uses its wealth of resources to maintain a greedy, competitive environment, permitting the accumulation of wealth for a few at the expense of the many. For those seeking the Promised Land of Freedom and all that it holds dear, this is the place.

Freedom, as practiced in the U.S., exhibits our species' animal level of caring for a chosen few. It thrives on limited caring, greed, corruption, and it demands the freedom to ravage global resources (including workers' lives). Consequently, as the U.S. and other advanced cultures support Freedom globally, our species is becoming a threat to itself.

The Injection of God

The practices of selling and trading with the hope of having more wealth at the end of the day, and the greed to constantly accumulate wealth, have been around since pre-recorded history. For Jews and unlabeled Jews, however, these practices were empowered via Judaism. Judaism incorporated these practices and ideas into god beliefs. In other words, the injection of "god" has made these ancient practices very powerful and enduring. They have been fundamentals of our civilization for over a thousand years. In the 1800s these Judaic god beliefs became known as "capitalism" (free enterprise, free market, etc.). German economist-sociologist Werner Sombart of the mid 1800s stated: "It is not surprising, therefore, that the history of the capitalist spirit should be inextricably bound up with the history of churches and religious systems." (Sombart was primarily referring to Protestantism, whose practices are closely linked to Judaism.)

Nevertheless, it must be remembered that the fundamental beliefs and practices of Judaism are triggered from our species' animal genetic traits. This means capitalism's greed, selfishness, and inequality did not originate in Judaism or in any other religion. What Judaic beliefs seem to do is to facilitate the triggering of these traits from our species' genetic potential.

U.S. Freedom Foundations

Our culture's wealthy Anglo European Protestant Founders' affinity for Judaic beliefs triggered them to mold a foundation for Freedom. In the 1700s the Founders solidified their Conservative nature by focusing on securing comfort and wealth for their kind and inequality for the working masses. This was done when they assigned themselves the task of writing the nation's Declaration of Independence and the Constitution. From the start, the culture was founded on inequality.

We in "We the people of the United States" excluded the greater population of the culture: All people of the American (bronze) and African (black) races as well as European (white) men without property and all women. A wife was her husband's property, and so were the children. A woman did not have legal ownership of her children, property, earnings, or of any inheritance acquired before or during marriage. In fact, in the Declaration of Independence, Thomas Jefferson underscored the phrase "all men are created equal," which became a cultural favorite. Jefferson ignored inequalities brought about by slavery and the poverty that existed everywhere around him when he wrote the Declaration of Independence. The intent of the Declaration was to protect the government and political rights of wealthy European (white) men.

The Declaration's famous saying about securing "life, liberty and the pursuit of *happiness*" was copied from English philosopher John Locke's *Second Treatise on Government*, in which he wrote: "life, liberty and the pursuit of *property*." Thomas Jefferson changed "property" to "happiness," but scholars believe he considered the pursuit of property (wealth) to be the pursuit of happiness. (Property included slaves. Washington, Jefferson, and their rich friends owned thousands of slaves).

Both the Declaration and the Constitution did not reflect the interests of all women, slaves, people of the American race, and even European men without property. This might be why Founder Alexander Hamilton stated that no one could be so stupid as to think that a poor "white" man's vote was equal to a wealthy "white" man's vote. At the time, the idea that "all men are created equal" was fixed to mean wealthy men of the European race. Records of the Treasury Department showed that most of the fifty-five men who wrote the Constitution "were men of wealth in land, slaves, manufacturing, or shipping, that half of them had money loaned out at interest and forty of the fifty-five held government bonds" (Zinn, 2003, 90). It seems logical for the Founders to have focused on protecting the wealthy against nationwide taxation, labor, and slave revolts. The Founders' intentions were *not* to establish equality via democracy, although today's U.S. political liberals like to lie that they were. They fail to understand that the Founders' caring was limited to their own kind.

George Washington made a special effort to make it known that "all men" included Jews. In August 1790 he sent a letter to the Hebrew Congregation in Newport, Rhode Island accepting them as equals. Washington included the Jews because he, as the top representative of the culture's wealthy few, identified with the Judaic belief of being of god's chosen people. He probably also identified with their love of Freedom.

The fact that George Washington felt a dire need to protect his wealth (being the nation's first multimillionaire) was a major factor in creating the Constitution. In 1786, Shay's Rebellion awakened Washington's fear of losing some of his vast land holdings, which extended far into the west. Massachusetts' rebellious farmers (many were war veterans) wanted permission to farm unused land, and Washington's private militia was not enough to protect his property. In a famous letter to his Conservative friend, Alexander Hamilton, he wrote: "If we are to preserve our property, we'd better organize some sort of a federal structure, because we're faced with anarchy." This prompted Hamilton to begin writing the United States Constitution to give wealthy Conservatives what they needed, a tax-supported police and military force to protect property. In other words, Washington, Hamilton, and other wealthy politicians made sure laws and institutions were put into place to protect their "pursuit of happiness." Our Founders knew they were establishing inequality for the common people. They were intelligent Conservative men of the time programmed to protect their wealthy kind.

The Founder's establishment of inequality and the oppression of others not of their kind was not a malicious intent. Such beliefs were triggered from their genetic nature and reinforced by their Anglo-Protestant culture. They were simply interacting as wealthy individuals caring for their own kind. It would have been weird if they had established a caring equalitarian democracy.

Conservative political writers have stressed the importance of property to the extent that Paul Elmore wrote: "The rights of property are more important than the right to life" (Nesbit, 1986, 55). Elmore explained that it is essentially these thoughts on property that separate man from animal. Conservative philosopher Roger Scruton stated: "Through property man embraces his world... and begins to therein discover himself as a social being" (Green, 1987, 4). It is not surprising that up to the 1950s, the primary duty of most U.S. lawyers was to protect the property of the wealthy few from the common people. The writings of such prestigious Conservatives as Elmore and Scruton, read in universities throughout the 1900s, reinforced our culture's capitalist spirit.

The Essence of Freedom

It has been easy for those who scream out the holiness of Freedom and those who scream out the animalness of Freedom to agree on its essence. This is that Freedom demands a wealthy few, the exploitation of an infinite supply of workers, greed, and a money-powered democracy. Even a brief analysis of these factors reveals that the essence of capitalism is based on primitive animal caring traits. Such practices should now be recognized for what they are.

Freedom Demands a Wealthy Few

Since the birth of the nation, there have always been a wealthy few individuals who have controlled the political and financial development of the United States. For example, by 1870 John D. Rockefeller had set up the Standard Oil Company, and by 1899 his fortune was $200 million, which increased when he went into banking. In 1895 the U.S. was depleted of gold, but New York bankers, headed by J. P. Morgan, had $129 million in gold. They bailed out the U.S. government and ended up with a profit of $18 million (Zinn, 2003, 256–7). Social-political scientist Dr. Gore Vidal explains: "For 200 years, they've [the wealthy few] been governing the country…they run every God-damned bank in the country" (Drifus, 1987, 36).

Sociologist Dr. David R. Simon explains that the wealthy few continue to run our nation in the twenty-first century, but they now do so mainly through their multinational corporations. Simon explains: "A handful of corporations have virtual control over the market place. The decisions made by the boards of directors and the management personnel of these huge corporations determined solely by the profit motive affect employment and production, consumption patterns, wages and prices, the extent of foreign trade, the rate of natural resource depletion and the like" (Simon, 1996, 323). Their global corporations make worldwide profits from other cultures' resources. They also control and direct political policies in many foreign countries.

Most of us do not know whom the wealthy few are, and we cannot conceptualize their wealth. We have difficulty conceptualizing the value of a million dollars, and a billion dollars ($1,000,000,000) is inconceivable. Our ignorance about who the wealthy few are and how wealthy they are is demonstrated when we think of physicians and lawyers as being rich. We cannot realize that if they were rich, they would not be serving us common working slobs. A few statistics give us an idea of what it means to be wealthy. A 2006 research (reported on Yahoo Finance) surveyed some of our culture's lesser millionaires' lifestyles. These multimillionaires' annual incomes averaged only around $9.2 million. Some of them had their own jet airplanes. On the average each spent $30,000 per year on alcohol, $107,000 per year on spa treatments, $157,000 per year on hotels and resorts, and some $248,000 per year on jewelry.

Now let's take a brief look at multibillionaires. Back in 2001 Ted Turner's net worth as vice chairman of AOL and its largest individual stockholder, was estimated at $3.8 billion (he was ranked ninety-seventh on a list of U.S. wealthy by *Forbes* magazine). At that time, Turner owned two million acres in ten states and three homes in the choicest areas of California, Georgia, and South Carolina. In one year he gave some $50 million to his favorite environmental organizations.

In 2006 *Forbes 400* published a list of multibillionaires. Sheldon Adelson was not the highest on the list, but *Forbes* reported that he had made about one million dollars an hour since the 2004 *Forbes 400* was published. (This gives us an idea why most of us cannot conceptualize what it is to be rich.) The founder of Microsoft, Bill Gates, and his wife head the short list of multibillionaires. In 2005 they gave more than $1 billion to global health care.

There are good tax incentives for the rich to donate large sums of money. But Ted Turner's and the Gates's donations indicate that they tend to care for the welfare of the general environment. Most of the wealthy few, however, support Protestant religious groups, right wing politicians, and Conservative think tanks such as the Heritage Foundation, which formulates and promotes Conservative public policies, limited government, and Freedom.

Freedom Demands Inequality

In 2009 only half of one percent of the U.S. population of over three hundred million made up the rich. This half of one percent of the population owned a large part of the total wealth of the nation (One third of the group were Jews; the rest were unlabeled Jews). Such a vast monetary disparity between the wealthy few and the vast population of common people exists because the culture's capitalist system requires it. In a capitalistic system there can only be a few that can amass an infinite amount of wealth. The rest of us are placed in a stupor of hope by the culture's propaganda to believe that in capitalism any one of us can become one of the wealthy few.

The disparity of inequality between working families' wealth and the wealth of the rich is obscenely huge. Yet, the culture programs families to believe that they form a *middle class* between the rich and the homeless beggars who live on the sidewalks, alleys, and under bridges. The reality is that the income of working families is obscenely closer to what street beggars get than to what the rich get. This is true even for working families of two professionals, such as an accountant and attorney, a physician and professor, and so forth. In 2009 such working professionals' annual incomes of $250,000 to $350,000 were still obscenely closer to what homeless beggars get than to what the rich get. Only multimillionaire film, musical, and sport celebrities, corporate executive officers, etc., come close to being the nation's "middle class." However, most working families are convinced that they are the middle class because they do not comprehend what it is to be rich, but they do see the homeless in their neighborhoods. So common workers see themselves between the

> Pierre Proudhon, a French political philosopher, first used the term "capitalism" in 1861 to mean "an economic and social regime in which capital does not generally belong to those who make it through their labor"
>
> (Robbins, 2002, 32).

homeless and whatever notion they have of the rich. Since lying is systemic in the culture, making working families believe they form the nation's middle class is just one more culture-serving lie masking the obscene inequality that our culture's kind of Freedom demands.

Most U.S. citizens don't know that capitalism causes hundreds of thousands of working families to have difficulty keeping up with adequate health care, living expenses, college tuitions, and so on. Without the culture's inequitable monetary distribution, a wealthy few would not exist, and life for working families would be less stressful. (No other advanced capitalist culture maintains the level of inequality that exists in the United States, and no other nation lies so much about it. Other advanced nations such as Switzerland and Japan have less poverty and crime and keep their citizens more educated and informed.)

Freedom Demands the Exploitation of Workers

By the mid 1800s, Karl Marx was already warning of capitalism's troubling relationship with workers: "What is unique about capitalism is the rationale of systematic expropriation of labor for the sole purpose of capital accumulation." Over 150 years later, political scientists continue to warn workers about their role in capitalism. For example, Dr. Michael Parenti explains: "The ultimate purpose of workers is not to perform services for consumers, nor to sustain life and society, but to, make more and more money for the investor [the capitalist]" (Parenti, 1994, 73). Yet, most workers continue to be only vaguely aware of the nature of Freedom. This remains true even as they spend their lives at the center of capitalism. Most are unaware that Freedom mandates a closed group of a wealthy few and the exploitation of an infinite supply of workers. Like ants, working families spend their laboring lives maintaining the inequality of our insect-like few. For ants, it is for their queen mother. For us, it is for our culture's chosen few.

Workers spend their laboring lives supporting the "pursuit of happiness" for the chosen few. Everything workers live, work, fight, and die for is primarily for the benefit of the rich. Workers must continue selling their working lives at a fraction of what their labor is worth. Why? They do so because they are shaped and programmed by the culture to maintain Freedom for a chosen few. They bare the brunt of capitalism's inequality. Consequently, most workers are left with no other choice but to fantasize about a better tomorrow and to comfort themselves with the prospect of a spiritual "here-after." How stupid or how insect-like can we workers get?

The demand for a continuous flow of cheap labor triggered corporate powers to come up with the North American Free Trade Agreement (NAFTA) and the World Trade Organization (WTO). NAFTA brings together the three largest nations of North America—Canada, United States, and Mexico—to benefit corporate Freedom. The World Trade Organization (WTO) makes it easy for corporate powers to practice Freedom without restraints from governments' interference, globally. The WTO "has the authority to overrule or dilute any laws of any nation deemed to burden the investment and market prerogatives of transnational corporations" (Parenti, 2008, 167). Therefore, U.S. corporations can import workers from other cultures even when there are unemployed domestic workers. They can also setup their businesses in poor nations where they can exploit an abundance of cheap labor. When doing business in money-poor nations such as Mexico, Guatemala, and El Salvador, corporations have the freedom to forego workers' safety regulations, minimum wage standards, health insurance, and so on. Such organizations as NAFTA and WTO give multinational corporations the freedom to exploit cultures' resources and peoples' laboring life spans.

The exploitation of foreign labor does wonders for corporate profits abroad and domestically. Immigrant workers generally get paid less than domestic workers, but they will earn more money than wherever they came from. Our capitalist culture therefore wants skilled immigrants to come and compete with domestic skilled workers. It doesn't matter if domestic workers lose their jobs because immigrants will be paid less, and profits should increase. Unfortunately, it becomes much easier for workers to hate immigrant workers than it is to hate their nation's capitalist system.

In the U.S., the center of the Judaican way of life, the wealthy few enjoy a life of perverted abundance. The bulk of working families undergo all kinds of stresses. Working families and retirees suffer because they do not have the money for their essential needs. Some citizens become so overwhelmed and distraught from lacking essential needs that they decide it is better to kill loved ones, and voluntarily stop living. There are many situations similar to the following showing the overwhelming desperation and frustration suffered by some retirees and others due to Freedom's greed and inequality.

A 51-year-old man, in desperation, kissed and then killed his seriously ill 47-year-old wife by dropping her from their fourth floor apartment balcony. They did not have medical insurance to help with their accumulating debts. She had uterine cancer, was partially blind and her weight was down to seventy-five pounds. He was suffering from depression. After dropping her, he waited for the authorities to come and take care of them both (CNN.com, 8/16/2007).

In a similar case, the life of a retired elderly couple with illnesses and without adequate medical insurance ended with a murder-suicide. The husband kissed his wife good night and then shot her in the head as she slept. He then shot himself in the head. He left a note of apology and indicated that he felt he would die soon and did not want his wife to suffer alone (reported on the Internet, 2009).

Stupor of Hope

The U.S. culture feeds us workers false hope to distract us from the inequality and frustration that Judaic freedom forces us to endure. We are programmed to believe that we, too, might get rich, soon and suddenly. Our hope to be rich triggers many of us to gamble in the corrupted Wall Street stock market, in state-sponsored gambling lotteries, and in casinos. In most states workers need only go as far as the local grocery store, liquor store, or gasoline service station to buy lottery tickets. Surveys find that workers at the bottom of our culture's financial hierarchy are most addicted to the hope of winning lottery games.

> "For members of the culture of capitalism the key element is money."
>
> (Robbins, 2002, 6).

Televised money game shows are another way of keeping workers' hopes alive. In most programs participants succumb to screaming, jumping, hysterical laughter, crying, drooling, and possibly urinating (involuntarily) over the excitement of winning money. In other programs, participants might endure embarrassment, frustration, fear, repulsion, and pain to win money. Live studio audiences interact as howling monkeys as they fantasize with winning participants. Millions more around the globe watch and fantasize that they would also win a lot of money if they could only live in the Promised Land of the United States. Stories of individuals going from poverty to riches, whether they are true, semi-true or lies, are exaggerated, glorified, and propagandized. The culture's capitalist propaganda constantly triggers our hope for wealth.

We are conditioned to love the power of money. Our love for money influences our feelings, thoughts, and behaviors for our family and things in general. We want to give our children things that our parents could not give us. Our love of travel, hobbies, and wanting to make donations to our favorite charity and church reinforces our desire for money. We want money to keep up with changing fads to look like, smell like, and act like our favorite celebrities and the rich. Our culture's propaganda influences us to buy all kinds of things that quickly become waste products. We buy jewelry, fingernails, clothes, shoes, anti-aging creams, drugs, cosmetic surgeries, toys, junk food, and so on. Our buying frenzy includes buying the latest technology—cell phones, computers, games, and a vast assortment of other gimmicks and gadgets. We are pushed to buy more things than we can afford. We buy and buy to the point that we turn into waste products ourselves. (Freedom even demands that televised and radio propaganda for selling products be advertised at a louder volume than is set for regular programming.) The culture keeps us chasing money like panting dogs running after a rabbit that is unlikely to be caught. As far back as 1835, after visiting the United States, the noted French philosopher Alexis de Tocqueville wrote, "I know of no country where the love of money has taken a stronger hold on the affections of men."

If we are programmed to think that being rich is being a winner, what happens to the bulk of us over time? Well, we get stressed out and feel like losers. Most of us overcome depressing feelings about ourselves by identifying with fictitious characters, media celebrities, or with anyone or anything that gives us a feeling of being a winner. Fictitious characters such as Superman, Wonder Woman, 007, and so on became popular because so many of us identified with their power. Almost any man or boy can tell you about Superman. The less money we have the more we need to fantasize with fictitious characters because they become our perfect selves. Many more of us losers spend much of our non-laboring time identifying with winning sport teams, and top athletes. We identify with our favorite team with caps, shirts, posters, mugs, noisemakers, certain foods, and many other things that propagandize our team. We pay high prices to attend games and feel free to eat, drink, paint our faces and bellies, scream, curse, and so on to participate with our team. It is not surprising that sometimes we cap-off our participation as destructive mobs when our team loses or wins a championship.

By trying to be winners we often create problems not only for ourselves, but also for our families. Too many of us end up bitter, having private conversations with our god, in prison, or killed by the police. We often give up hope and take to narcotics to numb the effect of being losers. We get involved in a multitude of crimes to get what is "sacred, kingly, and divine." We become apt swindlers, deceptive embezzlers, bold thieves, and murderers. Too many of us even feel like winners by harming or killing people and not getting caught. Our frustrations cause too many of us to become dangerous. It is of little wonder that of all advanced nations, our U.S. culture has the highest crime rate, the highest number of people incarcerated, and the highest number of people executed. The stress of feeling like losers catches up with too many of us who began with good intentions. It is not surprising that of the advanced cultures Unitedstatens of all ages take the most legal and illegal drugs to make living tolerable.

Freedom means one thing for workers, but it is something entirely different from what it is for the rich. They have the freedom to have more and do more than the worker can even fantasize of having and doing. Of course, the rich are free from the fear of losing employment, health care, pensions, their homes, and their children's education. For the wealthy Freedom bells ring throughout their lives.

Freedom Demands Greed

A good capitalist has no qualms about expressing greed for money. U.S. capitalist Nelson Rockefeller was once asked how much money was enough for a rich person to accumulate. He thought about it and answered, "a little bit more." (One of his many workers would have probably responded "enough so I can do all the things I love for the rest of my life.")

Financier Ivan F. Boesky, in his 1986 commencement address to the School of Business Administration of the University of California at Berkeley, advised students with a few sentences that became well known. He told them: "Greed is all right, by the way. I want you to know that. I think greed is healthy. You can be greedy and still feel good about yourself" (Stewart, 1992, 261). Some years later, Boesky was caught in an illegal Wall Street money scheme. It is said that he agreed to pay some 100 million dollars in fines for his illicit activities. It is not known how much money he made, but one can assume that the fine of 100 million did not extinguish his desire to be greedy. It is in the nature of a good capitalist not to perceive being greedy as wrong. So greed is still OK; you can still feel good about yourself.

Freedom's Greed Endangers Life

Freedom's greed triggers limited caring for the welfare of people and the environment for the sake of profits. We recall what David Simon said about corporate powers (the pillars of capitalism), that their decisions are determined solely by the profit motive. No matter what kind of business, decisions on whether products and services are good or bad for people and the environment are secondary to making profits. (This is something most people living in the center of Judaic freedom are ignorant about.)

Freedom's greed for profit triggers many corporate executive officers (CEO) to interact as primitive animals without a conscience. The profit motive forces them to produce and sell unsafe and unhealthy products. Their conscienceless greed for profit creates an environment that exposes people to all kinds of dangers as indicated by some classic cases.

Corporate executives will often choose a product design that yields the highest profit, even if some customers will be killed or otherwise harmed by the particular product. Such was the case with Ford's infamous Pinto automobile. Ford CEOs apparently decided for higher profits, even if it meant turning some customers into screaming torches. Documentation revealed Ford executives knew the Pinto had a faulty gas tank with the propensity to burst into flames in rear-end collisions. To recall the Pintos and make them safe would have cost $11 per car. So the executives did some dollar-wise soul searching. They "reasoned that 180 burn deaths, 180 serious burn injuries, and

2,100 burned vehicles would cost $49.5 million (each dead person was figured at $200,000). But a recall of Pintos and making the $11 per car repair would amount to $137 million" (Simon, 1996, 125).

Union Carbide's deadly 1984 accident in Bhopal, India is another classic case of greed and lack of caring for others. The victims were told that the gas was not toxic, that washing their eyes and drinking plenty of water would be sufficient. Yet two days after the accident, thousands had died. By this time, scientists had detected cyanide in the blood of people exposed to the gas. Physicians and nurses began treating them with a remedy that counteracts cyanide poisoning. Corporate and Indian government officials, however, denied the existence of cyanide poisoning and ordered that the treatment be stopped. Private physicians who continued treating the poisoned victims with the cyanide antidote were arrested and their supplies were confiscated. Confirming that cyanide poisoning was the cause of the deaths would have made Union Carbide legally responsible for the death and illness of thousands of people. In 2004, twenty years later, India reported that over 150,000 victims and their offspring were still suffering from birth defects as well as lung, kidney, and liver diseases. Union Carbide had not yet reimbursed the victims for medical care. (The chief executive of Union Carbide in India retired to live in the United States.)

Hooker Chemical Company's poisoning of Love Canal is another case of harm to many people and the environment due to greed. During a period of some ten years, the company dumped more than 20,000 tons of deadly carcinogenic chemicals into Love Canal near Niagara Falls, New York. Then, in a smart business move, the company sold its dirt-covered toxic dumpsite to the local Board of Education for one dollar. An elementary school was built on the site, and a small community developed. In 1977 toxic sludge began seeping up into the school and nearby homes. The carcinogens in the toxic sludge caused death and crippling diseases to people living in the area. They suffered "miscarriages, chromosomal abnormalities, liver disorders, respiratory and urinary disease, epilepsy, and suicide" (Simon, 1982, 9). Many babies in the area were stillborn or born deformed. The company had known of the potential danger of the toxic land since 1958, but kept quiet about it because a cleanup of the tons of carcinogenic matter had been estimated to cost up to 50 million dollars. Similar to Ford's Pinto recall, Hooker determined that cleanup was greater than the estimated cost of any possible legal suit that would develop from the toxins left buried. (These examples of Freedom's greed and lack of caring demonstrate why corporate powers want the U.S. and other governments to set limits or caps on the amount of money for which the public can sue corporations.)

Many corporations do not clean up their toxic wastes, or they get rid of them in the cheapest way possible. They hire the least expensive waste company to rid them of their toxic wastes and demand not to know how or where the waste is dumped. Some corporations get rid of their toxic products by selling them to developing nations. David R. Simon in his book, *Elite Deviance*, 1996, found that U.S. banned toxic products are exported to foreign nations each year. Some of these banned toxins such as pesticides come back to harm us in food products exported by U.S. food corporations based in these foreign nations. These food products are sold in our markets. We certainly cannot detect residues of pesticides and herbicides that are sprayed on or soaked into our food, which also kill some of our brain cells. So it doesn't matter if our food is farmed here, in Chile, Mexico, Brazil, Argentina, or wherever, it gets to our plate saturated with toxins.

Animal beings in control of corporations cannot identify with the men, women, and children poisoned, burned, deformed, and so on. Their cultural environment triggers them to focus on what is good for the corporation's well being. So they identify with the corporation's health. Their animalistic lack of conscience for the welfare of people is supported by Freedom's ideology of "greed is all right."

"Consumers Beware"

It should be the responsibility of the culture's government to make safe and quality food available to all its citizens. However, in our capitalist culture, this is not the case. Decisions made by the U.S. Food and Drug Administration (FDA) too often benefit corporate profits rather than consumers' health. For the milk industry, the FDA allows cows to be injected with growth hormones so that they will produce abnormal amounts of milk. For the beef industry, the

FDA allows livestock to be injected with antibiotics to make them gain weight by retaining water. The long-term effects of these hormones and antibiotics on our health are unknown. The FDA also allows the beef industry to irradiate meat in order to retard spoilage and provide longer shelf life. Irradiated meat has been found to contain toxic chemicals that can cause cancer and genetic defects (Parenti, 2008, 99). In addition, Food corporations are permitted to "help" the FDA determine permissible amounts of toxins in foods. This is why pesticides, lead, arsenic, and other toxins are allowed in all kinds of foods in various amounts. (Arsenic is fed to chickens because it makes them lay more eggs.) The corporations that make profits on these products decide what toxins are allowed and the quantity. This is our culture's Judaican way, the freedom to accumulate wealth with as little restraints as possible .

How many of us know that chickens, cows, and other animals that we eat are kept in small areas wallowing in their feces until slaughtered. How many of us eat "fresh farm-raised fish" not knowing that they swim in confined areas in their feces and eat their feces along with the hormones fed to them? How many of us know that cows are fed tons of old candy, dead animal parts, sawdust, and sewage sludge? These are some examples of why some nations have refused some food products from the U.S. However, the U.S. has pressured these nations to accept the products or face trade sanctions. As for us U.S. citizens, we are conditioned to eat what Animal beings in charge of the food industry put out. We eat their ink-stamped "U.S. Choice" slabs of beef, and so forth without qualms. Yet, these Animal beings are incapable of identifying with the long term health of the nation's citizens due to their narrow spectrum of caring.

In the late 1980s the "English mad cow disease" (Bovine Spongiform Encephalopathy or BSE) killed many people that had eaten contaminated meat. The disease, which destroys the brain, started with cows that were fed all kinds of things that cows should not eat. Contamination was passed on to other cows and, eventually, was passed on to people who ate the diseased parts of the cows. The disease spread all over the world because England was intentionally slow in warning nations that were importing its contaminated beef. Corporations were fearful of a possible significant drop in the price of beef leading to a reduction in profits. However, the time came when research confirmed that the contaminated beef killed the first person in England. The meat industry could no longer stall the ban on beef with the excuse that more time was needed for research. Of the 157 people who had eaten the meat and had an agonizing death, 148 were English citizens.

Decades later, the English Mad Cow disease was still causing nations to closely monitor beef and cattle feed. Diseased cows were found in Canada and in the United States, causing other nations to put a ban on importing meat from these nations. In December 2005, Japan lifted its two-year ban on importing U.S. beef. Yet in January 2006, just six weeks after lifting the ban, Japan reinstated its ban. The U.S. meat industry became upset, fearing other nations would follow Japan's food safety standards. In this case, the ban on U.S. beef was not because it was contaminated. The beef had been banned because vertebral parts with the spinal cord had inadvertently been left in the beef shipment. These parts would increase the risk of people getting Mad Cow disease. The U.S. takes risks with its citizens' health, because the beef industry's profit is prioritized over the health of citizens. However, for advanced nations such as Japan, the nation's health is top priority. This might be because, unlike the U.S., most advanced nations pay for their citizens' medical health expenses. There is therefore an extra incentive to protect their citizens' health from known risks.

It is difficult to know how damaging the accumulation of toxins and chemicals we get from food is to our health. However, the National Center for Health Statistics reported that infant mortality rose for the first time in the early 2000s (during the Bush–Cheney regime). Nevertheless, U.S government agencies keep telling consumers that the toxins and other inedible products injected into our foods are not harmful in the amounts permitted. They want consumers to ignore the fact that the small amounts of toxins permitted in each product accumulate to large amounts of toxins when the toxins in many food products are consumed daily. Could it be that the accumulation of toxins and other injected chemicals in our foods are increasing illnesses, including thought and behavior disorders in the U.S. population?

Most U.S. citizens will never know how corporate greed endangers their health and their children's health. They will never know because the CEOs of the food industry and chemical corporations have the money-power and the conscience of primitive animals. Therefore, without any misgivings, they tell us that we are eating the safest and best food in the world. (Most politicians of both political parties support their claims. They cannot afford not to.)

Corporate Corruption without Punishment

Greed for profit triggers corporate corruption. However, those involved in the corruption are often exempt from punishment. In a culture directed by Freedom, such as the United States, most corporate chief executive officers (CEOs) don't go to prison for criminal acts that would ordinarily land common workers in prison for decades or life. Laws governing corporations are such that corrupted CEOs are protected from being prosecuted as criminals. They are shielded by the corporation's "legal shield," and the Constitution's 14th Amendment protects their corporations.

The 14th Amendment was added to the Constitution after the Civil War in 1868 to protect freed African slaves' rights as U.S. citizens. It states: "Nor shall any State deprive any person of life, liberty, or property, without due process of law; nor deny to any person within its jurisdiction the equal protection of the laws." Soon after the 14th Amendment became law "the Supreme Court began to demolish it as a protection for blacks and to develop it as a protection for corporations" (Zinn, 2003, 260). By 1886 the Supreme Court ruled that a private corporation is a "natural person" and that it has all constitutional rights that are given to an individual.

Exempting corporate criminals from due punishment was obvious in the culture's infamous savings and loan (S&L) scandal (1981 to 1989). At the time, it was reported as the largest theft in world history. When the Reagan–Bush administration changed regulations for the savings and loan industry, restraints on Freedom were eased so much that S&L owners, CEOs, and other investors began borrowing huge amounts of money with the intent not to repay it, as indicated once the scandal was exposed. U.S. taxpayers ended up having to pay over $1.4 trillion to restore the money stolen by CEOs, lawyers, and accountants in their orgy of Freedom. (Yet, Ronald Reagan was able to finish his two presidential terms and remain the most glorified of Republican presidents to this day.) In 1990 the FBI had some 7,000 S&L related fraud cases. Some 331 executives, lawyers, and accountants were found guilty, and the "average jail term was two years" (Simon, 1996, 50). With good behavior, jail term was reduced to a few months.

Some twenty of the S&L criminal schemes were connected to joint activities by international crime figures and U.S. secret services. Furthermore, it was not the FBI that made the shocking discovery of the Mafia-CIA connection to the S&L schemes, but *Houston Post* reporter Pete Brewton. Brewton almost single-handed exposed the Mafia-CIA merger and their activities (Simon, 1996, 53).

> "The genius of capitalism consists precisely in its lack of morality" (Lapham, 1985).

In another classic scenario of corporate crime without punishment, tobacco CEOs, standing tall and proud lied to a U.S. investigating congressional committee. The lineup of about a half dozen tobacco executives raised their right hand and swore under god Judaic that what they said was the truth and nothing but the truth. Facing Old Glory and god, they solemnly swore they had not known tobacco was harmful. It was later confirmed that these overfed, expensively dressed executives had lied. Did these overfed liars see the inside of a prison? No, the rich liars and their families went on to live in splendor. It seems that those in power determined that the tobacco industry and its liars were only guilty of being good Freedom lovers.

In 2002 corrupted activities by Enron CEOs included lying to shareholders and prospective investors that Enron was making profits when in reality it was losing hundreds of millions of dollars. The consensus of most journalists reporting on the scandal was that such crimes are not only extremely difficult to investigate, but convictions are almost non-existent. In 2003 other corporations stole huge sums of monies from workers' investment funds. Although profits were down, CEOs were giving themselves generous bonuses and salaries. The orgy of corporate greed and corruption during the Conservative Bush–Cheney regime left many workers without pensions. They could only dwell in the fantasy perpetuated by the chosen few that "things will get better."

These examples of capitalism's greed and corruption provide a glimpse of the animalness encoded in our species that is triggered by our capitalist culture. In other words, capitalism triggers us to interact as the animals in Wislawa Szymborska's poem (1995):

> The Buzzard never says it is to blame
>
> The panther wouldn't know what scruples mean; ...
>
> A jackal doesn't understand remorse.

Freedom's Money-Powered Democracy

The U.S. culture's money-powered democracy was set during the Founder's era. At the 1787 Constitutional Convention, Charles Pinckney, a wealthy landowner, proposed that only someone with at least $100,000 should qualify to be president, an amount that disqualified almost all men of the time. This proposal was not included in the Constitution. Yet, wealthy men have been running the country since George Washington was president. In modern times most presidential candidates have been multimillionaires (Parenti, 2008, 231).

The wealthy continue to run it even if they are not elected officials. Sociologist David R. Simon points out that they are the owners of a handful of corporations that have virtual control over the market place. Richard R. Robbins describes them as "individuals or groups who control economic resources that everyone depends on but who are accountable to virtually no one" (Robbins, 2002, 97). In essence, the culture is by and for this "privileged minority."

Since the culture is a money-powered democracy, there is little difference in how the two political parties running the nation affect the status quo. The Republican Party, although open about its preference for the wealthy, still gets a lot of support from ignorant workers who identify with the wealthy few. The Democratic Party supposedly represents working families, but it cannot forsake its ties and loyalty to money-power. So while Conservative Republicans' alliance to the wealthy is made on solid ground, liberal Democrats' alliance to the workers is made on shaky ground. This is because most politicians are controlled by the culture's ideology of money-power. For example, liberal Democrat President Bill Clinton, on PBS's *News Hour*, is quoted as saying, "I want to create more millionaires in my presidency" (Parenti, 2008, 231).

In other words, both political parties run on the same (unspoken) creed—maintain the culture's money-powered democracy. Politicians of both parties identify with the culture's money-power. They cannot afford not to.

Our culture's money-powered democracy forces government policies to support the status of the wealthy few. Although some liberal politicians may voice working families' concerns, they cannot go against their culture's system that demands that a chosen few remain in control at the expense of working people. This is because it takes money-power to campaign competitively. Political campaigns cost millions of dollars. The higher the political office the more money is needed by the politician and by his or her political party. The entire democratic agenda of being heard is controlled by the ideology of money-power. There is more voice and more action favoring the will of the wealthy. The culture's so-called democracy therefore tends to be a fraud because it cannot represent the welfare of the bulk of its citizens, the workers, "the people." Yet most workers are unaware that politicians' priorities have to be in the interest of the wealthy few because they support and control the culture's money-powered democracy. Therefore, they are much more concerned about interests of the wealthy few than they are about workers' interests. However, during political campaigns candidates of both political parties attend to workers' interests with a lot of verbiage.

Simply having political elections doesn't make a culture a democracy. Dictatorships can have people vote and elect individuals who continue to support the status quo of the dictatorship. Even if a culture has multiple political parties it can function like a dictatorship, the results of the elections continue the status quo of those few in power. Similarly, the results of our U.S. elections maintain the status quo of the wealthy few.

※　　※　　※

Early U.S. capitalists did not hide the fact that the culture had to be a money-powered democracy. By 1776 (the same year of the Declaration of Independence) Adam Smith had written about Freedom in his book, *An Inquiry into the Nature and Cause of the Wealth of Nations*. Smith explained that for capitalism to exist it needed "self-interest and economic freedom." By the 1880s,

U.S. capitalist Andrew Carnegie was demanding: "We must accommodate ourselves, great inequality of environment, the concentration of business, industrial and commercial in the hands of a few, and the law of competition between these, as being not only beneficial, but essential for the future progress of the race" (Kronenwetter, 1986, 43). (Carnegie was famous for his wealth and monopoly of the steel industry.)

Today capitalists and their politicians are not as open about the culture's money-powered democracy as they were before the 1930s. No doubt they sense that it is better to keep the bulk of the citizenry ignorant about living in a money-powered democracy. The culture keeps its citizens ignorant by feeding them much garbage and nonsense via its new technology. Yet it would be befitting for the most powerful nation of the globe to use technology to educate and produce a well-informed citizenry. However, most politicians favoring the power of the wealthy know that the more ignorant people are about the culture's money-powered democracy, the better it is for Freedom.

Dr. Mortimer Adler found that peoples' ignorance keeps the culture from developing a true democracy and that our U.S. culture's educational system is clearly inadequate for the purpose of democracy. He explained that, "If we don't solve the educational problem, if we have only the kinds of citizens we have now, forget it" (Kidder, 1987, 5). Adler also indicated that the twenty-first century would see if our nation could expand, or maintain the degree of democracy it now has. It can be assumed that the nation will not significantly expand its democracy because educating the masses is not a priority for our capitalist culture. Good education for the masses requires equalizing financial distribution, and this is not on a capitalist culture's agenda. This is why democracy in the U.S. is unlikely to expand into what Adler envisions is a true democracy.

It is pathetic that people who have worked as long as forty, fifty, or sixty years for our capitalistic system are not guaranteed adequate health care upon retirement. Yet, the president, Supreme Court judges, generals, admirals, senators, and congressmen and their spouses are guaranteed the best welfare health programs for life. For them, their social welfare pensions and health care for life are not considered *socialism*. Yet if an elected politician brings up the idea that workers should also have similar programs upon retirement, the idea is negatively termed socialism. Most of us are ignorant about what socialism is, and we have been culturally programmed to think of it as something evil. Ignorance keeps us workers in the same pathetic condition generation after generation.

As we live, work, and retire in our culture, some of us become aware of the negative effects capitalism had on our parents, ourselves, our children, grandchildren, and will have on their descendants. However, by the time such realizations are upon us, we have spent our laboring lives perpetuating Freedom's animalness. Some of us angrily question why the richest superpower on earth has so many of its workers, war veterans, children, and elderly retirees in need of basic essentials.

In 2006 it looked as if retirement funds for workers would take a turn for the worse. Conservative President George W. Bush was for placing workers' Social Security money into the stock market (Wall Street). If this were to happen, the trillions of dollars for funding the retirement of the working masses would create one of the last big hurrahs for our culture's systemic greed. Putting this money in the stock market would bring on a gigantic Freedom orgy that *would not* be for the welfare of the workers. Yet such an orgy may be what is needed to set in motion events that would bring an end to the old Promised Land story.

Capitalists Who Tell It as It Is

There has been no shortage of politicians and social leaders who have identified the animalness of capitalism. Some have clearly stated that a capitalist culture demands inequality and limited caring for the welfare of people and the environment. George Kennen, as head of the Policy Planning Staff of the U.S. State Department in 1948, made it clear that as a nation "We need not deceive ourselves that we can afford today the luxury of altruism and world benefaction—unreal objectives such as human rights, the raising of living standards, and democratization" (Loewen, 1995, 210). Kennen indicated that it is our culture's nature to have greed, inequality, a wealthy few, many underpaid workers, homeless and hungry people. He also indicated that some politicians delude themselves into thinking that it is in the culture's nature to actually care about other cultures' democracy, equality, and human rights. Kennen, an advocate of capitalism, was honest to say that capitalism was not a social caring system. What Kennen said of our culture some sixty years ago is still true today.

Dr. Ayn Rand is considered the most honest and knowledgeable advocate of capitalism. Rand expounded the true meaning of capitalism as: "Freedom…means freedom from government coercion. It does not mean freedom from the landlord, or freedom from the employer, or freedom from the laws of nature…It means freedom from the coercive power of the state and nothing more" (Rand, 1967, 192). Michael Kronenwetter, in agreement with Rand, explained: "The less the government, or any other authority interferes with the private economic competition of individuals, the better for everyone" (Kronenwetter, 1988, 23). Rand and Kronenwetter were clear about Freedom's demand to acquire wealth without the interference of laws, taxation, and morals.

Rand was also clear about what has kept capitalism alive and what is destructive to capitalism. She was explicit about capitalism needing greed in order to exist. She saw greed as being of the true nature of mankind. The idea that greed is okay has been transmitted for generations. For the sake of capitalism's survival, she pleaded with readers to read her papers entitled *The Virtue of Selfishness* because the expansion of caring for the welfare of others and the environment brings death for capitalism. In her book, *Capitalism—the Unknown Ideal,* Rand warns that the expansion of social caring, in any form and by any name (altruism, socialism, communism, humanness, etc.) is destructive to the spirit of capitalism. Rand also warned Conservatives to stop hiding their greed and limited caring for others with god beliefs, and to stop masking capitalism with such words as *liberty, democracy,* and *the American way.* She referred to such denials as sickening cowardice. Furthermore, she thought it unwise to hide selfishness and greediness with religion because the enemies of capitalism will represent reason, while those for it will represent mythical faith without rational arguments. (It seems Ayn Rand overlooked the fact that capitalism as practiced in the U.S. is triggered from Judaic god beliefs.) Rand's theme was that the true nature of capitalism must not be masked, but faced and understood if it is to survive.

Alan Greenspan, who controlled the vast money interactions of the United States economy for nineteen years (U.S. Federal Reserve Chairman from 1987 to 2006), was a disciple of Rand's philosophical ideas on Freedom. During his swearing-in ceremony to the chairmanship in 1987, he expressed that he was most devoted to the two women who had accompanied him, Ayn Rand and his mother, Rose Goldsmith. Wall Street and the chosen few appreciated Greenspan's chairmanship and were happy that his successor in 2006, Ben Bernanke, promised to follow the ways of Greenspan. (On university campuses, students are still discovering Ayn Rand's honesty of what capitalism is and what it requires.)

Thomas L. Friedman, an advocate of global capitalism and author of *The World is Flat* (2005), expresses joy that not only will the U.S. continue to enjoy Freedom, but also that soon the whole world will be awash with it. Friedman believes this will cause people to be more competitive, greedy, and brutal, but he is for such a nature. To explain what one needs to come up on top in such an environment, Friedman tells about an African proverb written in Mandarin that he saw posted in a friend's business in China for employees to contemplate:

> Every morning in Africa, a gazelle wakes up. It knows it must run faster than the fastest lion or it will be killed. Every morning a lion wakes up. It knows it must outrun the slowest gazelle or it will starve to death. It doesn't matter whether you are a lion or a gazelle. When the sun comes up, you better start running (Friedman, 2005, 114).

For capitalists the proverb is to trigger people to identify with Judaic freedom by reducing their thinking to the world of common animals where you take or are taken. Therefore, Friedman advises readers to prepare themselves in order to come out on top.

In a televised program, Friedman and a U.S. senator, who had written a book on capitalism with a liberal slant, were interviewed on their opposing views. The senator decried the loss of U.S. jobs to areas of the world where foreign and U.S. companies have children working for ridiculously low wages in deplorable conditions. Friedman agreed that that happens, looked down at the table to show his concern and added something about capitalism being brutal. Then he lifted his head and stumped the senator by asking him: "But what is the alternative?" The senator could not respond that, perhaps, capitalism's animalness had to be stopped or reduced. He could not say that a dash of socialism, as practiced by some Western European nations, would help. No, he could not. Such offending ideas would have been political suicide for the senator in a nation horrified at the mention of socialism. Friedman was happily aware of this. All the senator could come up with was that we (capitalists) should care more about the welfare of others. On the other hand, Friedman, confident as most Conservatives are about their beliefs, was adamant that we either have capitalism's mandated inequality or worldwide equal poverty.

In his book, Friedman included what an emotional event it had been for him to leave his oldest daughter at a university. He pointed out how his child was entering a world much more dangerous than it was when he was her age. Friedman cares dearly about his children, but can't care about the welfare of someone else's children. The animalness of capitalism is okay if you and your kin come out on top.

Protecting Freedom

Unlike Jewish groups of yore in Europe that had to bribe kings, dictators, and the like to protect their Freedom, today the wealthy few and their corporations have guaranteed protection. Now, the civilization's most powerful cultures, the U.S. and the U.K., protect Freedom globally with money and military power. Favoring and protecting the wealth of the few over the welfare of the many is a major commandment of Freedom "a la Judaic." In fact, the U.S. has a unified power that is called the *national security state,* which includes the CIA, FBI, National Security Agency (NSA), the president, Joint Chiefs of Staff, and other government agencies. The primary purpose of this conglomerate of powers "is to defeat advocacy groups at home and abroad that seek alternatives to free market globalization" (Parenti, 2008, 148).

The U.S. has the greatest military complex with "an ever-flowing stream" of money to protect Freedom globally. The U.S. gives its secret organizations such as the CIA and NSA plenty of tax monies to protect Freedom. Only a small special congressional committee, whose members are sworn to secrecy, knows about the huge budgets allocated to the NSA and CIA.

Our nation spends billions of dollars and thousands of soldiers' lives to protect the cultures of Freedom-friendly kings, queens, shahs, princes, and other Conservative dictators. In return, Freedom-friendly dictatorships have given the U.S. perpetual rights to their culture's oil resources, harbors, air-bases, and other resources. As long as dictatorships play the Freedom game, the United States supports them. (The U.S. culture's hatred for a one-party rule is limited to liberal socialist-leaders such as Cuba's Dr. Fidel Castro who refused to be bought.) If they do not play the Judaic game, they are over-thrown or assassinated. However, even when people of a nation overthrow the Conservative dictator, the U.S. keeps rights to the resources that the ousted dictator gave it. This is why the U.S. claims Guantanamo Bay in Cuba and many other military bases in other nations. All that citizens of these nations can do is control their frustration and rage towards the United States.

It is the culture's nature to deal with global conflicts with its military. It therefore allocates a huge budget to the Pentagon whose primary purpose is to protect and ensure profits for military industrial complex corporations. These huge corporations are involved in producing war products (Chomsky, 2002, 75). And, the Pentagon is not required to report to the public or to the IRS the billions it gives to the war-profiteering corporations. So a few contracted corporations constantly create new weapons to replace old weapons. It is expected that some weapons given away or sold yesterday are being used against U.S. personnel today, but the profit motive is not affected. Dr. Noam Chomsky, one of the most knowledgeable authors of our culture's nature, explains that in the name of national security taxpayers' monies maintain the Pentagon's military industrial complex. In short, the purpose of the Pentagon is *not* to protect the lives of U.S. taxpayers; it is to protect corporate Freedom. (Except for World War II, the nation's many warring and military interventions have been primarily dictated by capitalism's greed.)

In his farewell speech of 1961, President Dwight D. Eisenhower, a five-star general in WWII, had the insight to warn the nation about the dangers that our military industrial complex could bring about. The following paragraphs are from his speech:

> In the councils of government, we must guard against the acquisition of unwarranted influence, whether sought or unsought, by the military industrial complex. The potential for the disastrous rise of misplaced power exists and will persist.
>
> We must never let the weight of this combination endanger our liberties or democratic processes. We should take nothing for granted. Only an alert and knowledgeable citizenry can compel the proper meshing of the huge industrial and military machinery of defense with our peaceful methods and goals, so that security and liberty may prosper together. Today, the solitary inventor, tinkering in his shop, has been overshadowed by task forces of scientists in laboratories and testing fields. In the same fashion, the free university, historically the fountainhead of free ideas and scientific discovery, has experienced a revolution in the conduct of research. Partly because of the huge costs involved, a government contract becomes virtually a substitute for intellectual curiosity. For every old blackboard there are now hundreds of new electronic computers.
>
> The prospect of domination of the nation's scholars by Federal employment, project allocations, and the power of money is ever present…and is gravely to be regarded.
>
> Another factor in maintaining balance involves the element of time. As we peer into society's future, we—you and I, and our government—must avoid the impulse to live only for today, plundering, for our own ease and convenience, the precious resources of tomorrow. We cannot mortgage the material assets of our grandchildren without risking the loss also of their political and spiritual heritage. We want democracy to survive for all generations to come, not to become the insolvent phantom of tomorrow. (Public Papers of President Dwight D. Eisenhower, 1961, 1035–1045)

President Eisenhower's military and political experience coupled with his caring for the welfare of the nation triggered him to identify the potential dangers of a possible out-of-control Pentagon and military industrial complex. Eisenhower warned: "Only an alert and knowledgeable citizenry can compel the proper meshing...so that security and liberty may prosper together." But instead of having an alert and knowledgeable citizenry, the bulk of U.S. citizenry is known as the most ignorant of the advanced cultures of the globe. Therefore, the culture's leaders have easily ignored Eisenhower's warning, and instead have increased profits for the military industrial complex. They also continue to use secrecy under the label of "national security." Any chance of the people becoming alert to an out-of-control Pentagon and military industrial complex is nullified. (President Eisenhower's warning should be in every high school's curriculum.)

Presently, and into the predictable future, U.S. secretaries of defense serve as pimps for the Pentagon and the military industrial complex. Therefore, in spite of the heinous, bloody war with Vietnam (1959–1975), which took the lives of nearly 60,000 of our fighting men and women, in June 2006 U.S. Secretary of Defense Donald Rumsfeld met with Vietnam's Defense Minister Pham Van Tra. They agreed to expand "exchanges at all levels of the military and in various ways further strengthen the military-to-military relationship." Rumsfeld, however, told reporters, "We have no plans for access to military facilities [bases] in Vietnam." Yet the United States government plans to make Vietnam dependent on its military industrial complex for weapons. The Pentagon will begin shaping Vietnam's dependency with its International Military Education and Training program, which will start with free English training for Vietnamese military officers to be held in a military base in San Antonio, Texas.

On October 30, 2006 a memo obtained by the Associated Press reported that teams of news experts would "develop messages" and produce 24-hour news to "correct the record" of what was said about the Pentagon and related activities. This permitted the Pentagon to slant the news in a way beneficial to the industrial military complex. President Eisenhower's fears have become a reality, and even worse than what he had imagined.

Backlash to Freedom

The backlash to Judaic freedom in New York City (9/11/2001) made many of us aware that our culture's worldwide Freedom cultivates rage from many cultures. Underdeveloped nations produce young men and women that brave certain death to hurt us Freedom lovers in whatever way they can. Yet, when these warriors give up their lives to hurt us, most of us are surprised and outraged that anyone would be that angry with us. After the 9/11 attack, many of us innocently cried out: "Why? We didn't do anything to them." (Ironically, the date of the attack, 9/11, matched the nation's 911 emergency phone number for help.) Here, we recall what Marx and Huxley concluded about the practice of Judaic freedom, that it brings a backlash of contempt.

After the Islamic commando suicide raid of 2001 on New York City, the Conservative Bush–Cheney regime disregarded the Geneva Convention standards for international law and human rights. Thousands of Islamic individuals were kidnapped from various nations and imprisoned in secret sites to determine if they were Islamic warriors. All were abused and many were brutally tortured. The Bush–Cheney regime created an "illegal prison" (as defined by the international community) at the U.S. military base at Guantanamo Bay, Cuba. Suspected Islamic warriors were imprisoned without being legally charged of a crime. The Bush–Cheney regime also determined that the suspected Islamic warriors were not war prisoners but "enemy combatants" and could be tortured. The Conservative duo then denied the U.S. Red Cross and the International Committee of the Red Cross access to all suspects held by the U.S. in secret sites in various countries and at Guantanamo. Throughout the regime's administration, attorneys, Amnesty International, and representatives from Geneva, the European Union (EU), and the UN were also denied access to the prisoners. Even family members were not allowed visitations. According to this Conservative duo, so-called enemy combatants did not merit the rights that war prisoners have under the Geneva Convention.

In the end, what should not be forgotten is that Bush and Cheney did not have to pay the price for the killing and torturing of an unknown number of men and women that went on under their leadership. (Bush and Cheney should not be pardoned for what international law determined were crimes against humanity. This duo's punishment could serve as the beginning of a new era where political criminals are punished regardless of their top positions and the global status of their nation.)

There have been other backlash attacks against our nation's self-serving practices, but its money-powered mighty military has easily squelched them. Such attacks have occurred in our culture's global outposts and in underdeveloped (poor) cultures. Such backlash attacks have targeted U.S. tourists, U.S. embassies, and our military bases that dot the globe. Retaliations should be expected to continue as our culture continues to forcefully maintain what is globally seen as a militaristic, money-powered political system in need of an overhaul.

More of us need to become aware of what our U.S. culture stands for and what it has done and does to others in the name of democracy and Freedom in its pursuit of happiness. When foreigners who hate us for what our culture's practices have done to them succeed in attacking us, as they did on September 11, 2001, we will not be ignorant and confused. We should not be surprised if our culture's Freedom triggers other jarring backlashes from other parts of the world. (For centuries, Jews in Europe dearly enjoyed Freedom, but they also suffered brutal backlashes more than once.) Our culture's capitalist profiteering at the expense of others' welfare and their resources has awakened people of underdeveloped cultures to try to put a stop to our culture's Freedom in any way they can.

The U.S. culture has historically interacted with other cultures with its self-endowed Manifest Destiny belief, that it is the "chosen nation" of god Judaic. Humane organizations such as Amnesty International are becoming aware of what it means when our culture's self-endowed idea of being god's "chosen nation" is led by Animal beings.

Summary

It is taking too long for most of us to realize that the so-called U.S. "American way" is actually the "Judaican way." There is nothing American about the U.S. Judaican way. It is just plain old Anglo-Judaism in action, which has been the essence of our Unitedstaten culture from day one. The Judaican way, under the alias of capitalism, is rampant throughout the globe under U.S. corporate powers. It remains protected by the mightiest industrial military complex on earth. Focusing on the destructive power of our U.S. culture's Freedom does not mean it is the worst culture of our species. It is just that it is earth's top gorilla that can break any other culture's back, and it will remain earth's military superpower into the foreseeable future.

The culture's limited caring, via Judaic freedom, has a huge negative effect on the stability and well being of the world. Social-political scientist Dr. Michael Parenti tells us: "The U.S. capitalist system squanders our natural resources, exploits and underpays our labor, and creates privation and desperate social needs, serving the few at great cost to the many, leaving us with a society that is less democratic and increasingly driven by wealth and want" (Parenti, 2008, 23). Environmental sociologist John Bellamy Foster puts it this way: "It becomes evident that capitalism is unsustainable—ecologically, economically, politically, and morally—and must be superseded" (Zinn, 2003, 219). Such intellectuals are warning us that it is absurd and dangerous to think that our self-centered Judaican way can be responsible for the welfare of our species. A global leadership with the morals of capitalism does not have the potential to care for the wrenching problems facing our species globally.

Up to this point, we have seen how our species' animal levels of caring through racism and Judaic Freedom hinder us from identifying with our species as a family and sharing earth's resources. In the following chapter we will see how religion follows this trend.

11

God Reality

"The enduring paradox of religion is that so much of its substance is demonstrably false, yet it remains a driving force in all societies"

(E. O. WILSON, 1975, 561).

Countless mythical beliefs perceived as real have dwelled in our species' genetics throughout its evolutionary journey. However, no other mythical beliefs have been treated and maintained for so long a time as our beliefs in gods. Gods have remained real for most of us because they have been at the forefront of our species' belief-reality in helping us cope with the environment. Therefore, we are assured of the reality of our god and of his protection.

Experts on animal interactions suggest that our beliefs in gods are rooted to animal instincts. This is not to say that groveling to a particular god was triggered from our species' inherited animal nature since day one. What it means is that our species' inherited nature predisposes us to grovel to an alpha entity that we call "god." We perform all kinds of rituals showing respect and reverence to appease "It" or "Him." We lower our head and body as our way of looking up and licking up to our god, somewhat like dogs and other animals appease their alpha leader. At times, we fear our god's "bite" if we don't conform to certain

Lions and lice don't
waver in their course.
Why should they, when
they know they're right?

(Wislawa Szymborska)

feelings, thoughts, and behaviors. Believing in and groveling to an alpha entity for guidance and protection are instincts forming our species' belief-reality. This is similar to many animal species' belief-reality.

God reality endures almost completely undisturbed by logic and scientific information. It is no surprise that god beliefs remain "a driving force in all societies."

Our beliefs in gods emerged "from a certain kind of ignorance and a certain degree of helplessness" (Huxley, 1941, 278). Early in our species' evolution we were spooked by anything that awed, startled, or killed us. We were instinctively triggered to worship and grovel to something for protection. However, with our species' multispecies potential we went beyond an animal species' potential of worshiping or groveling only to the group's alpha leader. We moved on to grovel to other things in the environment. In many cases it was a nonliving entity such as thunder, a huge boulder, a volcano, and so on.

As we got wiser, instead of having a *boulder god* or *volcano god*, we created gods that we could carry in our imaginations wherever we had a mind to go. We soon created imagined alpha leaders or gods with more wisdom than our mortal leader could ever have. We created gods to help us cope with the known and the unknown of our expanding environment. They ranged from simplifying existence for the shallowest among us, to exorcising the "heebie-jeebies" from the toughest among us. Their character ranged from "do not count too much on me" and "do your own thing" supernatural-types, to "I'm it, depend on me" and "I know it all and do it all" super-unnatural types. The dominant idea was to have a god with super powers to help us.

Throughout the ages, many of our created gods and their supporting stories lost out to those with better scripts. Or, they lost out to gods with powerful military supporters who forced us to worship "their" god. Eventually some god believers of northeast Africa came up with the idea that there was only one god, and that *their* god was it. In time, most peoples of the area accepted the idea of one god, but with different supporting stories for the concept of "one" god. In this case, the supporting stories to Judaism's belief of one god created Christianity and Islam.

Our Civilization's God Belief

Our civilization will be known as the one that emerged from a thousand-year-old myth based on a Hebrew chieftain's fantasy. According to Judaic stories, Abraham, chieftain of a wandering Hebrew (*Hapirus*) tribe, came up with the founding script for Judaism. After having spent a long, hot, day in the dusty desert, he heard a voice speak to him in Hebrew. He knew it was the father of all gods because of what the voice told him to do, which was to create a special tribe. Abraham sensed the potential for this to evolve into something big. So, the story was a wrap.

Abraham's story that he had been chosen as "the man" to father the chosen people of god Judaic was successful in attracting women to produce a tribe of the chosen. Abraham may have suffered from hearing voices, perhaps from too much sun, but he was no slouch. He was a good businessman and somewhat of a gifted hustler. It seemed to have been a simple "con job" (deception) for Abraham to sell the idea that god Judaic had placed an order that he had to fulfill. The story doesn't mention anyone else witnessing god Judaic's placement of the order. We need to remind ourselves that this all happened some three thousand years ago, and the *Hapirus*, the dusty ones as they were called, were wandering desert tribes. They were quite ignorant, gullible, and fearful of the unknown, as most people of that time were. They were easily seduced and controlled by a gifted hustler like Abraham.

During that time, it was not rare to create gods and supporting background stories. In fact, it can be said that besides tribal warring, it was the main thing for groups to do. It is impossible to know who or what actually existed, but we can assume that some aspects of the stories must be true (certainly the towns and land areas named are real). The essence of the stories is the identification of Jews as god Judaic's chosen people. Put another way, Judaic scriptures display our species' inherent animal instincts of favoring a select few at the top of a hierarchy.

Many of us might be perplexed as to how the Jews came to be the chosen of a god. Yet what perplexes most rabbis is why their god chose Abraham to father the chosen few. Why not someone much more kosher, someone in the likes of Jesus? After all, biblical stories about Abraham tell how he interacted like an Animal being with little caring even for his immediate family. He permitted his firstborn son, Ishmael, and his mother, Abraham's slave, to be sent out to the desert to die. The mother died, but the infant supposedly survived to initiate the Islamic religion. Abraham also loaned his loyal wife Sara to a wealthy man in exchange for some goats. (Abraham had introduced his wife as his sister to the wealthy man.) In another occasion, Abraham was willing to butcher his son to prove his allegiance to god Judaic. No matter how often and how many rabbis question and debate Abraham's interactions, they always conclude that Abraham's script is true. The possibility or probability that Abraham fabricated his story to get his period of glory is unimaginable. The probability that Abraham was a gifted hustler fulfilling his need to be a leader is unimaginable. No such thoughts enter the wondering brains of mullahs, priests, and rabbis.

To think that Judaism might have emerged from a sharp hustler or from a man otherwise suffering from the desert heat would pull "the chosen" cover right off the Jews. This would erode the Judaic foundation from under the god stories of Islam and Christianity. There is too much to unravel and too much to reveal. As such, the god Judaic belief has been patched up and kept going throughout the centuries by Jewish scholars. They must, however, continue to keep it simple—why Abraham? For their god belief, Abraham's simple script is more than enough substance for Judaism. It was enough to put the scriptures of Judaism at the foundations of our great civilization.

Moses further enriched Judaic scriptures. He, too, had personal conversations with god Judaic. Speaking with a god was still an expected happening for big name Jewish leaders. He enriched the scriptures with scenes in which he played major roles. Moses is best known as the Jew who walked up rocky Mount Sinai alone (with tools?) and came down with god Judaic's words mysteriously chiseled in stone some forty days later. In response to Moses' groveling for help in controlling his tribe, god Judaic supposedly carved out his advice in the form of the Ten Commandments on two slabs of stone. As commander in chief, Moses was concerned that Jews' intertribal problems stemmed from taking too many freedoms with each other. The Ten Commandments were guidelines for interactions among god Judaic's chosen people. (Jews, of course, were not expected to follow them in their interactions with non-Jews.)

We can rationalize that people of thousands of years ago were ignorant and gullible enough to believe Abraham and Moses' tales about god Judaic. Yet, even today in the midst of scientific knowledge, millions still believe such tales. With a better understanding of our species' nature, we can see that it is not simply a case of ignorance and gullibility. Now we can add that it's a case of the environment primarily triggering inherited animal instincts. This is much like triggering apes' instinctual need for an alpha leader's guidance and protection. For reasons similar to that of apes, it's impossible for most believers to think of god beliefs as instincts that help them cope with the environment. This is why god beliefs remain intact for most believers, regardless of science. As our species evolves, however, science will continue to change our species' inherited god reality.

God Beliefs Maintain Limited Caring for "Others"

Our god beliefs can trigger us to care for only those who believe in our god. Religious people have a long history of distrusting, hating, and killing others who are not their kind of believers. This is evident in the bestiality that oozes from Judaic biblical stories. Judaism's Old Testament is satiated with "holy" men's limited caring for others not of their kind. (Such limited caring is at the foundation of Christianity and Islam because they evolved from Judaism.) For example, biblical stories speak of holy men having the right to enslave, rape, kill, and take territory from others in the name of god Judaic. In Deuteronomy 2:32–35, Moses (creator of the Ten Commandments) recounts how god Judaic lends him and his tribe a holy hand in massacring non-Jews. This holy holocaust was a god-given right for Moses and his tribe.

> Then Sihon came out against us he and all his people, to fight at Jahaz. And the Lord our God delivered him before us: and we smote him, and his sons, and all his people. And we took all his cities at that time, and utterly destroyed the men, and the women, and the little ones, of every city, we left none to remain.

Moses was quite the ethnic cleansing agent, often warring against other tribes of the northeastern African deserts. After defeating the army of the Midianites, in which all the men had been killed, he commanded his group to continue killing. "Kill every male dependent, and kill every woman who has had intercourse with a man, but spare for yourselves every woman among them who has not had intercourse" (Numbers 31). Moses' commands were "identical in result to the aggression and genetic usurpation by male langur monkeys" (Wilson, 1975, 573). It should not surprise us that any man, holy or unholy, has the genetic aggression and reasoning of a male langur monkey. This monkey's aggression and reasoning is in our species' inherent animal nature. Moses, like a normal langur monkey, was genetically programmed to kill all men and boys ("every male dependent") and to proliferate genes of his own kind with unused females.

Dr. Michael Parenti, social-political scientist, points out that the Jewish Bible (Old Testament) "shows there is one ethical code governing relations among one's own people [one's kind] and another for outsiders, whose extermination is seen not only as an unfortunate necessity but an elevated endeavor, a carrying out of god's will" (Parenti, 1994, 117). Here, we need to recall which god was supporting the deeds of Moses and Abraham. It was not Jesus. On the other hand, it was natural for god Judaic to help *his* own kind in their bloody orgies. This god was not about to let his treasured chosen people down.

Such brutal ethnic cleansing based on Judaic beliefs continued. In 1948 Zionist leaders were thinking of reasons and ways to take the Palestinians' homeland—land the Jews needed to create *their* homeland nation of Israel. To remind himself of what was needed, Zionist leader Ben-Gurion wrote in his diary on January 1, 1948, "There is a need now for strong and brutal reaction. We need to be accurate about timing, place and those we hit. If we accuse a family—we need to harm them without mercy, women and children included. Otherwise, this is not an effective reaction … There is no need to distinguish between guilty and not guilty" (Mearsheimer and Walt, 2007, 99). The birth of the Israeli nation became a reality with the help of the U.K. and the U.S. in 1948. Even as of 2010, the bloody orgy continues in the "holy land."

Christian holy men also have a history of not caring for those *not* of their kind. In the 1500s, Catholic priest Martin Luther, significantly influenced by Judaic beliefs, favored a select few over the welfare of the impoverished masses. He made this evident in 1525 when German peasants rebelled against their exploitation at the hands of a wealthy few and their Catholic clergy supporters. The peasants' rebellion triggered Martin Luther to find his true Animal being calling. He urged "everyone who can to smite, slay, and stab [the peasants] secretly or openly, remembering that nothing can be more poisonous hurtful, or devilish than a rebel. It is just as when one must kill a mad dog." As Luther denounced the rebellious peasants and asked his god to go against them, he had his dear holy book on hand to justify his command to kill peasants. Luther was "a man of god" who could not care for the downtrodden. (This is not surprising if your image of god is god Judaic, not god Jesus.) By the mid 1500s Martin Luther was kicked out of the Catholic Church. (In the 1600s English Protestants came to glorify him as the founder of Protestantism.)

Similar to Luther, Pope John Paul II was a "holy" Christian who could not identify with suffering lives of the poor and oppressed of the world. He was incapable of caring about their impoverished, unsanitary conditions. In 1998 Pope John Paul II guided the power of the Vatican against some of the world's most downtrodden working poor by attacking the Liberation Theology movement. The movement, by caring Catholic *padres* (priests) of Brazil, was to help the working poor with more than just prayers.

The padres identified with the working masses' destitute living conditions—lack of food, medical care, education, legal help, and unsafe working conditions. The padres felt it was uncaring of them to simply tell the suffering poor that a good relationship with Jesus through prayer was all that was needed. The padres gave the people information to improve their lives. They helped them get organized to bring about political changes for a better future for their children. The padres knew the religious lifestyle of these people had been to focus on future heavenly rewards rather than on their deprived lives on earth. Especially in poor nations with large populations of Catholics, the working poor are conditioned by Catholicism to accept their deprived conditions with such religious verses as, "Happy the afflicted, for they will be comforted; Happy the undemanding, for they will inherit the earth," and so on. So the padres helped the people in reality, to find ways to reduce or get out of their impoverished conditions. (Businesses and Conservative Christian clergy saw the movement as communistic and urged Pope John Paul II to stop the Liberation Theology movement, which he did.)

Pope John Paul II decided that caring deeply about those in need was a priestly duty, but to actually do something to change reality for the needy was wrong. The priests could participate with working families in groveling to god, but not in helping them get essential needs. The Pope's objective was to make these people good Christian god believers. His nature was not that of Jesus or of the priests who annoyed him. He could not identify with the priests' level of caring for the welfare of families that have been suffering for many generations. This pope believed that god takes care of things in his own mysterious way or does not take care of things in his own mysterious way. However, the Conservative Pope did not want to accept the priests' humane efforts as god's mysterious way of helping. Instead, he transferred them to rural non-poverty areas and threatened others if they picked up the cause. It was beyond the Pope's caring potential to identify with the priests' humanness, or for that matter, with Jesus' humanness.

Pope John Paul II had been honest about his Conservatism. He had favored right-wing religious groups such as Legionaries of Christ, Opus Dei, and Liberation Group of Italy. He had also favored priests that led right-wing religious groups, ignoring their inappropriate behaviors. For example, Father Maciel was a pedophile, but he was great at raising money for the church. Pope Paul canonized Father Escriva who was known to have praised Adolph Hitler. Similar to historical and current Conservative Protestant leaders, the Catholic Pope interacted (felt, cared, acted, etc.) much more like god Judaic than like god Jesus.

Not surprisingly, Cardinal Ratzinger was chosen to be the Pope after Pope Paul's death in 2002. Ratzinger had worked closely with Pope Paul on many Conservative moves such as overseeing the destruction of the Liberation Theology movement in South America. He also silenced or dismissed over one hundred liberal theologians involved in the movement. He replaced the Liberation priests with Conservative priests from right-wing religious groups.

Pope Paul's and Pope Ratzinger's interactions clearly indicated their non-Jesus nature through their limited caring for the poor.

These Popes' lack of caring for the poor is no surprise. After all, popes live a luxurious and pampered life, much like the ancient living gods (pharaohs) of Egypt. However, the media often makes popes appear as saints. They are pictured in their gleaming, expensive costumes blessing believers from their throne or praying in the most humble position they can portray. However, no matter what holy position Animal beings hold or what god they idolize, their caring remains within animal nature's range of caring.

Judaic, Islamic, Protestant, and Catholic Conservative leaders, as any other Conservatives, counter ideas of liberalism, socialism, and humanism. They are forked-tongued about caring for the welfare of others. Although they can exhibit caring through charities they control, they viciously oppose government social caring programs for the welfare of all citizens.

God beliefs Support Wars

"All religions are oppressive to some degree. The tendency is intensified when societies compete, since religion can be effectively harnessed to the purposes of warfare and economic exploitation" (E.O. Wilson, 2002, 561). Judaican god beliefs, for example, are fundamental to our U.S. culture's capitalism. Capitalism is a major cause of wars, oppression and exploitation of other cultures' peoples and resources. Even millions of U.S. families are kept in a state of poverty due to the culture's capitalist system.

"Holy" wars between believers of different religions and between believers of the same god have been going on for thousands of years. These wars have involved Protestants against Catholics, Protestants against Muslims, Protestants against Buddhists, Catholics against Jews, Muslims against Orthodox Catholics, Jews against Muslims, and so on. Primitive animal instincts of caring for our kind and not caring for others are

> I distrust those people who know so well what God wants them to do, because I notice it always coincides with their own desires.
>
> Susan B. Anthony, Woman's Rights Activist, 1820–1906

so strongly imprinted in our species that it does not matter if god believers worship the same god. It did not stop English Protestants from asking *their* god to help them butcher Irish Catholics. Nor did it stop Irish Catholics from asking *their* god to help them butcher English Protestants. It has not stopped Muslim Shiites from asking *their* god to help them kill Muslim Sunnis, and so on. Little has changed from the days that we would cut off body parts from each other in battle with heavy metal axes. Now, we can kill and mutilate many more without heavy axes. Just as in those days, we continue to thank god for helping us kill those others.

Religions continue to support legions of young female and male patriotic zombies who are programmed by their culture to destroy others and be destroyed for god and country. Such believers know that god is on their side in times of bloody conflicts with others. They know in their hearts that they are right in the eyes of god. However, they are unable to realize that the eyes of god and their own are the same pair.

Julian Huxley tried to awaken believers from their religious stupor by explaining: "The disappearance of god means a recasting of a fundamental sort. It means the shouldering by man of ultimate responsibilities which he previously pushed off on god" (Huxley, 1970, 238). However, since god beliefs are at the foundation of our Judaic-Germanic civilization's interactions, and since most of us are Animal beings, we cannot be shaken out of our god reality. We cannot believe that god reality maintains much of the animalness in and about us.

God in Our Image

We might be indoctrinated with the same god beliefs, but our idea of god is whatever each of us is intellectually capable of conjuring. Each believer becomes his own imagined god. We each perceive and create god "in our image." Our god has the level of understanding and caring that only we can imagine is possible. This makes god as dense or enlightened, as uncaring or caring as each believer is capable of imagining. Therefore, it is impossible for most of us to escape from our self-delusion.

At the dense end of our species' god-belief spectrum we find believers with limited levels of understanding on how genetics and the environment profoundly affect our interactions. Their ignorance combined with god beliefs gives them mystic perceptions of why things happen. President Bush Jr. seemed to be such a believer. He was known to feel extremely enlightened whenever he contemplated that "things happen for a reason." As the case is for such believers, Bush believed that whatever happened to him was because of a script written for him. His script was that he get married, become a drug addict (alcoholic), become drug free, be heavily dosed with religion, and then become a U.S. president. In short, the less god believers know about science, the less they know about "why things happen" in and about them. As a result, their mystic perceptions of why things happen remain stagnant throughout their lives.

At the other extreme of the god-belief spectrum we find enlightened individuals such as scientists. Their god beliefs are separated from or replaced by beliefs based on science. Reality helps them cope with the known and unknown. As a group they have expanded perceptions of why things happen. They study interactions in and about them to increase their understanding about why things happen. They look for and study relationships and contingencies in existence. What they discover helps the rest of us expand our knowledge of reality. At the same time, they burden some of us with new things about reality that concern them.

Many scientists who study and decipher the awesome interactions of the universe come to perceive the entity of the universe as god, as physicist Albert Einstein did. When asked if he believed in god, he answered: "The universe is my god." In this sense, god is existence, which includes all interactions, everything that happens whether considered good, bad or ugly.

God Beliefs Maintain Our Greed

Presently, in our U.S. culture there are *holy* men (men-of-god) who make themselves wealthy with god reality. These men-of-god are mostly righteous evangelical Conservative Protestants. Many of them claim to have been "touched by almighty god." Such men-of-god can be called "god hustlers" because their goal is to make money preaching about their god. We recall that when Protestantism branched off from Catholicism, it took in more from Judaism's Old Testament than Catholicism had. Most Protestants claim to worship Jesus, but they tend to follow Judaic beliefs. They believe that being financially successful is the essence of being blessed by god.

Many Protestant ministers righteously exhort billions of dollars from millions of believers. They do so by telling them stories about Abraham, Moses, David and others from the Jewish Old Testament. God hustlers convince believers that they (the hustlers) have the power to make god help them with the scary known and unknown alike. In this manner they control god-believing addicts in the "here-now" and convince them that their help will continue throughout the "there-after." The more they convince believers of their powers, the more money believers give them. This in turn makes the hustlers expand their exaggerations about their connections with god Judaic.

Successful god hustlers get rich from (tax-free) donations. Most god hustlers claim that they use donations for altruistic businesses, which are often fraudulent. For example, Protestant evangelist Robert Tilton promised miracles to those who would send money to help orphanages that did not exist. He preached: "If you want to get rid of that dump you live in, that car that breaks down, you have to have faith. I've been supernaturally blessed by god to help… Yes, the Lord's ministry gets a portion of it but you get most of it" (Parenti, 1994, 47). Tilton got believers to put their money where their faith was in return for god's help in obtaining material wealth. His portion, as "the Lord's ministry," was enough to buy his family a $4.5 million house—with cash. He also had some $60 million in bank deposits, real estate, and other investments. Tilton knew what was important. He knew how to live well and he saw little need to share the root-of-all-evil (money) with his "non-existent" orphanages.

There are plenty of documented cases of Protestant preachers' moneymaking shenanigans. The well-known televangelist Oral Roberts took advantage of his celebrity status and believers' addiction. He preached that "god" (no doubt god Judaic) would kill him if he did not come up with over $8 million for missionary scholarships. As Michael Parenti points out, this would make god "an extortionist and a murderer" (Parenti, 1994, 47). Another Conservative preacher and television celebrity, Reverend Jimmy Bakker, spent some time in prison because of his improper use of believers' donations to do god's work. According to accountants, some $92 million that was to be used for god's work was missing. What happened was that Bakker collected $129 million for the lord, but greedily spent too much of it on the lord within himself. Reverend Bakker and his make-up caked wife Tammy lived in a glorious estate. Luxury ranged from gold-plated bathroom faucets to an air-conditioned doghouse for the outside dog. Naturally, upon release from his brief jail term, a "time-out" from his shenanigans, Reverend Bakker cried real tears about how sorry he was and returned to serving the lord. After having time to meditate, no doubt he became aware of what to improve upon next time. For such hustlers the only true god is in the image of their Conservative nature, and it is not Jesus.

God hustlers' enthusiastic use of god reality to fulfill their greed for money is part of our beloved capitalistic system. However, Michael Parenti notes that the U.S. Council of Better Business Bureaus has cited some god hustlers and their churches or associations for improper charitable solicitations. Among those cited were the reverend Moon's Unification Church, Billy Graham's Evangelistic Association, the Christian Anti-Communist Crusade, and Children of God (Parenti, 1994, 46). Readers are reminded about what Sociologist Werner Sombart explained about capitalism, that the history of the capitalist spirit "should be inextricably bound up with the history of churches and religious systems."

Protestant organizations have become global free enterprises with billions of dollars invested in the free market. It is reported that televised ministries and other religious organizations have billions of dollars invested in businesses ranging from war armaments to the media. Their profits from investments are free from state and federal taxes. To make it more inviting for believers to give money, their donations are tax deductible. Not surprising, it is common sense for students interested in becoming Protestant ministers to get college degrees in business management.

No doubt telecommunications and the Internet make it easier for Protestant hustlers to increase their profits by recruiting believers worldwide. Evangelist churches send out hundreds of thousands of young recruiters globally. Many of them are sent to places where evangelism has not taken hold, such as in Spanish speaking American nations, Eastern Europe, Asia, and Africa. This is why intelligent political leaders of some nations are weary of Christian groups that come to their nations "preaching the word of the lord."

Susceptibility to Myths

In the U.S. culture, our susceptibility to believe in fantasized characters as being real is triggered and reinforced throughout childhood just as god beliefs are. For example, there is a similarity between *Santo* Claus and god. (*Santo* is the masculine form of Santa. *Santa* Claus is correct if a female or a transvestite is playing the role.) Some might say that comparing the fantasy of Santo Claus to god is absurd because Santo Claus is a mythical character for the fantasy of children. Yet try telling that to a child who dearly believes in Santo Claus and is expecting wonderful gifts from him at Christmas. We often stop believing in Santo Claus, either because we find out who was leaving the gifts, or we are told that we are too old to continue with the farce. We could also be told that our god is a fantasy created by ancient primitive people to cope with their environment. Yet try telling that to an old man who dearly believes in god and is soon expecting wonderful things from him. Most psychologists would advise to "Stop lying to the kid, but let the old guy be." Unlike our Santo Claus reality, as we age our god becomes ever so much more real. There is much more riding on his existence.

Summary

For thousands of years billions of individuals from all over the world have groveled to some kind of god. This indicates that god reality is a programmed instinct in our species. Consequently, our relationship with god is similar to the relationship between an animal and its alpha leader.

Having explored the major role god reality has on our species' nature, several factors emerge indicating the negative effect it has on us. God reality maintains greed and animal levels of caring for others, even for believers of the same god. This is evident in "holy wars." Wars between religious groups have a long and bitter history. Now, weapons of mass destruction have made wars extremely dangerous for the survival of our species. Animal being leaders who make warring decisions based on the belief that god is on their side become the most dangerous creatures of our species. The Bush–Cheney regime (2001–2009) was an obvious example of such leadership. It should serve as a warning that in the near future the next Conservative president could well be that of a Cheney, not that of a Bush.

Our stagnant beliefs in god reality as well as our evolving beliefs in science exist because we are members of a transitional species. However, the longevity of stagnant god beliefs in the midst of advancing interactions in science indicates the stranglehold animal nature continues to have on our species. This suggests that our god reality is a lifetime reality for many of us because it is genetically based. As a result, our beliefs triggered by our god reality supersede those of science or they reject science.

Up until now we have examined racism, capitalism, and god reality as major interactions triggered from our species' animal nature and how they are exhibited in our culture. Although our animal nature continues to be dominant, the advancement of Human nature is the most significant thing in our species' evolution. This is the essence of what identifies our species as a transitional species. The evolution of *Human nature* is explored in the next chapter.

Part V:

On Becoming Human

Darwin made us aware of our species' animalness.

Marx made us aware of our species' humanness.

Jesus showed us what it is to be Human.

12

Human Beings

There is nothing more significant separating us from animal species than our species' potential to evolve humanness. For no animal can be humane.

The term "human" is defined as caring, kindhearted, merciful, benevolent, compassionate, and altruistic in dictionaries. Most of us Homo sapiens claim to have these caring traits, but scientists claim apes, elephants, porpoises, and other advanced animals also exhibit these traits at the same levels that most of us do. In other words, the potential to care for others at the levels of advanced animals does not make them or us *Human.* Neither does simply calling ourselves *human* make us Human. ("Human" is capitalized to distinguish the term from simply meaning a member of our Homo sapient species.)

We recall from previous chapters that most of us are Animal beings, interacting with only the caring potential of animal nature. However, there are some people among us that are not Animal beings. They can interact with a level of caring beyond that of Animal beings. Therefore, a rationale for being *Human* or *humane* is having the genetic potential to care for the welfare of life and its environment beyond that of common animals and Animal beings. For no animal can be humane.

At this juncture of our species' evolution, science has not detected a genetic difference between a Human being and an Animal being. However, scientists are continuously trying to decipher the nature of our species by comparing it to its ancestral heritage. Geneticists and biologists compare our physiological relationship to animal nature, and ethologists compare animal interactions with our interactions. While scientists have long confirmed the animal nature of our species, its "Human nature" has not been scientifically identified. However, humane caring has not gone unnoticed. For example, since 1943 psychologists such as Dr. Abraham Maslow were beginning to identify a level of caring in a few individuals that was significantly beyond the level of caring exhibited by most of us.

Humanness can be seen in a minority of individuals who are expanding our culture's social caring, and our animalness can be seen in many individuals opposing the expansion of social caring. The discrepancy between humanness and animalness brings to mind the exchanges between liberal Supreme Court Justice William Brennan and Conservative federal Judge Robert Bork in 2009 on how the U.S. Constitution should work. Brennan stated: "The genius of the Constitution rests not in any static meaning it might have had in a world that is dead and gone, but in the adaptability of its great principles to cope with current problems and current needs." In contrast, Bork stated: "The framers' intentions with respect to freedoms are the sole legitimate premise from which constitutional analysis may proceed." In other words, while Bork revealed our animal nature by wanting to retain the status quo of yesterday, Brennan illuminated our Human nature with his desire to expand ideas for the betterment of our present day world. This is why the rationale for being Human emerges from an observable disparity between the caring potential of Humans and that of Animal beings.

Our species' humane evolution is evident in the social caring progression that has occurred in our civilizations over thousands of years. What is not as evident is that this caring progression is our species' Human evolution and that it has been and continues to be maintained by a minority of Human beings among the bulk of us Animal beings. Also not evident is that for thousands of years Animal beings have violently opposed our species' evolving humanness.

Two Ancient Humans

Now that we have a rationale for what it means to be Human, we can identify individuals whose interactions many of us have sensed indicated a level of Human caring. We begin with the most renowned Human beings, the Buddha and Jesus. The Buddha (the Awakened One) lived among us some three thousand years ago in southwest Asia and taught *ahimsa*, which means caring for all living things. He taught that one must feel love for all living things like a mother feels for her only son. Although Buddhists do not refer to the Buddha as a god, the Buddha represents the model of humane caring for millions of people.

We will take a broader look at Jesus, since he is the dominant model of humanness for our present great civilization. Yet, while alive and among us, Animal beings violently opposed his humanness.

Although legend has it that Jesus was of a Jewish ethnic group, he could not accept the Judaic belief for one group to be favored over others. He was too ultraliberal, too equalitarian to identify with a godly chosen few. He also rejected the pursuit of material wealth. Jesus sensed the corruption and greed that capitalistic interactions bring about and didn't hide his repulsion toward them—"And Jesus went into the temple of God, and cast out all them that sold and bought in the temple, and overthrew the tables of the moneychangers, and the seats of them that sold…" (Passage Matthew 21:12). Jesus might have been born to a Jewess, but he could never have become a Jew.

Jews indubitably saw him as anti-god and evil to have rejected the "sacred, kingly, and divine" birthright bestowed on Jews by Abraham's god Judaic. (To this day many Jews view Jesus as a Marxist or a communist, a fact that most Christians are ignorant about.) As the biblical story stands, Jesus' humanness was so unbearable to Animal beings that free enterprise (Freedom) was used to end his life. A business contract was made, money changed hands, and a rare Human being was tortured to death. His last words, "Forgive them for they know not what they do," convey his awareness of the Animal beings around him and their inability to identify with him. How could Animal beings identify with such a Human being?

It was natural for Animal beings with the vigor of mad dogs to have despised Jesus' Human nature while he was alive and among them. They could not tolerate his humanness and instinctively feared the changes he could bring. Yet hundreds of years after Jesus was killed many Animal beings began to idolize him as a god. They instinctively began to perceive Jesus' "top dog" status, similar to how a pack of wolves perceive their alpha leader. This is why they continue to identify Jesus as a "Lord" and "King of kings." This is within their nature. Animal beings cannot even imagine that Jesus would not want to be a lord or king. They do not have the genetic potential to identify with Jesus' humanness. After Jesus' death, his followers sensed they had a story with a potential of being the greatest story ever told. It was a wrap. It caught the whirlwinds of evolution and became the most told story of all time.

Nothing else of what Jesus stands for supersedes his humanness. Yet only a minority of believers can identify with his caring. Most believers can only identify with his birth and his agonizing death. His birth date is eagerly anticipated and celebrated annually via Judaic freedom's commercialism. His suffering and death, via his crucifixion, are portrayed in every church. But do believers know that it was the animalness in our species that was triggered to kill the humanness that Jesus stood for? This animalness is still triggered in today's Animal beings.

Today, most of us Christians claim a love for Jesus because we think of him as a god that can help us with good health, wealth, miracles, and so on. We only have to go to church and pray to him. So, we enter god houses, lower our head and pray, sing, scream, or mumble verses from holy books. We re-read, re-tell, and re-listen to what Jesus is supposed to have said and done. We wear sacred trinkets, chant prayers, and bless each other with godly phrases. Most of us Conservative Christians can proudly say, "Hey, we're god-fearing people." Some of us have advanced to saying, "Hey, we're god-loving people." Most of us can claim a love for Jesus and idolize him as a god, but in reality we don't have the potential to identify with the ultimate do-gooder and advocate of equality that he was. Since we cannot identify with Jesus' caring, we idolize the holy status we have given him with rituals and lavish god houses.

To this day Animal beings would not want Jesus among us, and some would again have him killed. They don't want a Jesus or any other Human being trying to remove animalistic greed and the inequalities among us. Life for humane activists, as it was for Jesus, has always been difficult in an environment dominated by Animal beings. Animal beings continue to hate and often kill Human beings. Jesus' caring was incomprehensible to Animal beings of ancient times just as it is for today's Animal beings.

Although Jesus is worshipped as a god, he was not a super-unnatural entity. He was not an angelic, sexless, emotionless, painless being. He was real. He was a member of our Homo sapient species whom we should recognize as a Human being who awoke many of us to humane caring. However, worshipping Jesus as a god makes most of us think that his level of caring cannot exist in any of us mortals. This is something that a humane individual as Jesus would not want us to believe.

> "I like your Christ, I do not like your Christians. Your Christians are so unlike your Christ."
>
> Gandhi

Humanness among Us

It is difficult or impossible for most of us to perceive people who spend much of their life advocating humane caring to be as caring as Jesus. Yet Jesus' caring is still in our species. These caring people are Humans taking action against poverty, racism, lack of health care and education. In our Conservative culture they are derogatorily called "ultraliberals" and "bleeding hearts." Similar to Jesus' interactions, their interactions are evidence of our species' evolving humanness.

Human beings work alone as well as in groups and in organizations such as Amnesty International, Greenpeace, and Medicine Without Frontiers. We have cultures that focus on expanding social caring and reducing inequality among their citizens. Their goal is to establish forms of governments to increase social caring for all its citizens. These cultures, with noticeable degrees of socialism, seem to be our species' best efforts in expanding humane caring.

While Humans consider equality and social caring as basic things to strive for, Animal beings find these things undesirable and things to avoid. They see social justice and equitable social caring as unnecessary, unless they see some benefit for themselves or for those they hold dear. Some are as primitive animals in the sense that they are instinctively against whatever they sense is humane, even if their life depends on receiving social caring. Therefore, humane efforts whether by individuals, organizations, or cultures are confronted by Animal beings. In fact, we will see that it is difficult to talk about our species' humanness without mentioning our animalness against it.

Individuals' Humane Efforts

In 1943 psychologist Dr. Abraham Maslow was one of the first researchers to begin to identify humane caring in individuals. He labeled these individuals' ultimate level of caring in his Hierarchy of Needs as "self-actualization." Maslow identified Mrs. Eleanor Roosevelt and a few others as having reached self-actualization. In wondering about these few individuals Maslow asked: "Could… self-actualizing people be more human, more revealing of the original nature of the species?" (Lefrancois, 1980, 292) He believed, as almost everyone else believed, that all members of our Homo sapient species were "human." He therefore wondered whether persons like Mrs. Roosevelt were "more human."

The Humans among us globally must be in the millions. However, we become aware of only those who have become well known. The following are some examples of such individuals.

After his presidency, free from the shackles of the culture's Conservatism, President Jimmy Carter and his wife Rosalynn formed humane organizations. Their Habitat for Humanity builds homes for the working poor, and the Carter Center focuses on worldwide health care and establishing democracy. Former Vice President Al Gore has devoted his time and energy to making us aware of the need to expand our caring for the global environment, which in essence is to care for the welfare of our species. Bill and Melissa Gates have donated millions of dollars around the world to help children suffering from epidemic diseases and to improve education. Progressive activist Ralph Nader has tirelessly informed us about the need for major social changes to our culture's systemic corporate greed. Senator Robert Kennedy brought attention to our culture's inequalities. He created many government programs that addressed the needs of the poor and non-Europeans, including people of the American race.

Dolores Huerta served a key role, alongside Cesar Chavez, as a labor organizer and advocate for the welfare of farm workers. Her humanness almost caused her death. In 1988, while demonstrating peacefully against the policies of candidate George Bush, she was severely injured when police clubbed her and other demonstrators. After recovering from this life-threatening attack, she returned to working for the farm workers' union. Now, in her eighties, she continues to educate workers nationwide on their rights.

South African activist Archbishop Desmond Mpilo Tutu risked his life for many years in his opposition to Dutch apartheid. After the Dutch oppression ended in 1994 and the African National Congress took over, Tutu coined the term "Rainbow Nation" as a metaphor to accept South Africa's racial diversity instead of calling for punishment against Europeans' (whites) maltreatment of Africans. His humanness has been acknowledged: He received the Nobel Peace Prize in 1984, the Albert Schweitzer Prize for Humanitarianism in 1986, and in 2007 he was awarded the Gandhi Peace Prize. Former Russian president and 1990 Nobel Peace Laureate Mikhail S. Gorbachev advocated: "We need a new system of values, a system of the organic unity between mankind and nature and the ethic of global responsibility."

Linguist Dr. Noam Chomsky and historian Dr. Howard Zinn are two of our culture's most admirable Human beings. Both are known as passionate activists and educators for social justice; as advocates for the poor and downtrodden; and as committed intellectuals who do not compromise. They are known for speaking the truth about our culture, explaining what we should know aside from the propaganda on Freedom fed to us. They have provided explanations, clearing confusion caused by the conflict between the reality of the culture's Conservatism and its self-serving misleading image. Zinn was once asked "why he continued to fight, write, and speak for peace and social justice when it all seemed so hopeless." He answered: "I couldn't live with myself if I didn't" (Branfman, 2010, 76). He died on January 27, 2010.

Michael Lerner (a highly regarded rabbi and editor of *Tikkun*) has also been one of our U.S. culture's strongest advocates for humanness. He has been a prolific writer and lecturer on the subject of humanness. Similar to Gorbachev, Lerner makes his readers aware of the importance in understanding that our well-being depends on the well-being of all others on the planet. He lectured on the need to change from a discourse of selfishness to humane caring. While speaking in a synagogue in San Diego, California, Lerner advocated the removal of the constant search for material wealth as the dominant discourse of life. In short, he asked Jewish peers to disregard a cherished trait of Judaism. It was not surprising that a few in the audience compared Lerner's notions to Jesus and Marx's altruism. Such a comparison should have been a strong hint to Lerner that most Jews and unlabeled Jews cannot accept humane notions. This is because people who believe that the essence of life is the acquisition of material wealth will inevitably develop a lifestyle with a "dominant discourse of selfishness." This is disconcerting for humane individuals if they are ignorant that our species' dominant caring is that of animals. Not knowing that most of us go through life as Animal beings causes humane individuals to believe that simply pointing out our animalness will make us expand our caring for others. A Human being who finds himself in Lerner's position may wonder: "Am I a disciple for evolving humanness, or am I a humane caring façade for my group's god beliefs' sea of selfishness?" In other words, it might be that some Humans remain in a perpetual conflict between their animal and Human natures.

There are Humans who have spent their life's energy in bringing about equality and social justice for those being oppressed. Cesar Chavez devoted much of his life advocating caring for the welfare of oppressed workers. Chavez, a migratory field worker of the American race from the San Joaquin Valley of California, opposed agriculture corporations' greed and injustices against field-working families. Through hardships of poverty and physical exhaustion, he founded the National Farm Workers Association, which later became the United Farm Workers (UFW). In 1965 Chavez led California grape-pickers in a strike for higher wages. It took five years for the movement to win the first major victory for U.S. field workers. He put his life on the line for others by going on three hunger strikes to protest migrant workers' low wages and unsafe working conditions. For example, the pesticides sprayed on grapes and other fruit were causing cancers among field workers and their children. The pesticides were also endangering the health of millions of children eating the fruit. At the time of his death, Chavez was protesting the use of pesticides by agri-corporations and leading a boycott on grapes.

Dr. Raphael Lemkin, a Polish Jew, unselfishly devoted twenty-five years of his life to outlaw genocide globally. Lemkin coined the word "genocide" and drafted a treaty for the United Nations to have genocide outlawed. It was supported by the major nations of the world, but failed to pass because the United States vetoed it. Lemkin died in 1959 of a heart attack, penniless and alone. (It is notable that although the U.S. is a staunch supporter of Jewish interests, it opposed having genocide outlawed.)

Similar to Jesus, some of today's Humans have been killed because Animal beings found their humane actions intolerable.

Our U.S. culture's civil rights leader Reverend Dr. Martin Luther King, Jr. spent his short adult life advocating welfare for the deprived and the working poor. King preached that people everywhere should have three meals a day, education, dignity, and equal rights regardless of wealth or social status. Material wealth would not get you something better. He advocated nonviolence, not only in the United States, but globally. He was among the first leaders to speak out against the massacring of the Vietnamese people by the United States. In one of his speeches he stressed using love as a weapon and to understand those who hate us. Because of Dr. King's influential potential, he was one of the FBI's main targets to discredit. It blackmailed him, threatened him, and suggested that he commit suicide. According to a U.S. Senate report, the FBI's goal was to stop Dr. King (Zinn, 2003, 462). King was assassinated on April 4, 1968, the day before he was to lead a march in support of the Memphis sanitation workers' rights for equality.

Mohandas (Mahatma) Gandhi struggled and suffered for many years trying to achieve India's freedom from the United Kingdom's brutal military occupation. Instead of using the English oppressors' killing methods, Gandhi confronted them with massive nonviolent demonstrations; he was a practitioner of *ahimsa*. A Hindu nationalist and a co-conspirator against Gandhi's ideals of social justice assassinated him in 1948. Gandhi's biographer wrote of him: "Gandhi showed the world that the love of one's people need not be inconsistent with the love of humanity. He strove to free the downtrodden from the shackles of injustice, slavery and deprivation. But he was also obsessed with the future of the human [Homo sapient] race" (Chadha, 1997, vii). Renowned physicist Albert Einstein identified with Gandhi's humanness. He wrote for Gandhi's seventy-fifth birthday: "Generations to come, it may be, will scarce believe that such a one as this ever in flesh and blood walked upon this earth" (Chadha, 1997, 1). Albert Einstein himself was a pacifist and a socialist who expressed that a worldwide humane government was needed.

Catholic Archbishop Oscar Arnulfo Romero of El Salvador was killed by Animal beings because of his humane efforts. From 1977 to 1980 he defended the rights of the oppressed working poor from the brutality of a dictator supported by a U.S. fruit corporation. The Archbishop spoke out against the dictator's death squads and asked U.S. President Jimmy Carter in a letter (February 1980) to stop military aid to the El Salvadoran government. A month later the Catholic Archbishop was gunned down in his deeply Catholic nation. Some fifteen years later it was reported that the Archbishop's assassination was linked to the U.S. Central Intelligence Agency (CIA). The assassination plot included a right wing leader named Robert D'Aubuisson, who was protected by the El Salvadoran deputy minister of defense, Nicolas Carranza. Carranza was on the CIA payroll at $90,000 a year (Zinn, 2003, 590).

It has been and continues to be deadly for some Humans to advocate social justice, equality, and caring for the welfare of our species in a world dominated by Animal beings. Animal beings can easily be influenced to kill in a Conservative cultural environment. The animalness in our U.S. culture triggered the assassins of Dr. King, President J.F. Kennedy, and Senator Robert Kennedy to emerge. To know our culture is to know that too many Animal beings would have done the same thing given the assassins' opportunities.

Our U.S. culture, as well as other Conservative cultures, is hostile and aggressive toward influential humane individuals who go against the culture's nature of greed and inequality. Therefore, it is not surprising to find that our domestic secret police (FBI) has a history of secretly monitoring individuals who seriously advocate alternatives to the culture's greed and inequality. The FBI kept copious files on field labor leader Cesar Chavez, music conductor and composer Leonard Bernstein, physicist Albert Einstein, Dr. Martin Luther King, Jr., and others labeled as ultraliberals or communists.

Without a doubt, if Jesus were to reappear in the United States to continue his humanizing efforts, the FBI, NSA, CIA, and the SS would document his interactions to see what could be used to discredit and destroy him. Jesus would be in greater danger if he went outside the United States where its international secret police agencies would be more comfortable to torture or assassinate. Once again, money would change hands to stop his efforts to humanize us.

Most humane individuals do not become well known. Some humane individuals have been relatives or friends whose humanness we took for granted until they were no longer with us. We realized then that they were different from us and regret not having been able to return their kindness and love.

Humane Politicians

Individual humane Politicians need to assert their humanness. For some it will mean the end of their political career, but this is what they need to do. Compromising among humane politicians is practical and desirable. However, it is late in our evolution for Humans to compromise with Animal beings on proposals, policies, etc. meant to improve the welfare of people of our community, nation, and planet. When Human beings compromise with Animal beings, caring for the welfare of people is limited to what animals consider just and feasible. In the U.S for example, compromises inevitably favor Animal beings' solutions because it is they who maintain the culture's old, established Conservative ways. On the other hand, Human beings' solutions are to replace the culture's animalness (Conservatism). In compromises between Animal beings and Human beings, inevitably, the culture's animalness is maintained. Such compromising, in reality, is a confrontation between our species' dominant animal nature and evolving Human nature. This is why it is extremely difficult to change the course of an old established culture.

Humane politicians, usually identified as ultraliberals, simply have to stop cowering when attacked for their attempts to expand national and global humane policies. It is cowardly for them to compromise their humanness in order to get elected. For example, it was known that Al Gore had written one of the most insightful books on the environment before being elected, yet he did little for the environment as vice-president. Gore also ignored his deep concern and commitment for the global environment during his presidential candidacy campaign in 2000. Why? He feared being labeled "ozone man." In other words, our species' animalness in and about him caused him to compromise his humanness. He masked his humane caring in an effort to be elected president of the most animalistic culture of the advanced nations of the globe. He did so because he expected the bulk of U.S. citizens to reject his humane concerns. This trend is unlikely to change anytime soon in our Conservative culture.

Organizations' Humane Efforts

Human beings organize and participate in humane organizations. There are a number of humane organizations, and their mission is to help people in need or to promote global caring. Medicine Without Frontiers is a humanitarian international medical organization that delivers emergency aid to people affected by disasters. Other humane organizations include the United Nations World Food Program, Partners in Health, United Nations Children's Fund, Greenpeace, World Watch, Amnesty International, Habitat for Humanity, Buddhist Peace Fellowship, the Global Marshal Plan, the Tikkun Community, and others. To date, the UN is the largest organization created to care for our species as a family. Although the UN is a primitive step in global caring, it is a significant attempt at collective humane efforts.

It is important to note that animalistic regimes undermine UN humanitarian efforts. In the establishment of the UN, for example, the Conservative U.S. culture obtained the undemocratic system it wanted. Any one of the five permanent members (U.S., U.K., France, Russia, and China) can veto decisions made by the rest of the world's nations. Although headquartered in the U.S., the relationship between the U.S. and the UN has not been a warm one and has been combative under Conservative U.S. presidents. This was especially evident under the Nixon-Ford, Reagan–Bush, and Bush–Cheney regimes. Under the Bush–Cheney regime, the U.S. invaded Iraq against the United Nations' efforts to prevent the war.

A minority of Human beings and organizations urging expanded caring here and there is not enough in a world dominated by Animal beings.

Although individuals' and organizations' humane efforts improve the lives of many of us, their humanness is constantly at odds with their cultures' animal nature. However, we begin to see the effects of humanness when social caring is supported by the culture.

Cultures' Humane Efforts

The nature of a culture influences and shapes its members' and institutions' interactions. At this stage of our species' evolution, a culture can be the strongest supporter for the evolution of humane caring or the strongest barrier. Epigenetic research indicates that the environment can activate (turn on) or deactivate (turn off) genes and that these genetic changes in the plant, animal, or person can be heritable.

We can speculate that a social-caring cultural environment can turn on caring in some of its members who otherwise would not learn to care for others beyond the caring levels of animals. According to sociologist Dr. David Simon, "Social democracy or economic democracy is a politico-economic form of organization dedicated to full human equality, cooperation, participatory democracy, and meeting human needs" (Simon, 1996, 322). Such a system focuses on lessening the huge socio-economic gap between Freedom's chosen few and its workers by reducing greed and inequality among its citizens. However, it takes generations for a culture striving toward socialism to educate and shape its members to accept and practice humane caring. All aspects of a socialist culture's foundation, its educational system, laws, beliefs, technology, mass media, and so on, must work in unison to develop a dominant discourse of humane caring. In this manner, most Animal beings can be programmed to live cooperatively in a social caring environment.

A culture's educational system can be a major factor in shaping its members toward humane caring. For instance, a Unitedstaten school principal's experience with Nazism and the Holocaust made her aware of the importance of educating students to care for the welfare of others. She had seen men, women, and children shot and burned in huge ground pits and infants used for experiments by nurses and physicians. She therefore pleaded to her teachers to have their students become humane. In doing so they will not produce learned monsters, psychopaths, and educated Eichmanns. She added that education is only important if it teaches children to be humane.

It depends on the nature of the culture if such pleas for teaching humane caring will be supported or ignored. For example, in a culture with a dominant discourse of selfishness and inequality pleas to teach children to be humane will be listened to and not much more. But in a socialist culture whose evolving nature it is to try to meet the social needs of all its citizens such pleas will most likely be attended to.

It is difficult to establish social caring cultures for various reasons. Political leaders who begin with the intent of establishing socialism give up trying, or are corrupted by business interest groups, or are inept in bringing about change. Social caring leaders not only encounter resistance from their culture's Animal beings who want to keep the status quo, but they are also threatened or attacked by the top Conservative nation's CIA. For the U.S is well known for detesting and assassinating political leaders attempting to install degrees of humanness via socialism.

Our U.S. culture programs its members to detest even the mention of socialism because ideas of equality and humanness conflict with capitalism's ideas of greed and inequality. This was evident in the summer of 2009 when liberal President Barack Obama tried to implement affordable medical care for all the nation's citizens. His attempt to have the government directly involved in medical health care in order to reduce the greed of corporations involved in health insurance, pharmaceuticals, and the like, was vehemently opposed, even by those who would benefit from the government's help. Conservative business leaders, politicians of both parties, and more than half of the citizenry protested his proposed medical plan because they viewed it as socialism. The culture has programmed its citizens to fear or hate whatever evil thing *socialism* has come to mean to them. Yet, Social Security and Medicare are socialist caring programs benefiting workers and small businesses.

In 2010 President Obama was able to pass a government health care program that still left more than 23 million U.S. citizens without health care. The program didn't even begin to reach the level of health care of other advanced nations. "Rather, ... this [U.S. health care] legislation, which was written with heavy input from private health insurance and pharmaceutical lobbyists, further privatizes the financing of our health care and further enriches and empowers the very industries that are the problem" (Flowers, 2010, 14). Nevertheless, the health plan was considered a historical advancement in caring for its citizens in light of the culture's historical Conservatism.

At this stage of our species' evolution, cultures with significant degrees of socialism (i.e., reducing inequalities in health care, education, financial distribution, etc.), beyond that of capitalist cultures such as the U.S., seem to be our species' best efforts in advancing humanness.

Socialist Efforts Confronted by Capitalist Animosity

Capitalist cultures as the U.S. have opposed socialism since Karl Marx introduced his theory on our species' social caring evolution. He theorized that our species' cultural evolution would go from Kingdoms, to capitalism, to socialism, and finally to communism. Marx's theory on cultural evolution, indicating that socialism would replace capitalism, triggered fear and animosity in capitalist cultures.

No other nation has detested and hindered the evolution of socialism in developing nations as much as the United States. The government and its multinational corporations have used blackmail, subversion, military intervention, assassination, and paid political puppets to deter the development of socialism.

Efforts in establishing socialist cultures, except for the Russian effort, have not been surprises to the U.S. government. The U.S. has secret agencies such as the CIA and NSA especially for the purpose to spot and kill any movement by organizations or individuals supporting social caring efforts that threaten Freedom. These agencies and affiliated agencies are found in every nation of the world. In addition, the U.S. has special military forces based in most nations of the world. The U.S. culture gives its vast secret agencies and military forces huge allowances to maintain Freedom at home and abroad. Through these agencies the president and his administration get secret information on foreign governments and on leaders' personal interactions.

Leaders who attempt to establish socialism are considered enemies of

Freedom because they want control over their own culture's resources. They want the culture's elected officials to meet their citizens' essential needs, not the profiteering needs of multinational corporations. This is why U.S. capitalists strongly oppose even a hint of the development of socialism. The U.S. culture's opposition to developing socialist cultures is evident in how it aggressively confronted such nations as Russia, China, Vietnam, Cuba, Chile, Nicaragua, and El Salvador because of these cultures' efforts to install degrees of socialism. It is important to know that all of these nations' previous governments were dictatorships, friendly toward U.S. Freedom's greed and inequality. The United States had not considered them threats to its Judaican way.

The Russian Socialist Effort

Russia's revolutionist Nikolai Lenin (1870–1924) was the first to try to install socialist ideas soon after World War I in 1918. Lenin, however, did not follow Marx's theory of moving from kingdoms to capitalism. He believed his beloved Russian culture, which had been led by czars (kings) for thousands of years, could skip capitalism and move on to socialism. Lenin's plan was to overthrow the biggest Animal being dictatorship in the world, the Czar of Russia (Nicholas and his royal family).

In 1918 the U.S. rushed in to help the Czar's military forces, but by the time U.S. troops arrived, the Czar and his henchmen had already been removed from power. The U.S. withdrew its troops, but U.S. propaganda and subversive operations against Lenin's attempt at socialism went into full swing. Lenin died in 1924, at the age of fifty-four, before he was even able to stabilize his Bolshevik political party's attempts to establish socialism in the civil war-torn Russian nation.

With Lenin's leadership gone, Conservative Joseph Stalin bullied his way into power. This Animal being turned Lenin's dream into a nightmare for the Russian people and for neighboring nations. After WWII, Stalin claimed over half a dozen nations that Russia had freed from German Nazi occupation. Under the pretense of turning them into socialist states, he created the Union of Soviet Socialist Republics (USSR). In the early years of Stalin's USSR regime, the people believed Stalin's propaganda that they had achieved the socialism Lenin and Marx had championed. Many intellectuals worldwide fantasized that groveling to a chosen few was over, that an era of "do-gooders" had started at last. In reality, "no-gooders" were still very much in control. Under Stalin's brutal dictatorship there were free elections only because the oppressed citizens did not have to pay to vote. (Regardless of free elections, the dictator always won.) Extreme secrecy and inequality were the norm, just as in the days of the Czar.

During Stalin's regime, U.S. propaganda spread the lie that Russia was a communist nation. In reality it was an attempt at socialism. After Stalin died (1953) the USSR crumbled, and different Russian ethnic groups began fighting and butchering each other. Violence and corruption surfaced all over Russia. Some groups were even asking for the return of a royal family. Nevertheless, Capitalists propagandized the lie that communism had failed. What had failed was Lenin's attempt at socialism, and what had prevailed was the animal nature of the culture, our species' dominant nature.

Various Russian leaders tried to live the farce that Russia could still become a democratic socialist nation. It took the intellect and courage of Russian leader Mikhail Gorbachev to end the Russian socialist farce in the 1980s. Gorbachev stated that Russia's socialist attempt would have been successful if it had approached the level of socialism that the people of Sweden and of a few other Western European cultures enjoy. If the Russian socialist effort had succeeded, it would have indicated that a dictatorship or a kingdom could transition into a socialist culture, and do so in a short time. Such a transition to socialism, skipping capitalism, would have surprised Karl Marx.

The Chinese Socialist Effort

Marx's ideas influenced Mao Tse-tung (1893–1976) and Chou En-lai (1898–1976). In 1945, after WW II ended and the Japanese had been driven out of China, these leaders brought their peasant forces down from the *sierra* to battle against dictator General Chiang Kai-shek and his forces.

Mao Tse-tung and Chou En-lai's obstacles were more complicated than what Lenin had encountered. Unlike in Russia, where U.S. troops were too late to help the Czar's forces, Unitedstaten troops arrived in China with plenty of time and billions of dollars in armaments to help the dictator stay in power.

However, by 1949 it looked like General Chiang Kai-shek would be taken prisoner. The U.S. Navy therefore transported the dictator and his armies to take over China's Taiwan Island. The U.S. government promised dictator Chiang Kai-shek that it would forever use its military might to protect his forces in Taiwan from China.

Similar to what Lenin tried to do, the leadership team of Mao Tse-tung and Chou En-lai decided to skip the capitalistic phase and transform the huge culture—one with a long history of feudal dynasties and dictatorships—to a socialist culture. However, Russia's failure awoke them to the realization that their ambitious plan would also fail if they did not plan well. So, they decided not to entirely rule out capitalism (Freedom). The huge port of Hong Kong was allowed to remain a capitalist outpost. (England had held Hong Kong as a naval military base since the era when it was the most powerful and brutal pirate nation in the world. When the English returned Hong Kong to China, Chinese capitalists fearful of losing their wealth fled to the U.S. and to the U.K.) In recent years, Chinese leaders have thought it wise to designate additional coastal areas of China as free enterprise zones and gradually shape the masses' interactions toward socialism.

Chinese leadership was wise to realize that whether we are Chinese, United-statens, Mexicans, Russians, Cubans, etc., most of us are individualistic, selfish, and greedy—great traits for capitalism, but not for socialism. Although China is taking part in capitalism, it is still trying to prevent the development of greed and corruption inherent to capitalism. China is demonstrating how difficult it is for cultures that are transitioning out of dictatorships to try to install socialism. Chinese leadership became aware that the huge culture must first join the world of constant combat for that which is "sacred, kingly, and divine."

Being aware of the abuses that citizens experience in their capitalist cultures, China has taken a strong hand against its corrupted capitalists. For example, in 2004 the Chinese government executed four bankers found guilty of fraud in the midst of a campaign against financial crime (*The Standard*, "Corrupt bankers executed," Reuters, 9/15/2004). This was shocking for many in the United States. In the U.S. it is highly unusual for top-positioned criminal capitalists to be even moderately punished. In Chinese justice it seems that the more responsible the position held by the criminal, the greater the punishment. Intelligent workers see this as a step in the right direction to control corruption. U.S. Freedom lovers do not.

In 2010 China was still expanding its practices in capitalism while trying to curb the corruption that is triggered from the greedy. As the breakdown of the global economy occurred, due mainly to U.S. capitalist institutions' corrupted practices in their unrelenting pursuit of increasing profits, China had no choice but to help out. Otherwise global instability would most likely have erupted in violence for many parts of the world, including in China. It is a very difficult social experiment that China is attempting by using some aspects of capitalism as a bridge to establish a socialist nation. However, if China were to develop a significant degree of socialism, the giant nation will have moved our species' toward the hope of achieving our species' first humane civilization.

The Vietnamese Socialist Effort

As far back as 1918, the young Marxist Ho Chi Minh (1892–1967) had asked Conservative U.S. President Woodrow Wilson for a conference on Vietnam's independence from European (French) control. Wilson ignored Ho Chi Minh's plea. After World War II, Ho Chi Minh decided that only the use of arms would free his nation from Judaic freedom's strangulation. In 1954, after nine years of combat, his armed peasants won a significant battle at Dien Bien Phu over French troops. France decided to leave Vietnam.

The United States had already perceived Ho Chi Minh as a communist and Vietnam as having to be saved from communism. It had to be saved for Freedom (capitalism). The U.S. assumed Ho Chi Minh was a communist because he did not respect money-power, he was not greedy, and he could not be bought. He was therefore a dangerous threat to Freedom. As usual, the U.S. counted on its money and military power to take control of the small nation by installing a dictator to squash Ho Chi Minh and his peasant army. In 1954 U.S. military forces and free enterprise mercenaries reinforced the Conservative Vietnamese regular army, which had previously been supported by the French. The Conservative Vietnam army was trained, supplied, and paid for by U.S. taxpayers. The U.S. also set up a series of professional puppet dictators in the southern part of Vietnam.

The first of such puppets was Ngo Dinh Diem, a former Vietnamese official who had been living in the U.S. In 1954 Diem was installed as dictator of southern Vietnam. Diem had the "right stuff." He was self-centered and greedy and loved our U.S. culture's kind of Freedom. His cronies were Judeo–Christian businessmen, landlords, and military officers that had supported the French over socialist Ho Chi Minh.

However, ten years later in 1964 the U.S. leadership lost patience with its series of puppet dictators and decided to "take the gloves off" and do the job right and quickly. With the lie that U.S. Navy destroyer the *Maddox* had been fired upon by peasants off the coast of northern Vietnam, our almighty money-powered military machine was unleashed. It was later reported that the *Maddox* had not been attacked. The report had been a lie. Howard Zinn puts it this way: "The highest [U.S] officials had lied to the public" (Zinn, 2001, 476). From 1964 to 1973 the United States bombarded the tiny area of northern Vietnam by land, sea, and air. The bombing made hamburger meat of men, women, and children. By the end of the war the U.S. Air Force had dropped 7 million tons of bombs on the northern part of this small country (Zinn, 2001, 478).

The U.S. military's brutal campaign against the Vietnamese people reached a level that triggered some U.S. citizens to deem the war unjustified. The military's massive butchering of peasant farmers and their families triggered massive demonstrations. The U.S. flag was frequently spat on, torn, and burned. "Hey, hey, LBJ, how many kids did you kill today?" was a slogan cried out against President Lyndon B. Johnson. During this period of high stress, liberal leaders President J. F. Kennedy, Reverend Dr. Martin L. King, Jr., Senator R. F. Kennedy, and composer John Lennon were assassinated. President Johnson refused to run for reelection. Conservative President Richard M. Nixon resigned in disgrace. Conservative President Gerald Ford then excused Nixon of all criminal charges. Actor Ronald Reagan, suffering from a debilitating mental illness, became the most popular Conservative president to date. Millions of Vietnamese died to get rid of capitalism and establish socialism. It is estimated that three to four million Vietnamese men, women, and children were killed as enemies of Freedom. Some 58,000 U.S. military personnel (men and women) died defending Freedom. The slaughter of Vietnamese gave the Unitedstaten culture ugly sores from which it is unlikely to ever recover.

For this animalistic one-sided destructive affair, the Nobel Peace Prize was awarded to United States negotiator Henry Kissinger and North Vietnam negotiator Le Duc Tho. Le Duc Tho realized the impropriety and contradiction of sharing a peace prize with Kissinger and refused his Nobel Peace Prize. Kissinger shamelessly took his.

In spite of the brutal mutilation of their small nation, the Vietnamese people succeeded in ridding their culture of foreign domination. The nation, now united, continues in its effort to become a democratic socialist culture. Miraculously, after some twenty-eight years of combating the French, U.S. Conservative Vietnamese puppets, and the "almighty cradle of Freedom," the peasant Vietnamese culture could now have peace.

The Cuban Socialist Effort

Fidel and Che were intellectuals whose initial intentions were to practice law and medicine, not to be socialist *guerrilleros* (amateur warriors without government support). Dr. Fidel Castro, a lawyer, and Ernesto "Che" Guevara (1928–1967), a medical student from Argentina, placed their lives on the line in their struggle to remove Cuba's dictatorship and install socialism. This began in 1956 when Fidel returned to Cuba from Mexico with a small force of guerrilleros. Che and Cuban workers joined them. By 1959 Fidel and his small force had brought down the U.S.–backed dictator, General Fulgencio Batista. Forced to flee Cuba, General Batista took much of Cuba's wealth and retired in a secret place in the United States. Batista's politicians, judges, police, military officers, bankers, international and domestic organized crime figures, and their families fled with him. Almost all fled to the United States, mostly to Miami, Florida, and Las Vegas, Nevada.

Prior to Che and Castro's takeover, like many other Spanish American nations, Cuba had a long string of brutal dictatorships installed and supported by the U.S. During the last dictatorship under General Batista, Havana, Cuba had been the choice place for the Italian Mafia and the chosen few. It was globally known to cater to the best of Freedom's perks such as luxurious hotels and casinos, child prostitution, money laundering, illegal drug traffic, and white slavery.

Castro put a stop to this Freedom because his intentions were to make Cuba a democratic socialist culture. Naturally this triggered an immediate hate campaign from the United States. The U.S. banned travel to Cuba and forced other nations to do the same. It also created a U.S. naval blockade to stop any possible success in establishing a socialist culture. The blockade, which has been easily maintained since 1962, immediately caused a shortage of medicine, food, information, machine parts, and other essentials. The blockade and other subversive activities have kept Cuba an isolated island nation. This destructive campaign against Cuba stopped it from becoming the first successful democratic socialist culture of South and North America.

Dr. Castro's hope for Cuba to become a socialist model for neighboring American nations is dependent on future leaders. Loss of the culture's socialist goals will permit capitalism to again rise to a godly status in Cuba. If this should happen, money power will once again control public opinion through ownership of the mass media. Again there will be marvelous estates, hotels, casinos, country clubs, and large banks for the chosen few. *Cuba libre* (Free Cuba) will once again become the Promised Island where gambling, corruption, all kinds of money schemes, and beautiful teenage girl and boy prostitutes are dearly enjoyed.

Animal beings had been certain Castro could be bribed or blackmailed into submission, but neither worked. There is no shortage of disclosed reports on U.S. secret police and military Special Forces' attempts to murder Castro.

The Chilean Socialist Effort

Conservative capitalists' reaction to the possible development of an equalitarian culture can be as overt as the Vietnam War or as covert as the murder of a socialist president. President Salvador Allende, an intellectual, was the first proclaimed socialist to be democratically elected president of an American nation. (We find democratic socialist nations in Europe, such as Sweden and the Netherlands, but none in America.) In the three years of his presidency, beginning in 1970, Allende moved Chile toward socialism by nationalizing some of the country's industry and by expanding social welfare service programs for workers. He continued expropriating land from global agri-corporations and returning it to farming families faster than had the previous administration. Then in 1973, under the Nixon-Bush regime, the U.S. global secret police agency (CIA) spread the lie that President Salvador Allende had committed suicide.

Some twenty years later (in the 1990s), during the Bill Clinton presidency, CIA secret documents were released revealing some of the U.S. culture's subversive activities in Chile. These activities ranged from trying to keep Allende from being democratically elected to training and financing a bloody military coup, in which President Allende was murdered and Pinochet's dictatorship was installed. All this was initiated during the animalistic Nixon regime. Secretary of State Henry A. Kissinger and CIA Director James Helms were given an $8 million budget to restore control in Chile. Restoring control meant restoring Animal beings and Judaic Freedom back into political power. Kissinger (an immigrant Jew from Germany), for example, is reported to have said in his heavy accent, "I don't see why we have to let a country go Marxist [socialist] just because its people are irresponsible." In other words, Kissinger thought it irresponsible of the Chilean people to democratically elect a socialist leader to free them from the Judaican way of life. Animal beings as Kissinger and Helms proceeded with their plan to restore control. The plan included murdering President Allende and installing top Chilean military officer General Schneider as dictator. However, the courageous general could not be bought. He supported his president who had been democratically elected by the direct vote of the people. This was not about to stop the U.S. from defending Freedom. Both General Schneider and President Allende were murdered. The long murderous history of General August Ugarte Pinochet's regime in Chile began.

Under General Pinochet thousands of young people, especially university students, were tortured and murdered. Pinochet's brutal dictatorship continued throughout the terms of U.S. Presidents Nixon, Ford, Carter, and Reagan. These administrations never mandated a naval blockade. Nor did they support or create social unrest against Pinochet or plan to have the CIA murder Pinochet. Our U.S. culture's kind of Freedom loved what Pinochet stood for. The U.S. helped him stay in power for some seventeen years until he retired in

1990 due to illness and old age. Pinochet was one more Animal being dictator secretly installed and supported by the United States.

During his retirement Pinochet visited England. At that time, Spain asked England to arrest and send Pinochet to Spain to face murder charges. England refused. The mass media indicated that England's refusal was due to U.S. pressure. In the early 1990s, disclosed documents revealed that U.S. officials did not want Pinochet to face a trial. A trial would have implicated James Helms of the CIA and Henry A. Kissinger in the murder of Chilean President Allende. (It is not surprising to historians when repercussions of such acts "come home to roost.")

To date, no Chilean political leader has risen to challenge Judaic freedom as President Salvador Allende did in 1970. The lesson to be remembered from his assassination is that it is naïve for elected politicians advocating socialism (outside of Western Europe) not to expect opposition from the U.S. The U.S. secret police or its military special forces are likely to stop them in any way they see fit.

El Salvador's Socialist Effort

In 1979 U.S. special military forces countered El Salvadoran peasant workers, mostly of the American race, who had taken up arms to free their culture from Judaic Freedom. The workers wanted social equality. It was unlikely that this tiny, money-poor, poorly educated American nation would develop into a socialist democratic society to threaten the hold of Freedom. Even so, a U.S. global fruit corporation operating in the area was concerned that the American peasants would succeed. Its profits and huge land holdings in the small nation would be endangered by social and economic reforms. Conservative President Ronald Reagan responded to the threat by helping El Salvadoran dictator Jose Duarte control peasant workers protesting their suppression. U.S. money-power brought in advanced weapons, U.S. special military forces, mercenaries (mostly Jews from Israel), and the CIA. El Salvadoran American peasants refused to give up, even after some eight years of fighting. The U.S. culture maintained the war against them for four more years under the administration of another Conservative president, George H. W. Bush. Over

100,000 men, women, and children of the American race were killed during this uneven combat to save Freedom.

The killing stopped in 1992 because George H. W. Bush was not reelected. Liberal Bill Clinton became the U.S. president. President Clinton stopped the support to the Duarte dictatorship and helped negotiate a truce with the American peasants, but the dictatorship remained in control. The U.S. corporation dealing in bananas and pineapples, of course, continues to enjoy Freedom. (El Salvador is a good example of how violence against socialism is reduced during periods of U.S. liberal leadership.)

In 1993 the United Nations Truth Commission Report on El Salvador's civil war revealed the U.S.'s involvement. Two U.S. Conservative presidents from 1979 to 1992 had supported and protected Duarte's dictatorship in order to maintain Freedom. The report exposed thirteen years of lying by the two presidents who had concealed atrocities committed by dictator Duarte's right wing (Conservative) death squads. The report revealed that the death squads murdered entire village families (grandparents to grandchildren). The bodies were then laid out in the village streets so that friends and any remaining relatives could see them. This atrocity had a most debilitating effect on the peasant American warriors. It is believed that this mass killing style was learned in the School of the Americas at Fort Benning, Georgia. Yet, throughout the civil war, Conservative Presidents Ronald Reagan and G.H.W. Bush and the "free press" accused the peasant warriors of atrocities. They were blamed for the massacre of a group of U.S. Catholic nuns. The UN Truth Commission Report disclosed the truth, which was that Duarte's death squads had raped and murdered the nuns. The death squads had also murdered a female church worker and a Catholic archbishop. (Since the 1970s the CIA has supported certain Protestant religious groups in Spanish American nations where Catholicism is the dominant religion. This explains why members of the right wing death squads had no qualms about raping the Catholic nuns and murdering them and the archbishop.) The UN Truth Commission Report revealed a clear pattern of lying by two Conservative U.S. presidents about their support to the El Salvadoran right wing government. They supported him and his atrocities.

It is very difficult for a caring leader to remove multinational corporate powers' exploitation and oppression of his culture's resources and people in order to move his nation toward socialism. This is especially true if the nation is a poor, under-educated, and a non-Germanic European nation. As a rule, a socialist leader overthrowing a dictatorship of an underdeveloped nation needs to immediately break the control money-power has on the nation. The leader has to control the mass media. Permitting the money-powered "free" press to slant information against him and his ideas for the distribution of wealth and social equality is foolhardy. He also has to quickly remove the military and police leadership that supported the dictatorship if he wants to stay alive for any length of time. Chinese, Vietnamese, and Cuban socialist leaders stayed alive because they quickly replaced the mass media, the police, and the military of dictator puppets supported by United States' Freedom. All this takes resources and a core of educated individuals that underdeveloped nations such as El Salvador do not have.

In the early 2000s Venezuela and Bolivia became the latest American nations attempting to install degrees of socialism. Since 2005, Hugo Chávez, president of Venezuela, has been an outspoken proponent of what he called a "socialism of the 21st century" as a means to help the poor. Besides setting price controls on basic foods, he has also nationalized many of his country's major companies. He has opposed the globalization of the U.S. Judaican way. Also, in the early 2000s President Evo Morales of Bolivia led the political party called the *Movimiento al Socialismo*. Morales's Movement toward socialism established policies to give more power to the country's Americans by means of land reforms and redistribution of gas wealth. (President Morales is of the American race.) He accused the United States of trying to impede his political goals. As expected, the United States tried to keep these American nations from electing President Chavez and President Morales. The U.S. is not about to give up trying to destroy these nations and other American nations' socialist attempts.

In 2009 the U.S. was trying to prevent other Spanish American nations such as Paraguay, Guatemala, and Honduras from trying various forms of socialism. Honduran elected President Manuel Zelaya was kidnapped at gunpoint and flown out of the country by the military. The U.S. military has a base in this tiny banana country. To international observers it seemed that the U.S. endorsed the coup or initiated it via the CIA. The Obama administration, however, verbalized otherwise, that the U.S. government was unhappy about the coup. Yet it did not support other American nations insisting that the Honduran military permit President Zelaya to be reinstated. President Zelaya was kept out of office, and in 2010 a new president was instated. The Honduran military and the U.S. were satisfied with the new president. (Early in the Obama administration, it was indicated that hostility toward socialist efforts in the Americas would be more repressive than it has been in previous Democratic Party administrations.)

■　■　■

In the last hundred years or so significant degrees of socialism have emerged in Western European cultures—the most successful being in the highly educated cultures. Citizens of these cultures are well informed and have input in political actions. In most of these semi-socialist cultures there is not complete social equality with the removal of the chosen few. However, money-power is significantly harnessed for the welfare of all citizens. Dr. Simon explains: "The semi-socialist cultures of Western Europe have extremely high taxes to level material differences and provide the necessary services" (Simon, 1996, 331). The high taxes on the wealth of the chosen few and on corporate profits make it possible for all citizens to benefit from the culture's wealth and resources. All citizens benefit from socialized medical services, education, childcare, paid vacations, and so on. Even old capitalist England (mother nation of the United States) has modified its Judaican way with socialist ideas.

Although cultures in Western Europe have been successful in establishing various forms of socialism, most underdeveloped nations' attempts at socialism outside Western Europe have been stifled. Russia's attempt at socialism began in 1918 and dragged on for decades before collapsing. Now, with its oil wealth, it seems Russia is recovering and is incorporating aspects of capitalism to perhaps make a second attempt at socialism. Socialist attempts by Cuba, Vietnam, and China are still ongoing.

There are many other global socialist attempts that have been stopped by assassinations, corrupted leadership, etc. in the developing nations of Africa, Asia, North and South America. In most of these nations, dictatorships have been set up and protected by U.S. and U.K. military forces. For instance, in Asia "from 1979 into the 1990s, U.S. leaders aided the maniacal Khmer Rouge in Cambodia in order to debilitate the socialist-leaning government of that country, prolonging a civil war that took tens of thousands of lives" (Parenti, 2008, 87).

The world has predominantly been under capitalist control, so conflicts between socialist and capitalist cultures will increase as humanness continues to evolve globally. Humane political leaders will become convinced that compromising with Animal being politicians is not in the interest of caring for the global environment. Their animalism has kept a wealthy few in outrageous wealth, while billions of parents agonize over not being able to provide basic essentials for their children.

United States Socialist efforts

Although social scientists regard the United States as the most Conservative culture of the advanced nations, it has installed a bit of socialism, albeit by necessity. In the early 1920s, for a few years a small socialist party developed in the U.S. that helped organize social-political changes to benefit U.S. workers. This was brought about by the masses' extreme poverty and oppressed conditions. Workers were enduring extremely low wages and fourteen-hour to eighteen-hour workdays without overtime pay and without benefits. Preteen children were put to work in coal mines, a most dangerous job. Workers worked at the mercy of wealthy employers. They were abused and even killed, and their families suffered diseases from lack of food, health care, and shelter. The socialist political party helped the workers by organizing labor unions and strikes. These were the first big strikes against U.S. capitalism. Animal being leaders responded to socialists' help by having many of the strikers killed, including women, and children. Up to this historical period, our culture had what could be considered a pure form of capitalism; it was void of social caring.

Following the "roaring, happy 1920s," a time when those with money proudly displayed how Freedom had benefited them, the financial system was hit by the great economic depression of 1930. Wall Street stocks collapsed, thousands of businesses went bankrupt and millions were left unemployed. The depression triggered the election of the nation's first liberal president in 1933, President Franklin Delano Roosevelt (FDR).

President FDR introduced a bit of socialism (perhaps encouraged by his wife Eleanor) with his "New Deal." His New Deal included government social caring programs with the intent to help the nation survive the depression. It was a temporary plan that made the U.S. government the employer of millions of working families. Government work programs were created for the unemployed to work for wages building dams, bridges, highways, national parks, and other things for the nation. Most importantly, it established Social Security, a program for the welfare of the culture's working class. The New Deal helped millions of workers get through the early 1930s without having to depend on the whims of those with money to give them a handout. The U.S. government's bit of socialism was enough to stave off a possible violent revolution from workers, yet not enough to disrupt the nation's animalistic capitalist nature.

Although it took a bit of socialism to save the culture's capitalistic nature, Animal beings were rabid at President FDR's use of government resources to bring about social caring programs for millions of families. In fact, by 1939, work programs for thousands of unemployed artists and musicians had been stopped. To date, Animal beings continue to try to reduce or remove the bits of socialism that FDR implemented. Conservative politicians sense that increasing socialism for workers involves restructuring the culture with more equality and caring than the culture's nature can stand.

Nevertheless, the historical strikes, which caused the lives of many workers throughout the nation, and the government's bit of socialism helped the culture through the depression of the early 1930s. The strikes were forceful enough to have brought about an increment in social caring. Many of today's U.S. workers enjoy an eight-hour workday, paid vacations, minimum wage limit, overtime pay, unemployment benefits, strike provisions, safe working conditions, and other worker rights.

It is difficult for us U.S. citizens to perceive the reality of social humane caring. Our capitalist culture shapes and reinforces our feelings, thoughts, and behaviors with selfish beliefs. This makes it difficult to accept the idea that a socio-political humane system is possible and better than our old capitalist system. The bulk of us have been inculcated to believe that social caring programs are meant to benefit a minority of groups, including "undeserving others." In other words, our Conservative cultural environment triggers antisocial caring. But, we defend our selfishness and limited caring for others with the popular idea that more of our money will be taxed. When simple beliefs like these are backed by money-powered campaigns against social caring programs, they become sacred truths.

Even citizens at the bottom of our culture's social-economic hierarchy do not readily accept caring politicians' humane proposals. They are somewhat like chickens at the bottom of a chicken coop's hierarchy, programmed to accept their unequal status. It seems that many citizens at the bottom would find it weird *not* to have a "top rooster," or a "chosen few" above them. Without knowing about our species' animal heritage, it is impossible to understand why most workers tend to reject humane social caring, or why they continue to accept Conservative (Animal being) leadership that keeps them at the bottom of an animalistic hierarchy.

U.S. Conservative politicians at the top of the culture's animalistic hierarchy do not see a need for socialized caring benefits for working families. Yet, they have socialized benefits (life-long health care and pensions) for themselves and their families. So how can we, the working masses, expect creatures that are well taken care of by the culture's animalistic system to identify with our needs and lifestyles? They cannot feel our daily stress and concerns for adequate medical care, affordable housing, and education for our children and for our retired parents. As for their "socialized" care, it is "deserved" care because they are conservators of the culture's animalistic nature.

Evolution of Social Caring via Cultures

Our species has markedly expanded its interactions in many areas, but not in social caring for the welfare of others beyond that found in animals. We still have kingdoms, dictatorships, and capitalism with a chosen few living pampered lives, and with many of us living worse than apes at the bottom of their group's hierarchy. Nevertheless, our species continues to advance in social caring. Life for most common people is not as animalistic as it was thousands or even a hundred years ago. The advancement in social caring via the evolution of our cultures is ongoing. This is what gifted Karl Marx was saying over 160 years ago.

Karl Marx theorized about this phenomenon in the 1800s. He proposed that our cultures needed to evolve from the animal nature of kingdoms and capitalism to the evolving humanness of socialism and, finally, to the humane nature of communism. In other words, the cultural evolution from kingdoms to communism seems to coincide with our species' evolution of caring from primitive caring levels of animal nature to Human nature. Marx made clear the relationship between the evolution of social-political systems and the evolution of our species' humanness.

In **kingdoms** interactions are much like those of insects. The culture's dominant caring is limited to the welfare of the dictator, king or queen, and royal family. Information to the people is limited to the extent that extreme secrecy is the norm. If elections are held, as a rule they are a sham; the status of the royal family remains stagnated in its pampered lifestyle.

In **capitalist cultures** the focus is on the freedom to accumulate unlimited wealth by a wealthy few. Capitalist cultures have a money-powered democracy, which upholds greed and inequality. Lying to the people about socio-political issues, or keeping most of the people ignorant about significant issues is systemic. Capitalist cultures tend to maintain close relationships with kingdoms and Conservative dictatorships because of their similar nature.

Marx made intellectuals aware that the chosen few of capitalism use such terms as liberty, freedom, equality, and democracy as forked-tongue propositions. (Marx identified the animalness of capitalism in his *Manifesto* of 1848 and in *Das Kapital* in 1867.) Since Marx was aware of Judaism, he saw how Judaic/Christian religions and capitalist practices benefited each other. He saw religion as "the opium of the masses." Therefore, he referred to the effects of god beliefs as similar to the effects opium has on people. You feel good that things are all right as long as you have your beliefs (drugs) to depend on instead of facing reality. Marx sensed that dependency on god beliefs and capitalism was detrimental to the progress of our species' social caring cultural evolution.

Socialist cultures focus on providing essential needs for all members. In comparison to capitalist cultures, there is less inequality, secrecy, and less money-powered influence on democratic processes. Wealth distribution is significantly increased from that of a capitalist culture. Taxes are predominantly for the welfare of the working masses rather than for the culture's corporations (including military industrial complex corporations). Workers in socialist cultures are not dependent on hope and prayer or on charitable handouts as workers are in a capitalist culture. There is also more caring for the welfare of the global environment than there is in a capitalist culture.

As for the importance of socialism, Marx is to have said: "Socialism is an effort to try to solve man's animal problems, and after having solved the animal problems, then we can face the human [Human] problems" (Chomsky, Mitchell, and Schoeffel, 2002, 198). Our Culture's problems are primarily brought about by Animal beings' opposition to the advancement of social caring. Since Animal beings are the dominant members in our cultures, in numbers as well as in action, humane leadership has to become aware that they are going to be a hindrance to the advancement of Human evolution for some time. The fact that many members our species, not because of their choosing, can only interact with the limited caring of animals needs to be accepted as a natural phenomenon in our species. Then humane leadership might be able to confront Animal beings not as individuals of an opposing team, but as interactions (feelings, behaviors, etc) putting our entire species at risk.

Communist cultures, hypothetically, will interact cooperatively as a unit for the welfare of our species globally. In these cultures a democratic classless society by the people will have been achieved. Animal beings, cultural inequalities, and wars for territory and resources will be identified as our species' historical animalness. Our species' interactions will have created a global Human civilization.

Marx was an optimist. He believed that the social caring of his era, the 1800s, would not remain in animal-like stagnation, but would continue to evolve toward humane caring. However, he indicated that it would take revolutions to bring about changes. It is likely that he would have thought it natural to use the term evolution if more science had been available to him about our species. He was also aware that it would probably take thousands of years for us to evolve to communism's humane level of caring.

It is foolish to think that any present nation is even close to reaching Marx's meaning of communism. Yet capitalist Animal beings tend to use socialism and communism negatively and synonymously. They instinctively reject Marx's theoretical premise that our species' nature has the potential of expanding its caring. Marx saw the evolution of our species' caring through the evolution of our cultures. Animal beings consider such an evolution as utopian fantasy because their caring potential is limited to that of animals. Therefore, they perceive the nature of a kingdom or a capitalist culture as a permanent ideal that needs only minor adjustments. On the other hand, Humans perceive the expansion of our species' social caring as evolving beyond Animal beings' levels of caring, although moving as with the brakes on. At this time, cultures with degrees of socialism have the highest level of social caring.

Marx's ideas have stayed alive because they trigger an awareness of the dominant discourse of animal caring that exists in most cultures. Therefore, humane individuals continuously oppose capitalism's oppression of peoples and exploitation of resources for the benefit of a chosen few. On the other hand, Conservative political leaders relentlessly protect capitalism globally. They perceive humane cultural leaders as a dangerous threat to capitalism's global control. Not surprisingly, kingdoms and capitalist cultures continue to react with hatred toward socialist ideas.

We don't know how much Charles Darwin (1809–1882) influenced Karl Marx (1818–1883), but both are detested by Animal beings. Darwin confronted the animalness of our species' genetic evolution. Marx confronted our species' humanness with an ongoing cultural evolution. Marx made us face our animalness with our species' humane evolution similar to how Darwin made us face our animalness with our species' animal evolution. Or we can say that Darwin made us aware of our animal evolution, and Marx made us aware of our Human evolution.

Reflections

Conflicts among us, as a species, are generally triggered from the animalness in and about us. Conflicts arise even among members of the same group. There are conflicts within a family, within members of the same race, religion, or culture. There are conflicts between members of different races, religions, and cultures. As in animal species, such conflicts will exist as long as Animal beings' interactions are dominant over Human beings' interactions. If we were all Animal beings, our species would be marked an endangered species.

However, our evolving humanness is already proving to be a great tool in eliminating or minimizing our conflicts. We have the United Nations and the European Community dealing with conflicts between cultures. Amnesty International deals with eliminating torture, and so on. Even elementary schools train students in conflict management to reduce students' playground disagreements.

Yet, because we are a transitional species we are faced with something that no animal species has to face. We, as a species, have to confront our animalness in our evolution to becoming a Human species. The good thing is that this is already happening. More of us are becoming aware of our animalness as well as of our humanness. We can speculate that it won't be long before humane political leaders and scientists will become aware that the welfare of our species' survival depends on moving as fast as possible to de-animalize our species. This could be achieved perhaps through cultural environments and genetic changes.

Scientists will begin to identify what it is in the cultural environment that maintains and triggers animalism in us. They can then help humane leaders plan on how to incorporate the culture's educational, political, … systems to trigger and shape citizens' interactions toward humane caring. This is already being tried in cultures that have installed degrees of socialism. Only when this is accomplished can Humans focus on global social caring and preparing for the survival of our species on earth and beyond. Fortunately, evolution has indicated that changes in a species benefiting its survival eventually become dominant. In our species, Human beings will create such changes.

Although there is no known genetic marker distinguishing Animal beings from Human beings, there is a marked difference between the caring of Hitler,

Pinochet, and Stalin, and the caring of the Buddha, Jesus, and Gandhi. (No doubt over time genetic differences will be found.) One can speculate that all Homo sapiens are born with the "Human gene" and that the environment can only trigger (activate) the gene in some of us. Or, it might be that the "Human gene" is evolving only in some among us and can be triggered by the environment. In other words, humanness might be a genetic evolutionary change in our transitional species. The authors speculate that this might to be the case. If so, the environment, especially the cultural environment, becomes crucial in activating the Human gene.

As our species evolves, Humans' interactions will be more influential upon the rest of us, and we will be triggered to follow them. A preliminary step is for the bulk of us to become aware of our species' evolving humanness. We need to learn that social caring programs for the benefit of people are the results of humane efforts. We need to know that the expansion of social caring programs for all our nation's citizens and, eventually, for all people globally is a goal for humane leaders. We need to know that capitalism—its greed and oppression of others—is the outstanding animal problem facing humane leaders. This is because our species' most powerful culture nurtures and enforces an animal hierarchy of a chosen few of immense wealth over the welfare of the bulk of our species and the environment. Finally, we need to know that without Human beings there would be no hope of removing our species' animalness causing global suffering.

At this stage of our species' evolution, animal levels of caring have dominantly directed our cultures' interactions. As our species continues to evolve humanness, the next civilization will emerge with advanced social caring. At this time it appears that China and other Asian nations are forthcoming leading nations with the potential of becoming a global civilization. If this is to be the case, let us hope that our species has made great strides in its evolution of Human nature by the time Asian nations form the core cultures of a new civilization. This would mean that cultures' Animal being problems would be recognized as such. Efforts would be made to put social-caring programs, laws, and educational studies in place, enabling cultures to begin to transform our levels of animal caring to humane levels of caring. What would follow would be Human leaders' tremendous task of implementing a unified global responsibility to repair the destruction our animalness has caused.

As Humanness evolves, humane caring will be the measure of being civilized rather than what capitalist cultures have considered is being civilized. At this stage of our species' evolution, it is impossible for most of us to perceive humanness as the criterion for being civilized. Similarly, it is difficult to understand that our species' ongoing transition from animal nature to Human nature is as significant as the transition from dead entities' interactions to living entities' interactions.

Summary

The rationale for Human nature is based on our species' potential to care for the welfare of others beyond the potential of animals. However, because our species is transitioning out of animal nature, Human beings are a minority among the bulk of us Animal beings. Our species' caring evolution has been slow in comparison to our other traits. Nevertheless, it is ongoing.

We can detect our species' caring evolution by comparing the level of social caring of early cultures and civilizations to the level of social caring in present day cultures and in our Judaic-Germanic civilization. Even in the civilization's top Conservative capitalist culture, the United States, most of its citizens are experiencing a more social caring life than citizens had even one hundred years ago. Thankfully, there are now laws against child labor. Most people now have Social Security and other worker benefits. There are more individuals and organizations advocating care for the homeless, the ill, and the disabled. Finally, in 2010 a preliminary form of government-supported health care for citizens was put in place.

Culturally, the social caring disparity between humanness and animalness triggers conflicts between ultraliberals and Conservatives and between capitalist cultures and emerging socialist cultures. This is obvious by how the civilization's top capitalist culture has reacted negatively toward cultures attempting to establish socialism.

We have seen that cultural changes toward humanness are the responsibility of humane leaders. For as anthropologist Margaret Mead once said "Never believe that a few caring people cannot change the world. For, indeed, that's all who ever have." In other words, we should understand that it is because of our species' potential to evolve Human beings that there is hope for the survival of our species. Some of us are becoming aware that we need humane leaders to move our cultures beyond the caring levels of animal nature and to reduce or remove interactions harmful to the welfare of life. This cannot be over-emphasized if our species is to someday create a civilization that is no longer a keeper of animals.

Therefore, it is hypothesized that being *Human* or *humane* is having the genetic potential to care for the welfare of living evolution and of the universe.

For further discussions on this book see

www.becominghumanbook.com

GLOSSARY

Authors' terms*

African (black)—Racial identification of Africa's native people (unless otherwise stated)

Afro-Euro*—Biracial mixture of African (black) and European (white)

Amer-Euro*—Biracial mixture of American (bronze) and European (white)

America—The continents of South and North America—the Western Hemisphere

American (bronze)—Racial identification of America's native people (unless otherwise stated)

Anglo—Linguistic term identifying English speaking or English surnamed people, regardless of race; refers to cultures whose native language is English; originally people of the United Kingdom (UK)

Animal beings*—Members of our Homo sapient species who are genetically limited to interact with only the levels of caring for others found in animal species

animal nature—All animal species' collective interactions; the Animal Kingdom

Asian (yellow)—Racial identification of Asia's native people (unless otherwise stated)

Austra-Euro*—Biracial mixture of Australian (brown) and European (white)

Australian (brown)—Racial identification of Australia's native people (unless otherwise stated)

belief-reality*—A species' ready-set potential to interact with the environment

CERN— Conseil Europeen pour la Recherche Nucleaire (CERN) located in France; the world's largest particle physics center

Conservative*—With a capital "C" is used as another name for Animal being

dead entities*—nonliving particles that interact as individual entities.

domain of "nothingness"*—A speculated domain without timespace, without interactions

ethology—The study of our species' ethos and its foundation; the study of animal interactions (particularly of social animals such as primates, honey bees and ants); the study of comparative psychology (feelings, beliefs, awareness, behaviors, etc.) of Homo sapiens and animals

247

European (white)—Racial identification of Europe's native people (unless otherwise stated)

existology*—A proposed study unifying all interactions that create existence.

free will—The idea of being able to interact free from genetic and environmental influences

Freedom*—With a capital "F" is another name for capitalism, Judaic freedom, free market, free enterprise, money power

genetic-environment complex*—The evolution of reciprocal interactions between genetics and the environment; the environment continuously triggers interactions from living entities, in turn living entities trigger interactions from the environment.

Germanic—Refers to the family of languages including such languages as German, English, Austrian, Swiss, etc.; refers to cultures whose native language is a Germanic language; refers to people of these cultures regardless of race

god-reality*—Our species' instincts to believe in "gods," which are genetically programmed in our species' belief-reality

Hispanic (Hispano)—Linguistic term identifying Spanish speaking or Spanish surnamed people, regardless of race; refers to cultures whose native language is Spanish; originally people of Spain

Hominids—Refers to the branches of wise ape species (hominids) that split from common ape evolution

Humans*—With a capital "H" identifies members of our species with the genetic potential to care for the welfare of others beyond the caring levels of animal nature

Human nature*—Our Homo sapient species' genetic potential to care for the welfare of others and the environment beyond the caring potential inherited from animal nature

Indians—Citizens of India; People from the nation of India

indians*—A racist term used to identify people of the American race; it is written with a lower case "i" to mark the racism behind this term

individualized belief-reality*—An individual's ready-set potential to interact with the environment

instinctual interactions—Interactions that the environment triggers from a species' programmed interactions; in our species, interactions that take minimal effort and time

interactions—All actions, responses, behaviors, etc. of nonliving and living entities

Judaic freedom*—Capitalism, free enterprise, free market, Freedom, etc.

Latin—Refers to the family of languages including such languages as French, Spanish, Italian, etc.; refers to cultures whose native language is a Latin language; refers to people of these cultures regardless of race

learned interactions—Interactions that the environment triggers from a species' programmed interactions; in our species, interactions that take effort and time

matter—Anything that that occupies space; anything that has mass and energy

multispecies potential*—Our species' interactive potential, which seems to contain its entire ancestral heritage

Pre-Homo sapient species*—A hypothetical wise ape (hominid) species that evolved from Homo erectus species some 200,000 years ago; A hypothetical wise ape species from which our species emerged about 65,000 years ago

race—A genetic identification; there are five major races: African (black), Asian (yellow), Australian (brown), European (white), and American (bronze)

stagnant (static) **interactions**—Interactions that do not evolve beyond a species' genetic potential. Stagnancy is common in animal species, but is also seen in some of our species' interactions

Unitedstatens*—United States citizens

WASP—White Anglo Saxon Protestant; early immigrants from England to the U.S., Canada, New Zealand, and Australia

wise apes*—Our species' ancestral ape (hominid) species

BIBLIOGRAPHY

About CERN. CERN Website (2007).

"Afrikaner." *Christian Science Monitor* (December 14, 1987): 10.

"Agent Orange: Hue and Cry." *Science News* 138 (August 1990): 103.

Amnesty International USA Newsletter (1990).

An Interview with Danny Glover. *AARP* (May/June 2004).

Arvey, R.D., L. M. Abraham, T.J. Bouchard, and N. L. Segal. "Job Satisfaction: Environmental and Genetic Components." *Journal of Applied Psychology* 74.2 (1989): 187-192.

Attenborough, David. *The Trials of Life: A History of Animal Behavior*. Canada: Little, Brown & Co., 1990.

"Biology and Family, Partners in Crime." *Science News* 50 (July 6, 1996): 11.

Borowitz, Eugene B. "How is the Church to Confront Jesus' Jewishness?" *Moment* (April 1989): 40-53.

Bower, Bruce. "Australian Site yields Early Human Dates." *Science News* 137 (May 12, 1990): 293.

Bower, Bruce. "Babies Add Up Basic Arithmetic Skills." *Science News* 142 (August 1992): 132.

Branfman, Fred. "On Torture and Being 'Good Americans." *Tikkun* (March/April 2006): 34.

——"Long Live Zinn." *Tikkun* (March/April 2010): 76.

Buruma, Ian. "The Vichy Syndrome." *Tikkun* (January/February 1995): 44-50.

Bush, Lawrence and Jeffrey Dekro. "Jews, Money, and Social Responsibility." *Tikkun* (September/October 1993): 34.

Cahill, Thomas. *The Gifts of the Jews*. New York: Nan A. Talese Doubleday, 1998.

Carter, Jimmy. *Palestine: Peace Not Apartheid*. New York: Simon & Schuster, 2006.

—— *Our Endangered Values*. New York, NY: Simon & Schuster, 2005.

Cavalli-Sforza LL. "Genes, Peoples and Languages." *Scientific American* 205:5 (November 1991): 104-110.

Chomsky, Noam. *Understanding Power: The Indispensable Chomsky*, Ed. Peter R. Mitchell and John Schoeffel. New York: The New Press, 2002.

Christ, Michael and Peter Zheutlin. "Stop Playing the Nuclear Game." *Tikkun* (May/June 2001): 63.

Christian bible: The New Testament

Cochran, Rebecca Fawn. "Bear River Massacre." *Discovering Archaeology* (January/February 1999): 78-81.

Collins, Graham P. "Higgs Won't Fly." *Scientific American* (February 2001): 17.

Daley, Tad. "Nuclear Irony." *Tikkun* (July/August, 2006): 27

De Chardin, Teilhard. *The Phenomenon of Man.* New York: The Cathedral Library, Harper & Row, 1959.

Drlica, Karl. *Understanding DNA and Gene Cloning A Guide for the Curious.* New York: John Wiley & Sons, 1984.

Eban, Abba. *Heritage Civilization and the Jews.* New York: Summit Books, 1984.

Eberhart, J. "Pre-life Chemistry Found in Meteorite." *Science News* 124 (September 3, 1983): 150.

Edelman, M.W. "Putting Children First." Tikkun. 11 (1996): 40

Ehrenreich, Barbara. *Nickel and Dimed on (Not) Getting by in America.* New York: Metropolitan Books Henry Hold & Company, 2001.

Ezzell, C. "Brain Receptor Shapes Voles' Family Values." *Science News* 142 (July 1992): 6.

Feldman, G. J. and J. Steinberger. "The Number of Families of Matter." *Scientific American* (February 1991.).

"Final Report of the Tuskegee Syphilis Study Legacy Committee." Internet (May 20, 1996.)

Flowers, Margaret. "After the Reform: Aiming High for Health Justice." *Tikkun* (May/June 2010): 14.

Fortey, Richard. Life. New York: Alfred A. Knopf, Inc., 1998.

Friedman, Thomas L. *The World is Flat A Brief History of the 21ˢᵗ Century.* New York: Farrar, Straus & Giroux, 2006.

Giroux, Henry A. "The Politics of Lying, The Assault on Meaning in Bush's America." *Tikkun* (March/April 2006.): 36.

Gottfried, P. and Fleming, T. *The Conservative Movement.* Boston: Twayne Publishers, 1988.

Green, David G. *The New Conservatism.* New York: St. Martin's Press, 1987.

Green, R, ed. *Problems in European Civilization Protestantism and Capitalism: The Weber Thesis and Its Critic.* Boston: D.C. Heath & Co., 1959.

Griffin, Donald R. "Essay: Animal Thinking." *Scientific American* (November 1991): 144.

"Hands-on Babbling." *Science News* (March 30, 1991): 205

Hölldobler, Bert and E.O. Wilson. *The Ants.* Cambridge, Massachusetts: The Belknap Press of Harvard University Press, 1990.

"How Neanderthals Chilled Out." *Science News* (March 24, 1990): 189.

Huxley, Julian. *Man Stands Alone.* Freeport, New York: Books for Libraries Press, 1941.

——*Evolution, The Modern Synthesis.* New York: Harper & Brothers, 1942.

"In Kosovo, Uneasy Truce Among Neighbors." *Christian Science Monitor* (May 5, 2006): 4.

"Interview With Gore Vidal." *Los Angeles Times.* (December 15, 1991): Section M: 13.

Jewish bible: The Old Testament

Johnson. Dirk. "A Merit Badge in Murder?" Newsweek (March 15, 2004): 56.

Kidder, Rushworth M. *An Agenda for the 21ˢᵗ Century Interviews from The Christian Science Monitor.* Cambridge, Massachusetts: The MIT Press, 1987.

Kronenwetter, Michael. *Capitalism VS Socialism Economic Policies of the U.S. and the U.S.S.R.* New York, London, Toronto, Sydney: Franklin Watts, 1986.

Lapham, Lewis H. "Moral Dandyism." *Harper's New York* (July 1985).

Lefrancois, Guy R. *Psychology*: 2ⁿᵈ Edition. Belmont California: Wadsworth Publishing Co., 1980.

Lerner, Michael. The Destruction of the Planet. *Tikkun* (May/June 1989): 9-13.

——*Jewish Renewal: A Path to Healing and Transformation.* New York, Canada: G.P. Putnam's Sons, 1994.

——*The Left Hand of God: Taking Back Our Country From the Religious Right.* New York: Harper Collins, 2006.

Levinson, Sanford. *Our Undemocratic Constitution: Where the Constitution Goes Wrong and How We the People can Correct It.* New York: Oxford University Press, Inc., 2006.

Lewin, Roger. *Thread of Life, The Smithsonian Looks at Evolution.* Smithsonian Institute, 1982.

——"The Earliest Humans Were More Like Apes." *Science* 236 (May 1987): 1061-1063.

——*In the Age of Mankind A Smithsonian Book of Human Evolution.* United States: Smithsonian Institute, 1988.

Lipton, Bruce H. *The Biology of Belief: Unleashing the Power of Consciousness, Matter and Miracles.* Santa Rosa, CA: Elite Books, 2005.

Loewen, James W. *Lies My Teacher Told Me.* New York: The New Press, 1995.

Lorenz, Konrad. *Civilized Man's Deadly Sins*, Trans. M.K. Wilson. New York: Harcourt Brace Jovanovich, Inc., 1973.

——*Motivation of Human and Animal Behavior an Ethological View.* New York: Van Nostrand Reinhold Co., 1973.

——*On Aggression*, Trans. Marjorie Kerr Wilson. San Diego, New York, London: Harvest/ HBJ Book "A Helen and Kurt Wolff Book" Harcourt Brace Jovanovich, Publishers, 1966.

——*The Foundations of Ethology.* New York-Wien: Springer-Verlag, 1978.

Lovejoy, Owen C. "Evolution of Human Walking." *Scientific American* (November 1988.): 118-24.

Maddocks, Melvin. "Who Cares How the Other Half Lives?" *World Monitor* (February 1989): 10.

Malkin, Peter Z. and Harry Stein. *Eichmann in My Hands*. New York: Warner Books, Inc., 1990.

Mander, Jerry. "Economic Globalization and the Environment." *Tikkun* (September/October 2001) 16: 33.

Mayr, Ernst. *What Evolution Is*. New York: Basic Books, 2001.

Mearshiemer, J. J. and S. M. Walt. *The Israel Lobby and U.S. Foreign Policy*. New York: Farrar, Straus and Giroux, 2007.

Mora-Torres, Gregorio, ed. and trans. *Californio Voices The Oral memoirs of Jose Maria Amador and Lorenzo Asisara*. Texas: University of North Texas Press, 2005.

Morris, Richard. *The Edges of Science Crossing the Boundary from Physics to Metaphysics*. New York: Prentice Hall Press, 1990.

"Nurture Over Nature: Certain Genes are Turned On or Off by Geography and Lifestyle." Internet, *Science Daily* (April 23, 2008.).

Nesbit, Robert. *Conservatism: Dream and Reality*. Minneapolis: University of Minnesota Press, 1986.

Newsweek/Beliefnet Poll. *Newsweek* (September 5, 2005): 48, 49.

"On Torture and Being Good Americans." *Tikkun* (March/April 2006): 34.

Operin, Aleksandr I. *The Origin of Life On the Earth*: 3rd Revision, Trans. Ann Synge. New York: Academic Press Inc. Publishers, 1957.

Padilla, Genaro M. *My History, Not Yours: The Formation of Mexican American Autobiography*. The University of Wisconsin Press, 1993.

Parenti, Michael. *Democracy For The Few*. 8th Edition. Belmont, CA: Thomas Wadsworth, 2008.

——*Land of Idols Political Mythology in America*. New York: St. Martin's Press, 1994.

Parrinder, Geoffrey. *World Religions from Ancient History to the Present World*. New York, NY and Bicester, England: Facts on File Publications, 1983.

Peterson, Ivars. "Microsphere Excitement." *Science News* 125 (June 30, 1984): 408.

Powell, Corey. "Looking for Nothing." *Scientific American* (April 1991).

Powers, Samantha. *A Problem from Hell: America and the Age of Genocide*. Harper Perennial, 2007.

Raloff, J. "Roach Hormone: Clue to Human Ancestry." *Science News* (November 8, 1986): 295.

——"Is There A Cosmic Chemistry of Life?" *Science News* 130 (September 20, 1986): 182.

Rand, Ayn. *Capitalism: The Unknown Ideal*. New York: The New American Library, 1967.

Richey, Warren and Brad Knickerbocker. "Court: EPA Must Address Climate Risk." *Christian Science Monitor* (April 3, 2007.): 1, 10.

Riordan, M. and D. N. Schramm. *The Shadows of Creation Dark Matter and the Structure of the Universe.* New York: W. H. Freeman & Company, 1991.

Robbins, Richard H. *Global Problems and the Culture of Capitalism.* New York: Prentice Hall, 2008.

Rohlfing, Duane L. and A. I Oparin. *Molecular Evolution Prebiological and Biological.* New York: Plenum Press, 1972.

Ross, Philip E. "Compulsive Canines." *Scientific American* (July 1992): 24.

——"Hard Words." *Scientific American* (April 1991): 139-147.

Ruhlen, Merritt and Joseph H. Greenberg. "Linguistic Origins of Native Americans." *Scientific American* 267: 5 (November 1992): 94—99.

Sagan, Carl and A. Druyan. *Forgotten Ancestors.* New York: Random House, Inc., 1992.

"Seeking Hidden Messages in Stone Tool Technology." *Science* 236 (May 1987): 669.

Shlossman, Ruth. "Can You Teach Empathy?" *Tikkun* (March/April 1996): 20.

Simon, David. *Elite Deviance.* Massachusetts: Simon & Schuster Co., 1996.

Simon, Michael. *The Matter of Life Philosophical Problems of Biology.* Yale University Press, 1971.

Skinner, B.F. *Beyond Freedom and Dignity.* New York: Alfred A. Knopf, 1971.

"Skulls Reveal Dawn of Mankind." *Nature* 423 (June 11, 2003).

Sorbel, Dava, *Galileo's Daughter: A historical memoir of science, faith, and love.* New York: Penguin, 1999.

Soloman, A. "Rock Art in Southern Africa." *Scientific American* (November 1996.): 111.

Spindler, Konrad. *The Man in the Ice.* New York: Harmony Books, 1994.

Spotts, P. N. "Often Deleted: Global Warming." *The Christian Science Monitor* (January 31, 2007): 7, 11.

Stewart, James, B. Den of Thieves. New York: Simon & Schuster Paperbacks, 1992.

Stringer, Christopher, Robin McKie. *African Exodus: The Origins of Modern Humanity.* New York: Henry Holt & Co., 1996.

Summa, John. "Union Carbide." *Multinational Monitor* (October 1988).

Szymborska, Wisawa. *View with a Grain of Sand: Selected Poems,* Trans. Stanisaw Baranczak and Clare Cavanagh. New York: Harcourt Brace & Co., 1995.

Tattersall, Ian. "Out of Africa Again … and Again?" *Scientific American* (April 1997): 67.

Teilhard de Chardin, Pierre. *The Phenomenon of Man,* Trans. Bernard Wall. New York: Harper and Row, 1959.

Thomas, Hugh. *The Slave Trade.* New York: Simon & Schuster, 1997.

Tobias, Phillip V. *The Brain in Hominid Evolution*. New York-London: Columbia University Press, 1971.

Toobin, Jeffrey. *The Nine: Inside the Secret World of the Supreme Court*. New York: Doubleday, 2007.

Walker, Alan and Mark Teaford. "The Hunt for Proconsul." *Science News* (January 1989): 76-81.

Weinberg, Steven. *The Discovery of Subatomic Particles*. New York: W.H. Freeman & Co., 1983.

Wheeler, John Archibald. "Making the Quantum Leap." *Christian Science Monitor* (June 14, 1986): Section B: 4.

Wilford, John Noble. "In Ancient skulls from Ethiopia, Familiar Faces." New York Times: Late Edition (June 12, 2003) Section A: 1.

Wilson, Edward O. *Biophilia*. Cambridge, Massachusetts: Harvard University Press, 1984.

——*On Human Nature*. Cambridge, Massachusetts: Harvard University Press, 1978.

——*Sociobiology The New Synthesis*. Cambridge, Massachusetts: The Belknap Press of Harvard University Press, 1975.

Wolfram, Herwig. *The Roman Empire and Its Germanic Peoples*, Trans. Thomas Dunlap. Berkeley, California: University of California Press, 1997.

Yogesh Chadha. *Gandhi A Life*. New York: John Wiley & Sons, Inc., 1997.

Zinn, Howard. *A Peoples' History of the United States*. New York: Harper Perennial Modern Classics, 2005.